T0394005

Social Movements in the Balkans

From Slovenia to Turkey, social movements and protests have shaken the political systems of Southeast Europe. Confronting issues such as austerity, the provision and privatisation of welfare, public utilities and public space, corruption, bureaucratic inefficiency, environmental concerns and authoritarian tendencies, these revolts have also served as conduits for broader social and political discontent. Although they have contributed to the defeat of unpopular policies and practices and the fall of governments, perhaps their most significant impact has been in creating dynamic political and social actors and contributing to the realignment of the political space.

This volume sheds new light on the wave of protests and emerging social movements. Placing individual protests in a wider context, it highlights connections between different social movements and discusses parallels with similar movements from recent history. The contributors include both well-established scholars and up-and-coming researchers who engage with both activist and academic perspectives to identify the similar and varying dynamics of protests and the governments' responses to them.

Building upon studies of social movements, the book will be of interest to scholars examining political dissent, protests and mechanisms of mobilisation in the region.

Florian Bieber is a professor of Southeast European History and Politics at the University of Graz, Austria.

Dario Brentin is a university assistant at the Centre for Southeast European Studies at the University of Graz.

Social Movements in the Balkans

Rebellion and Protest from Maribor to Taksim

Edited by Florian Bieber and Dario Brentin

LONDON AND NEW YORK

First published 2019
by Routledge
2 Park Square, Milton Park, Abingdon, Oxon OX14 4RN

and by Routledge
711 Third Avenue, New York, NY 10017

Routledge is an imprint of the Taylor & Francis Group, an informa business

© 2019 selection and editorial matter, Florian Bieber and Dario Brentin; individual chapters, the contributors

The right of Florian Bieber and Dario Brentin to be identified as the authors of the editorial material, and of the authors for their individual chapters, has been asserted in accordance with sections 77 and 78 of the Copyright, Designs and Patents Act 1988.

All rights reserved. No part of this book may be reprinted or reproduced or utilised in any form or by any electronic, mechanical, or other means, now known or hereafter invented, including photocopying and recording, or in any information storage or retrieval system, without permission in writing from the publishers.

Trademark notice: Product or corporate names may be trademarks or registered trademarks, and are used only for identification and explanation without intent to infringe.

British Library Cataloguing-in-Publication Data
A catalogue record for this book is available from the British Library

Library of Congress Cataloging-in-Publication Data
A catalog record for this book has been requested

ISBN: 9781138052147 (hbk)
ISBN: 9781315167985 (ebk)

Typeset in Times New Roman
by Apex CoVantage, LLC

Printed and bound by CPI Group (UK) Ltd, Croydon, CR0 4YY

Contents

List of tables and figures	vii
List of contributors	viii

Introduction: social movements and protests in Southeast Europe – a new tragedy of the commons?   1
DARIO BRENTIN AND FLORIAN BIEBER

1 Divided they stand: peace building, state reconstruction and informal political movements in Bosnia-Herzegovina, 2005–2013   9
HEIKO WIMMEN

2 Maribor's social uprising in the European crisis: from antipolitics of people to politicisation of periphery's surplus population   30
GAL KIRN

3 The 'stronger state' and counter-democracy: Bulgarian street protests, 2012–2013, in the accounts of participants   48
VALENTINA GUEORGUIEVA

4 The spaces of social mobilisation in Greece   66
KOSTIS PLEVRIS

5 At the crossroads of cultural and ideological exchange – behind the visual communications of 2012–2013 Slovene protests   79
KSENIJA BERK

vi *Contents*

6 Social media and the 'Balkan spring'   96

ŽELJKA LEKIĆ-SUBAŠIĆ

**7 'Missing the forest for the trees': from single-issue protests
to resonant mass-movements in Greece, Turkey and
Bosnia-Herzegovina**   113

CHIARA MILAN AND LEONIDAS OIKONOMAKIS

**8 Are the Balkans different? Mapping protest politics in
post-communist Southeastern Europe**   131

MARIUS I. TATAR

**9 The international context of mass political unrest in the
Balkans – conceptual issues and perspectives**   158

MARK KRAMER

Index   188

Tables and figures

Tables

8.1	Protest participation in Europe 2008; regional variation in a comparative perspective	135
8.2	Dynamics of petitioning and demonstrating in SEE, 1998–2008	137
8.3	Explaining the signing of petitions in post-communist SEE (Exp (B) logistic regression coefficients)	152
8.4	Explaining participation in lawful demonstrations in post-communist SEE (Exp (B) logistic regression coefficients)	154
8.5	The measures	156

Figures

8.1	Trends of protest participation in post-communist SEE, 1995–2008	136
8.2	Quality of democracy and protest activity in SEE Europe (2008)	138
8.3	Economic development, quality of democracy and protest activity in SEE (2008)	139

Contributors

Ksenija Berk is an independent scholar and critic from Ljubljana (Slovenia). She holds a PhD in Aesthetics and MA in Historical Anthropology of Visual Arts. Her research interests are history of design in the Balkans, design and politics, visual culture of protest movements, dissent, social design and the politics of the street. She has a particular interest in understanding how design and material culture work as agents of social and political change and how they help us develop critical thinking on our values, ideas and processes.

Florian Bieber is a professor of Southeast European History and Politics at the University of Graz, Austria, director of the Centre for Southeast European Studies at the University of Graz and coordinator of the Balkans in Europe Policy Advisory Group (BiEPAG). He was previously a lecturer in East European Politics at the University of Kent, UK. He received his MA in Political Science and History and his PhD in Political Science from the University of Vienna, as well as an MA in Southeast European Studies from Central European University (Budapest).

Dario Brentin is a university assistant at the Centre for Southeast European Studies at the University of Graz. He is also currently completing his PhD thesis at the School of Slavonic and East European Studies at University College London, working on the topic of sport and national identity in post-Yugoslav Croatia. He obtained his MagPhil in Political Science and Eastern European History at the University of Vienna. He has taught at the University of Vienna and has since been a visiting lecturer at the University of Copenhagen and University of Brighton.

Valentina Gueorguieva is an associate professor at the Department of Cultural Studies of the University of Sofia 'St. Kliment Okrhidski' (Bulgaria). Her research interests are in youth cultures and social movements, and political anthropology. She authored a number of academic publications, as well as popular readings. Recently, she published the research monograph *The Multitudes of Discontent* (2017, in Bulgarian), based on her anthropological fieldwork on protest movements in Bulgaria 2009–2013.

Gal Kirn works at the TU Dresden as an open topic fellow. He holds a PhD in political philosophy from the University of Nova Gorica (2012). He was a researcher at the Jan van Eyck Academie in Maastricht (2008–2010) and a research fellow at ICI Berlin (2010–2012). He received a fellowship at the Akademie Schloss Solitude in Stuttgart (2015) and was a postdoctoral fellow of the Humboldt-Foundation (2013–2016). He has been teaching courses in film, philosophy and contemporary political theory at the Freie Universität Berlin and Justus-Liebig-Universität Gießen. Kirn published *Partisan Ruptures and Contradictions of Market Socialism in Yugoslavia* at Sophija (2014) and is a co-editor (with Marian Burchardt) of *Beyond Neoliberalism: Social Analysis after 1989* (Palgrave Macmillan, 2017). He is also the editor of *Post-Fordism and its Discontents* (JvE Academie, B-Books and Mirovni Inštitut, 2010).

Mark Kramer is the director of Cold War Studies at Harvard University and a Senior Fellow of Harvard's Davis Center for Russian and Eurasian Studies. Originally trained in mathematics, he went on to study International Relations as a Rhodes Scholar at Oxford University and an Academy Scholar in Harvard's Academy of International and Area Studies. He is the author of many books and articles about a wide variety of topics.

Željka Lekić-Subašić is a TV journalist and producer, currently working as the head of the ERNO (Eurovision News Exchange for Southeast Europe) Coordination Office in Sarajevo, Bosnia and Herzegovina and as the assistant professor at the Sarajevo School of Science and Technology, Department for Political Science and International Relations. She holds a PhD from London Metropolitan University, MA from La Sapienza University in Rome and bachelor's degree in journalism from the Faculty of Political Science, Sarajevo University. She is the winner of the 2014 Dr. Erhard Busek – SEEMO Award for Better Understanding in Southeast Europe.

Chiara Milan is a Post-doctoral Research Fellow at the Institute of Humanities and Social Sciences, Scuola Normale Superiore, where she is part of the Centre on Social Movement Studies (COSMOS) research team. She holds a PhD in Political and Social Sciences from the European University Institute (EUI) and in fall 2016–2017, was a Visiting Fellow at the Centre for Southeast European Studies of the University of Graz (Austria). Since 2010, she has conducted extensive research on the dynamics of mobilisation and collective action in the Yugoslav successor states, with a specific focus on Bosnia-Herzegovina. She also investigated grassroots initiatives in solidarity with refugees along the Western Balkans route and in Austria in the context of the 2015–2016 so-called refugee crisis. Her main research interests include contentious politics, urban grassroots movements, nationalism and migration. She has published articles in international peer-reviewed journals and chapters in edited volumes on the dynamics of mobilisation in the Yugoslav successor states.

Leonidas Oikonomakis holds a PhD in Social and Political Sciences from the European University Institute (EUI), is a researcher affiliated with the Centre on Social Movement Studies (COSMOS) at the Scuola Normale Superiore and is currently teaching at the Department of Sociology of the University of Crete. His research and teaching focuses on Latin American politics, social

x *Contributors*

movements, autonomy, revolutions, electoral politics and the commons. He is also a rapper with hip-hop formation Social Waste and a member of the editorial collective of *ROAR Magazine*. He is the author of the forthcoming monograph *The Zapatistas and Bolivian Cocaleros Road to Change: Political Strategizing with(out) the State* (Palgrave, Latin American Series) and has published articles in international peer-reviewed journals and chapters in edited volumes on social movements in Latin America and Southern Europe.

Kostis Plevris has effectuated his PhD thesis in the University of Paris 1 Panthéon-Sorbonne in the field of urban geography, studying economic uneven development in post-1989 Balkans and its analogues in the urban form. He has visited the cities of the peninsula multiple times as a visitor of universities and has proposed concrete modelisations of post-socialist urbanisation in different scales, taking into account empirical and theoretical issues that he analysed during his research. Currently, he is working as a civil engineer using his bachelor's degree in the construction field with Médecins Sans Frontières in international humanitarian missions.

Marius I. Tatar, PhD, is a lecturer in the Department of Political Science and Communication Studies at the University of Oradea, Romania. His research interests are in the nexus between various forms of citizen participation and democratisation in post-communist contexts. These topics have been analysed both in his MA thesis (2005, Central European University – Budapest) and PhD thesis (2011, University of Bucharest/Oradea) as well as during three postdoctoral fellowships carried out at the Institute for Human Sciences (IWM) in Vienna (2013), the University of Debrecen in Hungary (2014) and the University of Lausanne, Switzerland (2015–2016).

Heiko Wimmen is the director for Iraq, Syria and Lebanon at International Crisis Group, the independent organisation working to prevent wars and shape policies that help promote peace and prevent deadly conflict. Prior to joining Crisis Group, he was an associate researcher at the German Institute of International and Security Affairs in Berlin and the deputy director in the Middle East office at the Heinrich Böll Foundation in Beirut. His research focuses on political activism in divided societies, identity politics and institution building in post-conflict environments.

Introduction

Social movements and protests in Southeast Europe – a new tragedy of the commons?

Dario Brentin and Florian Bieber

Over the last decade, social movements have been at the very centre of political struggle in Southeast Europe. Tackling a wide range of issues and concerns (including austerity, the privatisation of public space, the (non-)provision of welfare and public utilities, poverty, corruption, bureaucratic inefficiency, environmental concerns and authoritarian tendencies), these protests have at times shook the very basis of established political systems from Maribor to Istanbul. Although often focusing on particular issues, the protests repeatedly served as conduits for broader political, social and economic discontent and are thus a serious challenge to ruling political elites in the region (and beyond). We continuously witnessed the transformation of ostensibly 'apolitical' opposition against tangible issues into an articulation of a much more fundamental disagreement with the reigning political culture. Heterogeneous in nature and impact, these past and present protest movements, however, have to be understood as part of a larger wave of social movements that took place globally: from Occupy Wall Street in the US to the Maidan Square in the Ukraine, from Gezi Park in Turkey to Tahrir Square in Egypt.

This edited volume aims to encompass, portray and analyse the diverse nature of Southeast European protests that took place over roughly the last decade in their heterogeneity and plurality.[1] At the same time, the contribution also tries to illustrate that there is something tying these protests together as a regional phenomenon. They share many characteristics with other movements around the world and particular in the Mediterranean region, from Spain to Egypt. Whereas some took place against the authoritarian regimes in the Arab world, others vented their frustration against democratically elected governments. We hence argue that by mapping the plurality of participants and the specificities of the individual protests in the larger Southeast European regional context, one can identify similarities that transcend one particular regime type. More significantly, we postulate that the protest movements in question all share a sense of grievance with the way the authorities administer the common good, public spaces and the state, both in authoritarian as well as democratic societies.

The study of social movements as a 'counterweight to oppressive power' and 'as a summons to popular action against a wide range of scourges' (Tilly and Wood 2016: 3) has established itself as a cornerstone in contemporary social studies drawing inspiration from a long academic tradition (see Tilly 1995; Diani and

2 *Dario Brentin and Florian Bieber*

Della Porta 2006; Della Porta 2013; Tilly and Tarrow 2015). Many of the case studies presented in this volume, however, represent social movements in the particular context of a European austerity regime in the continent's semi-periphery (Della Porta 2015). This distinguishes them from the previous global waves of protests as a wave of social movements that articulates political demands beyond the labour movement and the identitarian focus of the new social movements during the 1980s. As mentioned, the protests often used and adapted frames from other (global and regional) social movements and were furthermore in communication with one another. Sharing the context of (formally) democratic political systems, they mainly occurred in countries affected by the economic crisis and its aftermath (Della Porta 2015). The anti-austerity context in the region (and beyond) has thus led scholars to argue that there is a return of 'class' and 'capitalism' as both a category of analysis and an element of contestation (see Kalb and Halmai 2011; Della Porta 2015). The protest movements furthermore shared being held in the European (semi-)periphery, where the sense of powerlessness is compounded by an unresponsive elite and a (perceived) lack of agency over larger socio-economic processes.

Despite a number of studies by authors from the region itself (see Arsenijević 2014; Bibić et al. 2014; Horvat and Štiks 2015), more general publications on social movements in Europe regularly fail to systematically address developments in Southeast Europe (see e.g. Fominaya and Cox 2013; Fillieule and Accornero 2016). Whereas significant focus is dedicated to developments in Turkey and Greece, particularly the post-Yugoslav space is often omitted from the overall analysis. This edited volume hence aims to bridge that scholarly gap and offers a number of case studies that discuss parallels as well as differences in the recent wave of social movements and protests within the Southeast European region vis-à-vis a wider European and global perspective.

The struggle for the commons

Virtually every country in Southeast Europe has witnessed mass protests over the last decade. Although anti-austerity movements in Greece and the mass opposition to the development of Gezi Park in Istanbul and the subsequent attempts to violently contain protestors in Turkey have been the most prominent, no state has been left unaffected by the newest wave of social movements. Although many protests focused on fairly particular and tangible issues, such as public spaces, corruption, speeding fines or mining projects, demonstrations frequently served as conduits for broader social and political discontent, as rallying points for citizens to demand fundamental political and social transformation of their societies. As such, mass protests have over the years contributed to the fall of government in Slovenia, the resignation of Bulgarian Prime Minister Boyko Borisov and the defeat of certain unpopular policies and practices such as the Romanian healthcare bill and legislation increasing the threshold for anti-corruption investigations. Perhaps most significantly, they led to the creation of dynamic political and social actors and the significant realignment of political space.

Introduction 3

In 1968, Garrett Hardin wrote his influential essay 'The Tragedy of the Commons', in which he argued that common goods are easily depleted by individuals seeking to maximise their own short-term interests to the disadvantage of the common good. The modern answer for this collective action problem is the state, which can regulate the commons and prevent its depletion. The protests that have shaken governments in Southeast Europe draw our attention to a *new tragedy of the commons*: what if the state is unwilling or unable to protect the commons? The dilemma itself is by no means new and the abuse of the commons for the benefit of a few has existed in political systems around the world for decades. However, this dynamic has not been as central to social movements as it has in recent years. The wave of protests in the 1970s and 1980s culminating in 1989 was focused on authoritarian and totalitarian regimes, whereas recent protests focused on both democracies and authoritarian systems, which share an elite perceived to be depleting the common good for the benefit of narrow interest groups.

The protest movements arose over the use of common goods for private, often commercial interest. For example, the transformation of Gezi Park in Istanbul into a shopping centre and similar projects for Picin Park in Bosnia-Herzegovina's second largest city, Banja Luka, and in the Albanian capital, Tirana, triggered protests. In next door Skopje, the capital of Macedonia, architectural students and citizens protested against the transformation of the city centre through the government building project 'Skopje 2014'. In Maribor, Slovenia, protests were triggered in November 2012 after Mayor Franc Kangler signed a partnership with a private company to establish a traffic safety system – with most profits remaining with the company – that resulted in thousands of citizens receiving gratuitous fines. In Romania, the Roşia Montană mining project threatened to destroy the commons' countryside through open pit gold mining. Furthermore, there is the perceived failure of political elites to act in the interest of the common good. In the Bosnian-Herzegovinian capital, Sarajevo, protesters blocked parliament in June 2013 after it failed to pass a law to overcome an impasse over issuing ID numbers that prevented newborns from obtaining identity documents and thus passports to travel – a failure that was life-threatening for babies requiring medical assistance abroad. The protests erupted again in 2014, this time countrywide and more violent. Spreading from the city of Tuzla, where demonstrators protesting over unemployment clashed with security forces, the so-called 'Bosnian Spring' became a short-lived but intense protest movement demanding substantial change and the end of decades of political inertia. Similarly, in Bulgaria in 2013, two waves of protests shaped the country's politics. The first protests from January to March 2013 were directed against high electricity prices and the political elite more broadly for failing to represent citizens' interests. After early elections, the new government named a controversial media tycoon to the post of security chief, triggering a second wave of protests. These were directed against the political elite and their focus on private interests over the common good. Greece has seen multiple protest waves, especially between 2010 and 2012, against the austerity measures of the government. More recently, the citizens of Belgrade have

4 *Dario Brentin and Florian Bieber*

taken to the streets to protest the project 'Belgrade Waterfront' and the destruction of buildings in the adjacent Sava Mala district. Elsewhere in the region, football fans, disappointed with the way their clubs are run, engaged in various forms of social protest to protect or (re-)gain control of something they considered to be a common good.

Southeast European (non-)specificities

A striking aspect of the protests in Southeast Europe has been that they took place in democracies that have undergone profound transformation since the 1990s. Yet the grievances expressed in the protests highlight the inadequacies of democratic transition in these countries. The introduction of representative democracy and market economies has been unable to provide for good governance that focuses on the *common good*. In some cases, protests highlighted ideological differences over the role of the state and the degree to which the state should be privatised. In most cases, however, the dissatisfaction of protesting citizens was less ideological, but focused on the evident state capture by predatory political elites. Informal networks of private interest have particularly dominated parties and, by extent, the state in post-communist countries of the region. The discourse of Europeanisation or representing ethno-national interests has been utilised to disguise these private interests and led to a weakening of the state. This dynamic has been compounded by neoliberal reforms and a more social-democratic understanding of the state by most citizens in the region. The global economic crisis since 2008 has further been a conduit for the protests as economic hardship and austerity accentuated the gap between the social groups that gained from the state captures and those that did not. As such, the protests' success cannot be measured by the number of government resignations or a simple fulfilment of a particular demand – by these standards, most protests have been successful. Instead, the larger paradigm of democratic and economic transition has been challenged, but what is lacking is a clear alternative. In particular, the European Union (EU) and its integration process have not provided an answer as to how to control political elites and secure them to act in the interest of the common good. This is in part because the EU enlargement towards Southeast Europe has failed to sufficiently transform the polities of the region and also lacks mechanisms to monitor governance after a country joins the EU. Furthermore, the discourse of Europeanisation and EU integration has become so ubiquitous that it was shared by the Turkish government of Recep Tayyip Erdoğan and the protestors in Taksim, the ethno-nationalist elites in Bosnia-Herzegovina and those opposing them, and governments and their opponents elsewhere in the region. This broad consensus weakens the transformative capacity of the EU.

In the region itself, the process of Europeanisation, i.e. the adoption of norms and roles of the EU and the policy prescription of the core EU, has been described as the primary driver of reform in recent decades (Noutcheva 2016). Yet at the same time, this process has been presented by local elites as being without alternatives and thus serves as a useful guise to pursue self-serving interests. As a consequence, protests have sought to reclaim agency and choice. Manifested in their predominantly horizontal nature, it furthermore often resulted in a categorical refusal of protest groups to align themselves with established political parties and elites. The refusal and/or incapability to institutionalise opposition towards the dominant form of politics often led to experimentation with new forms of grassroots and direct representativeness, mainly through people's assemblies throughout the region.

Research on these new social movements reflects some of the dilemmas of the movements themselves. Scholars from the neo-Marxist perspective emphasise the shared scepticism of neoliberal policies and the consequences of the global economic crisis as a shared framework. On the other hand, scholars of democratisation processes are more likely to focus on the inadequacies of democracy and rule of law in the countries that witnessed mass protests. As a result, these perspectives lead to divergent views on whether the EU and the integration process are a cause of the social grievances through neoliberal reforms or a tool to remedy the inadequacies of unconsolidated democracies. Rather than viewing these two approaches as irreconcilable alternatives, we argue that they are commonalities. The critique of neoliberal policies helps explain how economic and political transformation has failed to deliver states that respond to citizens' needs and protect from predatory elites. Yet the emphasis on democratisation and rule of law highlight why some liberal democratic market economies have been able to mitigate the economic crisis and respond to citizen demands.

Leftist groups from some parts of the protest movements to the most prominent new left party in the region, *SYRIZA* in Greece, sought to challenge the EU and discuss alternative economic and political models. Yet these remained vague and much of the debate focused on what they oppose rather than on viable alternatives. They also neglected to recognise that market economy and representative democracy as such were not a problem, as demonstrated by a variety of these across Europe that are widely accepted by citizens. Instead, the core problem remains weak institutions that are easy prey to the dominance of strong parties driven by narrow interests. However, transforming the institutional landscape and new political alternatives that break with this pattern remain sketchy. As such, protests have largely subsided across the region although grievances persist. The new tragedy of the common remains: how to insure that the state seeks to define and then protect the common good.

Chapter overviews

The following chapters map and examine social movements and protests from a number of Southeast European countries: Slovenia, Bosnia-Herzegovina, Bulgaria, Romania, Greece and Turkey. Methodologically, the contributions encompass a variety of approaches, but predominately rely on qualitative datasets acquired through ethnographic material, interviews and surveys. They offer a bottom-up perspective, asking who are the people protesting and what are the triggers for protest while at the same time highlighting activist perspectives.

6   *Dario Brentin and Florian Bieber*

The volume opens with a chapter by Heiko Wimmen, who analyses the options and limits of non-formal protest movements operating within a dysfunctional system of institutionalised (ethnic) power sharing. Dissecting the rise of civic activism in Bosnia-Herzegovina (BiH) between 2005 and 2013, Wimmen examines how and to what degree these forms of engagement may compensate for the specific shortcomings of the BiH political system. He argues that despite limitations of the BiH power-sharing system, (spontaneous) social movements represent a significant potential to generate substantial change in the relationship between citizens, as well as in the country's political sphere.

Gal Kirn's chapter opens with the working hypothesis that political outbursts happening on the European (semi-)periphery should not be seen as pure coincidence, but rather a deeper historical sign and sequence of post-socialist transition. Kirn offers a historical analysis of the largest workers' protests in the history of socialist Slovenia, occurring in June 1988 in Maribor, and compares them to the outbreak of protests in 2012–2013. Following the process of the disenchantment with post-socialist transition and certain negative tendencies of capitalist modernisation, the second part of the chapter provides a political analysis of the irruption of mass protests. Kirn argues that the events were unexpected, with the complete absence of major established political parties illustrating the point. However, the democratic irruption and articulation of popular discontent of 2012–2013 powerfully illustrated the crisis of representative democracy and neoliberal answers to the economic crisis (austerity), but more importantly, opened a space for the emergence of new political groups and parties.

In a similar vein, Valentina Gueorguieva based her contribution on extensive ethnographic research conducted during the 2012–2013 protests in Bulgaria. She argues that although Southern European protesters and the global Occupy movement questioned austerity policies and neoliberalism as the doctrine of minimal state intervention, the Bulgarian case with its demands for a stronger state, political responsibility and citizens' control featured a certain degree of local specificity. Contrary to many other protests in the region, protesters demanded participation, but at the same time embraced a vertical organisation of their own movement, demanded the resignation of the government and engaged in the opposition parties' struggles for power. Paradoxically, the demand for citizens' control and the protection of public goods resulting from that strategy was juxtaposed with trust that the same bureaucratic apparatus of the state identified as corrupted and ineffective would provide for it.

The volume continues with a contribution by Kostis Plevris, who addresses the spatiality of social mobilisation during the peak of the austerity crisis in Greece. The chapter examines the intricate ways in which space defines, develops, but also restrains the articulation of protest. Plevris elaborates how the study of space has to be understood as a necessary condition to agree conceptual schemes with social reality, but also how it laid a central role in the reassertion of the right of each mobilisation to a distinct and particular space. Plevris argues that spatial claims culminated after 2008, diffused in society and evolved to certain awareness that social struggle is grounded in space and, in turn, only a particular space (working spaces, squares, etc.) enables social struggle to flourish.

Focusing on the visual aspects of protests, Ksenija Berk analyses how posters cannot only be described as a medium with which dissent is situated, but also as places of deeper cultural and ideological exchange. In her chapter, Berk explores the ideological underside of the Slovenian uprising in 2012–2013 and argues that these (posters, flags, banners, puppets, masks and other artworks) with their oftentimes ironic commentary on social reality contributed to successfully intertwining the protesters' mentality with a complex image discourse for a political cause. Berk demonstrates how the Slovene protests had strong connections to the nation's past, manifested in various visual symbols predominantly from earlier revolutions and the period of socialism, and concludes that the strength of the visual material was in the successful connections between various semantic levels to form a single unified message demanding resignation from corrupt politicians.

Željka Lekić-Subašić highlights the usage of social media platforms (Facebook, Twitter and YouTube) as an important distinction that prominently shaped recent protest movements in Southeast Europe. The chapter focuses on the JMBG protests in Bosnia-Herzegovina and the ways that social media was used to mobilise and communicate during the protests. Concluding, Lekić-Subašić argues that social media cannot be considered a tool of democratisation per se, but that these platforms nonetheless represent an important source of information for the wider public and, more importantly, a communication tool for the protest organisers, particularly in early stages of the protests.

In an effort to compare the triggers of protests in Greece, Turkey and Bosnian-Herzegovina, Chiara Milan and Leonidas Oikonomakis examine why some single-issue protests evolve into resonant mass protests and why others fail to convincingly articulate a more systemic critique of representational democracy. Exploring the cases of austerity measures in Greece, the destruction of Gezi Park and the failure of BiH authorities to distribute national ID numbers, they argue that these cases were all expressions of dissatisfaction with a political system deemed incapable of addressing issues of concern to the protesters. However, only in Greece and Turkey did the protests transcend the single-issue aspect and morph into a crisis of legitimacy of the representational political system as a whole. The reason for this lies in the pre-existence of significant political movement networks that could be activated, as well as the existence of movements with experience in horizontal decision-making and direct democracy.

Marius Tatar examines the dynamics and determinants of different forms of protest activities in Southeast Europe. He follows a longitudinal approach using statistical analysis of survey datasets, thereby capturing the dynamism of the phenomena allowing for both a single-country analysis and cross-national comparison. Tatar's contribution aims to profile different types of protesters and their elite-challenging protest action repertoire, as well as factors that may account for their preference for certain forms of protest actions over others. The chapter ultimately illustrates the implications for our understanding of how protest action repertoires are reconfigured in post-communist societies and their consequences for democratic governance in the region.

Concluding, Mark Kramer explores how the calculations and efforts of anti-regime protesters can be influenced by external actors, focusing on the mass

8 *Dario Brentin and Florian Bieber*

protests in Bulgaria, Romania and Turkey in 2013. These external actors include foreign governments, foreign media outlets, international organisations, transnational movements, foreign individuals and groups, and other entities, of which some affected the protests only inadvertently, whereas others took steps to instigate or fuel protests, and still others sought to prevent or curb unrest. Kramer illustrates the various ways in which the specific nature of political protest in the Balkans was influenced and discusses how external actors can affect the likelihood that a protest movement succeeds.

Note

1 This volume is based on revised contributions from the conference 'Rebellion and Protest from Maribor to Taksim: Social Movements in the Balkans', held at the University of Graz and organised by the Centre for Southeast European Studies.

References

Arsenijević, D. ed. 2014. *Unbribable Bosnia-Herzegovina: The Fight for the Commons*. Baden-Baden: Nomos Verlag.

Bibić, V., A. Milat, S. Horvat, and I. Štiks. eds. 2014. *The Balkan Forum: Situations, Struggles, Strategies*. Zagreb: Bijeli Val.

Della Porta, D. 2013. *Can Democracy Be Saved? Participation, Deliberation, and Social Movements*. Cambridge: Polity Press.

Della Porta, D. 2015. *Social Movements in Times of Austerity: Bringing Capitalism Back Into Protest Analysis*. Cambridge: Polity.

Diani, M. and D. Della Porta. 2006. *Social Movements: An Introduction*. Oxford: Blackwell.

Fillieule, O. and G. Accornero. eds. 2016. *Social Movement Studies in Europe: The State of the Art*. Oxford: Berghahn.

Flesher Fominaya, C. and L. Laurence. eds. 2013. *Understanding European Movements: New Social Movements, Global Justice Struggles, Anti-Austerity Protest*. Abingdon: Routledge.

Hardin, G. 1968. The Tragedy of the Commons. *Science* 162(3859): 1243–1248.

Horvat, S. and I. Štiks. eds. 2015. *Welcome to the Desert of Post-Socialism: Radical Politics After Yugoslavia*. London: Verso.

Kalb, D. and G. Halmai. eds. 2011. *Headlines of Nation, Subtext of Class: Working-Class Populism and the Return of the Repressed in Neoliberal Europe*. New York and Oxford: Berghahn Books.

Noutcheva, G. 2016. Societal Empowerment and Europeanization: Revisiting the EU's Impact on Democratization. *Journal of Common Market Studies* 54(3): 691–708.

Tilly, C. 1995. *Popular Contention in Great Britain, 1758–1834*. Cambridge, MA: Harvard University Press.

Tilly, C. and S. Tarrow. 2015. *Contentious Politics: Second Edition, Revised and Updated*. Oxford: Oxford University Press.

Tilly, C. and L.J. Wood. 2016. *Social Movements 1768–2012*. London and New York: Routledge.

1 Divided they stand

Peace building, state reconstruction and informal political movements in Bosnia-Herzegovina, 2005–2013

Heiko Wimmen

Introduction

Since the early 2000s, Bosnia-Herzegovina (BiH) has seen a growing level of civic activism, and a corresponding increase in its intensity. Groups of citizens are taking initiative and engaging in contentious action to influence governance and politics for the benefit of society as they perceive it, rather than marching at the behest and in support of political actors and agendas. On the one hand, growing numbers of mostly young Bosnians have begun to express discontent and a desire for change. On the other, local non-governmental organisation (NGO) professionals and external donors have come to see bottom-up citizen involvement as an effective supplement to larger strategies that attempt to work via 'civil society' to improve governance and accountability, and to reduce the political salience of ethno-national antagonisms (USAID 2008). By 2015, spontaneous, decentralised protests, which on some occasions grow into (ephemeral) informal political movements, have become a normal(ised) aspect of Bosnian politics. They provide an alternative (and often the only) mode of interaction with public affairs for citizens who are profoundly alienated by a political system that has recycled the same actors and impasses over the past two decades, while rampant unemployment, dilapidating infrastructure and corruption remain unaddressed.

This chapter investigates the rise and gradual normalisation of (mostly) informal civic activism in BiH between 2005 and 2013, and asks if, how and to what degree these forms of citizens' engagement may compensate for the specific shortcomings of the Bosnian political system. It discusses whether they contribute to a gradual process of replacing ethno-nationalist identifications with a shared sense of Bosnian citizenship, as proposed by peace-building theory and practitioners, and some local observers and activists themselves (e.g. Mujkić 2013; Štiks 2013). To this end, the chapter discusses the attempt to strategically initiate statewide citizen involvement undertaken by the NGO-coalition GROZD in 2005, the activist-led movement *Dosta!* [Enough!] launched in Sarajevo around the same time, and the first attempts at organised resistance against the semi-authoritarian rule of nationalist parties in Republika Srpska in 2010–2011. The summer of protest against high-handed local rule in the entity capital Banja Luka in 2012, and that

10 *Heiko Wimmen*

against the suspension of national identification numbers (JMGB) in Sarajevo a year later, serve as examples for the emerging pattern of spontaneous and increasingly broad protest movements that erupted in response to perceived moral outrage, but they also shed light on the narrow limits that the Bosnian power-sharing system, continuous ethno-political antagonism and external tutelage still impose on such forms of bottom-up participation.

Civil society and democratic state (re)construction in BiH

Since the early 1990s, the notion that liberal democratic systems provide the most reliable remedy for post-conflict societies has guided international attempts to address the fall-out of intra-state conflicts and pre-empt relapses into violence (Paris 2004).[1] Described by one analyst as a 'Leninist approach to state reconstruction' (Ottaway 2003: 315), the assumption took hold that external actors could, or indeed *should*, become involved in countries emerging from violent conflict, and 'engineer not only new political systems, but also a civil society to underpin those systems' (ibid).

Bosnia-Herzegovina after the 1995 Dayton Peace Accord constitutes a 'maximalist' attempt at such externally led 'democratic state reconstruction' (ibid). After the 1996 elections gave the wartime nationalist leaderships full control over the political process, and as the latter showed little intention to reconstruct themselves voluntarily, external engineers of democracy increasingly looked to 'civil society' for an alternative. Foreign-funded and often foreign-created NGOs developed into an 'indispensable complement to failing top-down strategies' (Belloni 2007: 110) that would invest the decrees of international bureaucrats with a semblance of democratic legitimacy and provide cost-effective service delivery. Civil society organisations (CSOs) were also considered 'schools for democracy in the Tocquevillian sense' and expected to reduce the hold of the nationalist political elites over the electorate (Fagan 2005: 7) by contributing to reconciliation. Cooperation between individuals of different ethno-national identification along shared issues and in interaction with society and political actors would create a unified Bosnian political sphere and constituencies for multi- or non-ethnic parties. Such high expectations, caustically described by Michael Foley (2010: 181) as 'the assimilationist prejudices of the American civil religion',[2] were concisely expressed by Bruce Hemmer (2009: 61) of the Democratisation Office of the Sarajevo OSCE office between 1998 and 1999: 'New civil society must be added that is voluntary, issue-based, multi-ethnic, internally democratic and liberal in ideology [. . .] These associations will eventually knit the society together across ethnic lines and undermine divisive ethnic politics'.

Thus, by the mid-2000s, a number of professionalised, locally run advocacy CSOs had emerged and were becoming involved in the governance processes, not least at the insistence of foreign donors and governments (Fagan 2005: 412f). This 'civil sector' has been criticised for many of the same flaws observed elsewhere (donor-dependence, lack of representativeness, etc.). However, for reasons that critics relate to the specific approach to state-building applied in Bosnia – in

Divided they stand 11

particular, transferring decisive power from locally elected to internationally appointed institutions (Belloni 2001), and re-defining political issues as technical questions of governance (Chandler 2005) – these strategies also fell short on some of the larger objectives that had motivated donor assistance: ethno-nationalist rhetoric would still trump any debate on government performance and quality of governance, and obliterate attempts to establish accountability. The overwhelming majority of Bosnian citizens, on the other hand, increasingly viewed politics and public affairs with cynicism and disdain, rather than engaging in 'active participation [. . .], buoyed by a strong, plural, associational base' (Smillie 1996: 13, quoted in Chandler 2000: 135), let alone building bridges of trust and shared interests across the ethnic divides.

Bottom-up, top-down: the inconclusive experience of GROZD

Motivated by this modest balance sheet, in summer 2005, a number of established Bosnian NGOs embarked on an ambitious project to turn this trend around and generate broad bottom-up engagement in public affairs through top-down initiatives (RI Mrđa 2011).[3] Upcoming 2006 general elections would be the occasion and lever to make political actors more responsive to their electoral basis, and thus initiate a virtuous cycle prompting more citizens to become active members of the polity. To upend the logic of zero-sum ethno-political competition, the *Građansko Organizovanje Za Demokratiju* [Citizens organise for Democracy (GROZD)] coalition promoted 'moving away from the nationalist rhetoric, and focusing on what matters [. . .] employment, better health care, a better education system' (RI Isanović 2011).

Accordingly, the first campaign phase focused on publicly establishing that a significant part of the Bosnian citizenry indeed considered such issues to be important. Two rounds of town-hall meetings, convened in nearly all of Bosnia's 143 municipalities, yielded 12 core demands of a predominantly social nature. As elections approached, signatures were collected under this so-called 'Citizens Platform', political parties were canvassed to commit themselves to it, research was commissioned to establish its feasibility, and working groups evaluated parties' programmes in its light (RI Bajić 2010). The findings were released and a demonstration held outside parliament at the end of the official campaign period on September 30.[4] The expectation was that linking performance on issues to electoral decisions would reduce the traction of nationalist rhetoric and convince the growing percentage of abstainers that their vote mattered.[5]

Initially, the strategy appeared to be a stunning success. The public debates attracted large audiences, and GROZD became a recognised name across the post-Yugoslav space (RI Šero 2010). From a core group of six NGOs, the coalition grew to more than 400 organisations fielding some 500 volunteers who collected more than 500,000 signatures under the 'Citizens Platform' (equivalent to nearly 40% of the turnout for the 2002 polls), while 30 parties committed to implementing the platform.

12   Heiko Wimmen

Despite this massive response, the impact on the 2006 elections fell short of expectations. Participation improved only slightly in the parliamentary and declined in the presidential ballot.[6] The two parties whose platforms fared best in the GROZD evaluation (SDP and NSRzB, both committed to a multi-ethnic Bosnia) achieved only marginal gains.[7] The party that had performed *worst*, SBiH, scored a resounding victory, nearly doubling its electoral support. The programme of the second big winner, SNSD in Republika Srpska, fared well in the evaluation (owing partly to coaching by international actors[8]), yet the party refused to commit itself to the 'Citizens Platform'. Post-electoral assessments concur that its success, just as that of SBiH, was primarily owed to the heated exchange of nationalist rhetoric between the two party leaders, Milorad Dodik and Haris Silajdžić. Although GROZD organisers quote the broad response to their campaign as evidence that 'we all have the same problems here, no matter what your nationality or religion is' (RI Isanović 2011), this did not translate into election results or leverage over political actors. In 2006, most voters still limited their desire for change to exchanging one nationalist option for the other.

This should not have come as a complete surprise. Because GROZD claimed to be an impartial platform for expressing 'what citizens really want', with the implication that a broad social consensus existed somewhere beyond the fray of ethno-national politics, it could not openly take positions against the nationalist parties, which most organisers considered to be unfit to govern. The hope that the public debates would nudge a sizeable number of voters towards the same conclusion turned out to be overly optimistic. At least in the short term, GROZD thus (once more) underlined the limits of a strategy 'to achieve heady political objectives but through using apolitical means' (Fagan 2005: 408). As one of the founding organisations concluded, 'the NGO sector had no strength or clear strategy to support a certain political option in a concrete way', preferring to 'stay "non-party-political"', and avoid engaging directly on party-political matters, which impedes the full unmasking of politicians' (NGO Infohouse 2006: 11).

Furthermore, to build as broad a support base as possible, GROZD studiously avoided antagonising the nationalist mainstream. Where the campaign material included attacks on nationalist *politicians*, such critique was carefully balanced to target representatives from all three ethnic communities,[9] while avoiding any positioning that could have been construed as favouring one of the three nationalist narratives over the others, or questioning the validity of nationalism as such – quite on the contrary:

> If we have to be nationalists in this country, let's be *more demanding nationalists*. I am Muslim, let's say, so I am a nationalist, but let me think how I live. *As a Muslim*, I will make pressure on my *Muslim* representative to have a better life.
>
> (RI Bajić 2010)

The GROZD strategy thus amounted to *side-stepping* the ideological agendas of nationalist politicians, attacking instead where the campaigners thought them

Divided they stand 13

vulnerable. On the mobilisation level, it mostly worked through *local* networks, meaning that it either remained confined to one ethnic community or relied on and reproduced locally conditioned patterns of ethnic relations, rather than creating the broad cross-cleavage cooperation around shared issues coveted by peace builders.[10]

The *Centar za promociju civilnog društvo* [Centre for Civil Society Promotion (CPCD)], the main interface between GROZD and the grassroots, was perhaps uniquely placed to achieve mobilisation in all three ethno-national communities. Originally established in 1996 as a publishing house providing documentation and translations of international norms and agreements, it had evolved into a resource centre for other CSOs and a sub-donor for USAID. By 2006, it had thus established a far-flung network across all of BiH, and its long-standing working relationships with local partner organisations obliterated the fact that CPCD itself was headquartered in Sarajevo, which otherwise leads many Bosnians with Serb or Croat nationalist orientation to label and reject organisations as 'Muslim'[11] (RI Mrđa 2011). Attempts to discredit the initiative as yet another Sarajevo-based machination to change the ethno-national status quo thus appeared less plausible than on other occasions.[12] After all, citizens of all nationalities in Bosniak, Croat and Serb-dominated areas alike were equally encouraged to ask their representatives to create jobs and reduce poverty, and this under the auspices of organisations with long-standing credibility in the (ethnic) polities that these politicians were supposedly representing. Working on the local level and through organisations with a developmental focus also helped to steer clear of the larger controversies of Bosnian politics, i.e. the questions of ethnic relations and state organisation. Thus, even Bosnians with nationalist opinions on all sides of the ethnic divides could subscribe to GROZD or be active in it without feeling at dissonance with, let alone disavowing, their mutually exclusive preferences for the organisation of the country.[13]

Thus, it remains questionable whether 'the fact that so many people of all ethnic backgrounds cooperated and signed a petition stating their main concerns for the future of BiH implicitly points to the possible emergence of a new pattern of identification and the possible development of a sense of Bosnian nationhood' (Touquet and Vermeersch 2008: 279, for a similar perspective, see Bodruzic 2010). Rather, GROZD achieved what could be described as a mobilisation that occurred *parallel to* rather than *cutting across* the dominant ethnic cleavage lines. According to the original plan, 2006 was supposed to be only the beginning – after the polls, the performance of elected Members of Parliament (MPs) would be monitored and measured against the Citizen Platform. Conceivably, this could have exposed the gap between the expectations of citizens and the performance of politicians elected on the account of overt nationalism, in hopes that the lesson would sink in before the next round.[14] However, after the elections, the coalition quickly dispersed, and although some of the participating organisations continue monitoring activities today, the public impact of these (often highly technical) accounts remains negligible (Evenson and Marchenko 2011). For many of the founders, GROZD had, in any case, not been about establishing yet another CSO,

14   *Heiko Wimmen*

but about jumpstarting a dynamic that would prompt citizens to take initiative on their own: 'The idea was to encourage people to *be* GROZD, to become active by themselves, not to wait for us to come and bring change' (RI Mrđa 2011). Such ideas had, however, already been put into practice beyond the world of formalised NGOs by a younger generation applying different forms of activism.

Dosta! and the ambiguities of 'informal' activism

By the mid-2000s, a new generation of activists entered the public sphere in Sarajevo. Their young age, lack of organisational structures, and non-conventional modes of operation – cyber activism, provocative street action, counter-cultural gatherings – led most seasoned CSO-professionals and the media to initially ignore the newcomers and underestimate their capacity to affect 'serious' politics. Interviews with activists conducted by this researcher indicate that a general sense of exasperation with the externally led state-building project took hold at the time, even or perhaps especially among well-educated Bosnians with good *individual* opportunities, and contributed to their decision to take initiative.[15] Some already had a history of engaging with specific issues that highlighted the shortcomings of institutions, prompting them to intervene more strategically in the sphere of politics. Says Darko Brkan, co-founder of *Zašto Ne*, a group that had campaigned for the right to conscientious objection (CO) to military service since 1999:

> We needed nearly six years to achieve something that the government should have fixed by itself.[16] That was an incentive to create the movement we have now. Let's try to raise the level of citizens' awareness, the power of civil society, form a civic movement that would make it possible for anybody to engage in issues.
>
> (RI Brkan 2010)

Likewise, interaction with international solidarity movements and cultural initiatives, facilitated by digital communication and proficiency in foreign languages well beyond the level of the older generation, familiarised a growing number of young Bosnians with new forms of collective action. In contrast, the bureaucratised and hierarchical world of formal NGOs was hardly attractive to people in their early 20s. What was missing, however, was an initiative to congeal lingering discontent into action.

> As a long term activist, I knew that a person or a group needs to show direct action. So I announced on the Internet forum Sarajevo-X that I would stand on the square outside parliament, and whoever wanted change should join me. For the first week, I was there alone, every day for one hour, and afterwards I wrote on the forum that I was there but nobody came.
>
> (RI Mahmutćehajić 2011)[17]

Divided they stand 15

Eventually, the numbers went up to a few dozen would-be activists in their mid-20s who met daily outside parliament, and who expressed their discontent with the slogan '*Dosta!*'.[18] In January 2006, the *Zašto Ne* group joined, bringing with them a largely informal network of activists across Bosnia. What was still lacking was a larger strategy. Occasionally, protests by disadvantaged groups at the same location, such as agricultural producers, gave an occasion to connect to wider social strata (Lombardo 2011: 61). In March 2006, a hike in energy prices and the first coverage in conventional media triggered a larger turnout (Touquet 2012: 155). The 2006 elections provided another opportunity to gain attention and take aim at the status quo. On one occasion, a convoy of yellow cars – yellow being one of the few colours not identified with any political party – toured the city blasting the sound of bleating sheep over a mounted sound system (RI Mahmutćehajić 2011) to mock uncritical support for non-performing parties. Rock concerts (a time-tested method of the CO campaign) featuring popular anti-nationalist bands from all parts of Bosnia generated large turnouts, underlining that a certain part of the Bosnian youth actively opposed the hegemonic narratives.

Yet how the urge for alternatives could be aggregated into a momentum for change remained controversial within the movement itself. Nationalist parties were clearly seen as adversaries, and similar to the more confrontational GROZD material, many saw their antagonistic posturing as charades staged to divert attention from corrupt wheeling and dealing. An invitation to join GROZD was nevertheless turned down, as most activists scoffed at the 'corrupt civil society' of foreign-funded NGOs organising the campaign. The top-down setup of GROZD and the generational gap between its leadership and the 20-something activists of *Dosta!* also made it unattractive for the latter to become 'foot soldiers' (RI Mahmutćehajić 2011) in a structure in which they would have little agency. It would also have been difficult to reconcile the confrontational and counter-cultural thrust of *Dosta!* with the strategy of maximum inclusiveness pursued by GROZD, which aimed to also reach moderately nationalist mainstream constituencies. Rather, its constituency was the explicitly anti-nationalist urban youth of Sarajevo and other Bosnian cities. Although some participants of *Dosta!* argued that the movement could be complementary to GROZD (RI Brkan 2010), the relationship remained uneasy, and occasionally turned acrimonious.

In addition, unlike GROZD, with its clear orientation on elections and political parties, *Dosta!* had an ambiguous position (or many different positions) vis-à-vis the formal political process. A significant part, perhaps the majority, felt disdain for Bosnian politics as such and argued for a boycott, seeking to build a resistance movement that would usher in a radical transformation towards forms of council democracy. On the other hand, an organisation like *Zašto Ne*, which provided paid employment for some prominent *Dosta!* activists, received a USAID grant to, inter alia, 'increase citizens' participation in the elections' (NGO Infohouse 2006: 8). Thus, although opposition to nationalism as an ideology – and not only to nationalist parties – was a central and consensual aspect of the movement, *Dosta!* refrained from endorsing any of the non-nationalist parties. It did not help that the

16 Heiko Wimmen

only plausible challenger to the nationalists – the Social Democrats – appeared very much as their mirror image, combining the communist legacy of bureaucratic conformism with a hierarchical leadership perceived as part of the political establishment (Lippman 2008) rather than an alternative to it.

Opponents of the boycott strategy felt vindicated by the results of the 2006 elections: 'We were arguing for change, but we did not have our message clear, so Haris Silajžić hijacked it. SBiH was the opposition, and they won by a landslide. And we lost what I think were a crucial four years for Bosnia' (RI Brkan 2010). This experience prompted a partial hiatus in protest action, as the activists were reflecting about more efficient methods to challenge the political establishment. An unexpected occasion occurred on 5 February 2008 when three teenagers fatally stabbed 17-year-old high school student Denis Mrnjavac in a Sarajevo street car. The crime, preceded by similar incidents, highlighted the negligence of the authorities (in this case, the Sarajevo Canton) regarding the problem of juvenile offenders. As so many times before, the *Dosta!* activists called a protest on the following Saturday, 9 February 2008. But unlike before, participation surged to several thousand, clogging much of downtown Sarajevo, and included a significantly broader cross-section of the population. On 13 February 2008 (marking one week since Mrnjavac's death), a new protest was organised in cooperation with NGO representatives speaking in the name of GROZD, explicitly calling for the resignation of the mayor and the cantonal government. Held outside the premises of the latter (conveniently flanked by two open spaces), the second protest drew an even bigger crowd, but turned rough when juvenile protesters pelted the building with stones and battled riot police. Interviews conducted by local media indicated that the issue of public security resonated strongly with many participants, and included expressions of empathy and a desire for collective responsibility,[19] as well as a disdain for the performance of the authorities that far exceeded the actual occasion.[20] Thus, a comparatively minor event generated a narrative with which a significant number of citizens with no activist history strongly identified, thus serving as a catalyst to convert cynicism and resignation into a strong desire to take action and assume responsibility. This mood, however, was completely misread by cantonal Prime Minister Samir Silajdžić (SBiH), who broke into televised rants, explicitly *rejecting* the responsibility demanded from him, and hurling abuse at protestors, who represented a cross-section of his voters. He resigned eight months later after his party suffered a crushing defeat at the municipal polls, for which the activists took credit (RI Brkan 2010).

After the second demonstration, differences arose regarding how to continue. Although some activists pushed to keep up the momentum and escalate the pace, perhaps taking aim at the federation government as well, or occupying the cantonal building (RI Bilić and Huzbašić 2011), others were wary about the violence, and warned against the dangers that the specific Bosnian environment created for contentious action.

> I realised that doing such things in Sarajevo would be welcomed in Belgrade and Banja Luka, and in other places openly calling for secession. If I can be

Divided they stand 17

convinced that at the same time, the same day, we can have similar masses on the streets in Banja Luka, Sarajevo and Mostar, then I would accept *any* kind of activity from those masses. Even open rebellion. But if it's just happening in Sarajevo, or just Banja Luka, it is counter-productive.

(RI Mahmutćehajić 2011)

The 2008 protests indeed failed to resonate beyond the city itself, let alone generate the kind of solidarity Mahmutćehajić was referring to. Although this may relate to the Sarajevo-specific character of the original cause, parallel demonstrations in Banja Luka against the independence of Kosovo underlined that concerns in other parts of Bosnia were still of a different, explicitly nationalist, nature. A significant part of the activists' efforts over the next two years thus went into building up support outside the capital, including the regions still dominated by Serb and Croat nationalism.

A second high-publicity event involving *Dosta!* occurred in early 2009 with a campaign against the prime minister of the Bosniak-Croat Federation, Nedžad Branković (SDA), accused of high-level corruption on many counts.[21] Although such narratives were circulating regarding many Bosnian politicians, they rarely ever damaged a political career, and arguably contributed to cynicism and apathy rather than causing the kind of outrage that would lead to action. Paradoxically, this equation was reversed by what appeared a minor case amidst the many tales of large-scale corruption in BiH: in 2000, Branković, then a member of the Federal Parliament and a chief executive with the state-owned energy provider Energoinvest, had purchased an apartment in the prestigious Sarajevo suburb of Ciglane for just 500 Euro.[22]

What we learned here is that you need something that people can emotionally relate to, that they feel can be part of their own life. An average person cannot grasp the concept of five million Euro. But when you live on 50 sqm with your whole family and he has 150, and when you paid 10s of 1000s of Euros for your 50 sqm and he paid 450 for his 150, everybody can get *that*.

(RI Brkan 2010)

Yet the manipulation itself had already become public in 2007, and received little public attention until, on 10 January 2009, graffiti appeared at the entrance of the building in question asking the 'thief' to return the apartment. Although not even named in person, the prime minister overreacted absurdly, threatened to resign and called emergency meetings over his personal security at a time when a sudden gas crisis amidst Arctic temperatures had thrown Sarajevo into an actual state of emergency. Within hours, a Facebook group by the name 'I am the hooligan who wrote the graffiti' gathered thousands of members who flooded police stations across Sarajevo with faxes and phone calls 'confessing' to the authorship of the graffiti. Crowdfunding provided the group with the means to purchase billboard space, on which they advertised a 'fantastic bargain': apartments ostensibly available for the same conditions that Branković had obtained in 2000. Within days,

18   Heiko Wimmen

the advertising agency pulled the ads under a formal pretext, generating further (free) publicity through speculations about who may have been pulling strings.[23] Sequences of an earlier video interview in which the prime minister, with a smug smile, insisted he had 'forgotten' the details of the deal but that all was 'handled legally', further served to turn Branković into a perfect icon for a class of politicians who had lost any connection to moral standards.[24] Thus, by letting himself be provoked into a blatant, almost comical display of the arrogance of power,[25] Branković became a symbol for all that was wrong in Bosnian politics; in June 2009, he resigned.[26]

Although ousting corrupt politicians must have been gratifying, and arguably created deterrents against future abuse of power, achieving lasting change in the behaviour of political actors nevertheless required broader and more reliably available forms of mobilisation. After the ouster of Branković, the activists attempted to establish an alliance with reformist elements in the largely co-opted Bosnian Trade Union Federation, aiming for a 'march of one million' on Labour Day (May 1) 2010 that would compel the government to open a serious dialogue with social actors. Yet the unions reneged on the alliance shortly before the advertised date, and without their mobilisation machine, the demonstration was reduced to a group of some 500 that barely filled one lane of the huge East-West thoroughfare bisecting the modern parts of Sarajevo. Thus, being unable to mobilise broad grassroots support except in a reactive fashion, by 2010, many *Dosta!* activists had returned to the electoral process, urging voters to measure politicians' performance against the promises made in 2006, checking political programmes against their own interests, and vowing to monitor politicians once parliaments were in session.

This did not only sound close to, but was, for all practical purposes, a continuation of what GROZD had already proposed in 2006. In 2010, the Centre for Civic Initiatives (CCI), originally a creation of the National Democratic Institute (NDI) and a constituent member of GROZD, coordinated a campaign mostly funded by the National Endowment for Democracy (NED), and recruited a host of youth-based, informal or barely formalised groups to push once more for the 2006 'Citizen Platform', evaluate the performance of politicians and get out the vote (RI Isanović 2011). Unlike 2006, however, the 2010 campaign was more explicitly directed against the (nationalist) parties in power, creating the impression that the real purpose was to give a boost to SDP as the one major party that had been in opposition for the past two election cycles. Close personal relations between individual activists and prominent party members, and a particularly close cooperation between NDI and SDP during this period, further nurtured such suspicion (RI Šero 2010; RI Gratz 2011).[27] Former members of SDP reject the idea of a coordinated campaign (RI Bajrović 2013), as do the activists themselves, while at the same time claiming credit for the massive swing vote from Muslim nationalist parties to SDP (RI Brkan 2011).[28] Yet although these results created some optimism that the formal electoral system could, after all, provide a mechanism for change, the performance of the party afterwards served to dash these hopes once more (Toè 2013).

Divided they stand 19

A silver lining in the heart of darkness: activism in Republika Srpska

Banja Luka, the capital city of Republika Srpska (RS), still figures as something of a 'heart of darkness' in many accounts on Bosnia. Seen from Sarajevo, the northern city appears as the centre of unreconstructed nationalism, where ingrained structures of the deep state protected Serb war criminals well into the 2000s, and nationalist parties exercised unchallenged hegemony. As opinion polls confirm, this does not mean that people in the RS are satisfied with the political status quo.[29] The 2006 GROZD campaign had shown that ostensibly non-political associations could potentially be turned into platforms for political demands. Banja Luka was also home to the NED-funded media platform *Buka* (Noise), established by a Bosnian veteran of the Serbian *Otpor* movement, as well as clusters of local dissidents, in particular at the university, some of whom responded to the initiative of the *Dosta!* activists to expand their network. After meetings in Sarajevo and Banja Luka, the activists agreed to create a formally independent group rather than a local chapter of *Dosta!* (as in Federation cities like Zenica, Mostar and Bihać) to avoid the stigma of association with Sarajevo.

Oštra Nula [Sharp Zero] organised street action around social issues starting in late 2009, and participated in the GOTV campaign for the 2010 elections. The first mobilisation for a sizeable protest against the nationalist political elite was, however, initiated from outside this activist milieu. On 3 February 2011, one Stefan Filipović was incensed when RS Prime Minister Milorad Dodik threatened war veterans who were protesting against delayed benefits. Filipović, a student of political science whose own father had fought in the war, created the Facebook group *Glas Naroda* [Voice of the People] and called upon 'the citizens of RS to take to the streets and show the political elite that the voice of the people must be heard'.[30] A flurry of supportive responses eventually led to a meeting with the *Oštra Nula* group, NGO activists and members of the local cell of *Naša Stranka*,[31] who had ventured into activism after the disappointing 2010 elections (RI Pejić 2011). The result was an impromptu alliance for a broad platform of social demands, and a demonstration of some 500 people on 6 February 2011 who marched down the main Boulevard of Banja Luka, shouting 'thieves' as they passed the National Assembly.

Encouraged by this response to a spontaneous and scarcely publicised initiative, the group planned a second protest for 19 March 2011. However, two days beforehand, the state-run news agency SRNA exposed connections between *Oštra Nula* and several Federation-based organisations, highlighting in particular the work of the Youth Initiative for Human Rights (YIHR) for the commemoration of the Srebrenica massacre. *Oštra Nula*, and with it the rest of the alliance, were hence portrayed as supporting the Sarajevo version of the war narrative, tantamount to national treason for the mainstream public opinion in RS.[32] Whether the low turnout on March 19 was related to the news (some bystanders shouted related insults and some organisers received calls from concerned relatives) or to bad weather is hard to judge. The coalition, however, broke apart as a result.

20   *Heiko Wimmen*

According to Filipović, 'with this image, nobody in Banja Luka can work with you' (RI Filipović 2011).[33]

The park and the people

A little more than a year later, a spontaneous wave of protest erupted over a building project for commercial and residential space in the centrally located Banja Luka neighbourhood of Nova Varoš. Although rendered as vacant space on the municipal map, the lot was used as a park by inhabitants of Banja Luka during the day and by street prostitutes plying their trade at night, earning it the nickname *Picin Park*. Yet the lot was never formally recognised as a park and was slated for development in the regulatory plan. Awarding the project to a close associate of Prime Minister Milorad Dodik certainly raised questions, yet all legal procedures were observed, including the mandatory public consultations in the *Mjesna Zajednica*[34] of the area. Persistent warnings of local activists against the accelerated destruction of green spaces had gone without public response. Thus, when the area was finally fenced in for work to begin, the coordinator of the *Centar za Životnu Sredinu* [Center for Environment Health (CZZS)] posted an exasperated comment on the NGO's Facebook page:

> This is exactly what you, the residents of our city, deserve. You do not want to be informed and to engage in activities to prevent further destruction of our city. And you have always elected those who have systematically destroyed the green areas in our city. Ask yourselves what may be the next thing that is irretrievably lost, and what you are willing to do to prevent that.[35]

However, a former *Oštra Nula* activist who came across the post decided that, rather than hoping for more activism in the future, direct action should be taken *now*. In a hurry, he created the Facebook group *Park Je Naš* [The Park is Ours], and added some photos from the CZZS page. Within two hours, the group drew some 2,500 subscribers, growing to over 40,000 within days (RI Ćocić 2013). By the late afternoon, hundreds of protestors were pouring into the park and took possession of the space.

CZZS had expected nothing of this sort, but tried their best to seize the moment. By publicising a list of procedural irregularities, they attempted to invalidate the project's legal status. Pre-established networks, in particular the coalition *re:akcija* established in 2010, helped to bring together some 15 NGOs who petitioned the municipality to put the project on hold (RI Dakić 2012). Yet city officials remained unimpressed and the destruction of the park proceeded apace, accompanied by a media campaign that accused the protesters of serving the political opposition and, inevitably, forces aiming to destabilise RS.

There is no question that the numbers necessary for confrontational tactics – such as establishing a protest camp in the park, or human chains to block the earth-moving machinery – were available, and some activists indeed pressed for such a course. In the end, the majority decided otherwise, and when the bulldozers

Divided they stand   21

moved in, only symbolic gestures were made. A major reason appears to have been the sense that Banja Luka, and perhaps all of BiH, is still a high-risk environment for contentious action:

> It would have given the police the mandate to move against us with force, and we are not willing to enter such a confrontation. These people have no qualms using violence, and there is so much violence in our society, so having this as a peaceful movement is a big achievement.
>
> (RI Dakić 2012)

To the amazement of the seasoned civil society workers, however, the support base established during the initial protest remained even after the park was destroyed. Over the summer, dozens and sometimes hundreds of people would meet at the *Stari Hrast*, a massive but dead oak tree serving as yet another example of official negligence for public spaces. From there, they would often walk as a group to sites of civic concern, expressing their determination to participate in public affairs by movement through physical urban space, a method that earned these groups the moniker *Šetači* (walkers).[36] As these actions were coordinated collectively in virtual space, the authorities could not identify individual leaders that could be pressured, and disproportionally strong police presence during the marches likewise failed to achieve the obvious objective of intimidation. Protests finally abated by the end of the summer, yet organisers such as Dakić insist that the atmosphere in the city has changed.

> It is the loss of fear concerning public participation in demonstrations against the authorities and sending, for our circumstances, the quite radical political message of dissatisfaction with the state our society is in; having in mind the deeply internalised fear of sanctions which regime authorities would be keen to impose on 'unruly' individuals or groups.
>
> (Dakić 2012)

The normalisation of civic resistance in a divided polity

Events in BiH over recent years point towards a normalisation of civic protest and resistance that frequently expands into non-formal political movements. Activist networks and registered NGOs – which overlap to some extent – serve as catalysts, resource bases and support networks for movements that erupt from a baseline of high and growing discontent around issues that epitomise the dismal performance of political and state institutions to the point of moral outrage. In some cases – like the campaign against Federal Prime Minister Branković – such public outrage was strategically generated. More often, activists have amplified the impact of events that occurred beyond their direct authorship, and jolted a hitherto passive and cynical public into practices of active citizenship.

This pattern became apparent once more in the *Bebolucija* [Baby-lution] protests that erupted in Sarajevo in June 2013. Nationalist posturing had led to a

22   *Heiko Wimmen*

suspension of national identification numbers, preventing the issuance of passports for children born after February 2013. By early June, this led to the death of a child in need of life-saving treatment abroad. Within hours, enraged citizens encircled parliament, vowing to trap the lawmakers inside until the problem was solved. Activists who had played central roles in the earlier protests participated actively and contributed networks and know-how. Yet most were in the street for the first time, and overcame their aversion to politics via the outrage of newborn infants being sacrificed for political machinations (RI Arnautović 2013).

Although these ephemeral protest movements, in most cases, achieve only a fraction of their demands, each round adds new recruits, networks and knowledge to constantly accumulating potentials and repertoires of bottom-up resistance. The result may be described as a consolidation of practices and structures of civic resistance that provide checks against authoritarian, corrupt or irresponsible rulers, which procedural democracy fails to achieve in Bosnia due to the powerful sway of nationalist rhetoric over electoral choices. By 2015, politicians in Bosnia knew that herding followers to the polls does not relieve them from heeding an increasingly watchful public. Understandably, this is not enough for Bosnians measuring their country against European standards of governance, yet it is clearly a positive development compared to where the country was in 2000, or 2006.

The 2013 protests were, however, also indicative of the limits that are still placed on bottom-up participation by ethno-national cleavages, the power-sharing structures that convert these cleavages into politics and governance, and external tutelage. Croat-nationalist politicians exploited them to conjure up threats to the safety of non-Bosniak representatives in the capital, once more making their case for further (ethnic) decentralisation in the form of a third (Croat) entity. Bosnian Serb media portrayed them as staged by Bosniak politicians to pressure representatives from the RS. At some point, rumours circulated that RS-based anti-terror units were preparing a commando operation to 'rescue' the besieged RS representatives, summoning the spectre of an inter-entity confrontation. Thus, the concerns over the inherent dangers of contentious action in the specific Bosnian context, as expressed by the organisers of prior initiatives, were vindicated. High Representative Valentin Inzko, for his part, quickly stepped in and brokered a temporary compromise to defuse the protests, once more sparing Bosnian politicians the need to measure up to a mess they had brought upon themselves. His move also showed that 'citizen empowerment', which goes beyond a circumscribed, merely supplementary role in technocratic governance processes, tends to be perceived as a security problem rather than a democratic asset.[37] Finally, as the experiences of the 2006 and 2010 elections have demonstrated, the 'electoral straightjacket' (Perry 2014) of Bosnia's power-sharing system severely circumscribes the extent to which change can be effected through the ballot box. On the other hand, activists who attempt to directly influence the competition between contests over political power risk finding themselves in an ambiguous area where the line between political partisanship and co-optation is easily blurred.

Contrary to the evaluations of observers with liberal/multi-ethnic (Mujkić 2013) or post-communist/anti-nationalist (Štiks 2013) preferences, the 2013

Divided they stand 23

protests also provide little indication that non-ethnic (or 'post-ethnic'[38]) notions of citizenship are on the rise. Participants from predominantly Serb and Croat areas who attended the Sarajevo protest were feted as living proof of its cross-ethnic appeal (thus implicitly underlining how preciously small the latter really was), and solidarity meetings were held in Prijedor or Banja Luka. Yet most if not all of these appearances were carried by the same courageous yet small networks of non- or anti-nationalist activists who established themselves in earlier cycles of contestation, and remain voices in the wilderness. When an unusually large protest march was held in Banja Luka in July 2013 (originally protesting the poor quality of student housing, it quickly grew to denounce a broad range of grievances), the leaders found it necessary to explicitly *distance* themselves from the 'Babylution' events occurring in parallel,[39] confirming that cross-entity solidarity is still a liability rather than a resource (Basta 2013).

These observations cast doubt on the expectations that civil society or civic action may become focal points for cross-ethnic solidarity that will 'knit the society together' (Hemmer 2009). Observations in Bosnia indicate that in the early post-conflict stage, these activities are carried out by people who *already* reject divisive politics, often dissidents or former supporters of leftist parties, who engage in activism in the absence of other political options. As the dysfunctional aspects of the post-conflict order become entrenched, general exasperation serves to recruit a younger cohort, who exert pressure on the political sphere rather than striving to enter it. With the normalisation of activism, wider circles become involved on account of specific issues and occasions, and some of these may gradually turn into regulars. Apart from the small core groups of anti-nationalist activists mentioned previously (who may experience some modest growth in the process), this does not, however, lead to a significant growth in inter-ethnic cooperation and cross-cleavage alliances. Due to the decentralised structure of the country, even activists with a Bosniak background – who are exposed to a much lesser degree of pressure for conformity to the nationalist mainstream – mostly direct their efforts at institutions and audiences in Sarajevo, Zenica or Tuzla. When civic action touches upon issues that involve institutions on the central state level (as was the case in the JMBG protests), the fact that these institutions are located in the Bosniak-dominated capital again affects the composition of the activist groups. In the RS, on the other hand, tapping into the significant repository of discontent that does exist below the surface of top-down conformism requires activists to downplay or even actively disown links across the ethno-national and entity divide. Those who do openly engage in such cooperation quickly put themselves outside the political mainstream, and remain in the position of (courageous) fringe groups.

These results indicate that civic activism may not, indeed cannot, serve the purpose of re-integration assigned to it by peace-builders, as it does not occur in a space removed from the power struggles of political actors, but engages with and thus becomes an integral part of a political process that is geared to maintain and recreate division. It may, however, still serve to gradually chip away at the spell of authoritarian conformism that nationalist political forces have cast over their societies, and force a democratisation and tolerance of

24 *Heiko Wimmen*

difference within the polity that may, in the long run, also extend to ethno-national difference.

> If there was a movement that says fuck off everybody from the Federation, we hate you, we are the Serbs, but there are internal problems here, we are against the dictatorship of this person (Dodik) – I would love it, even it would not go into ethnic issues. Ok, we are all Serbs, who gives a fuck, but we want social justice, development, people to get better education.
>
> (RI Brkan 2011)

Hence, the problem may lie not with the 'failure' of civil society to comply with the expectations of theoretically informed approaches to peace building. Rather, the idea that such a transformation could be 'engineered' at all in a society deeply traumatised by deadly conflict, and where the political heirs of the victimisers still hold the reins of power, may have been presumptuous in the first place. Adjusted to more realistic benchmarks, the gradual decline in the capacity of nationalist discourse to enable authoritarian rule and the consolidation of bottom-up civic resistance do not look like failure, and may be considered steps towards a genuinely pluralistic polity some years down the road.

Notes

1 As Paris (2004: 19) notes, despite involving a plethora of actors, peace-building missions in the 1990s 'all pursued the same general strategy for promoting stable and lasting peace in war-shattered states: democratization and marketization'.

2 As Foley (2010) points out, these notions go back to the (predominantly American) literature on social cleavages and political stability of the 1960s. In an influential contemporary reiteration, Varshney (2001) identifies a correlation between cross-communal associational structures and a low propensity for communal violence in India. Putnam's (1993) claims, whereby vibrant associational life supported good governance and democracy in north Italy and its absence in the south led to paternalism and exploitation, are also a popular reference (see for instance Smillie and Evenson 2003).

3 Although the idea was conceived locally, GROZD received some €1.5 million in funding from USAID, the Olof Palme Centre, OSI and other international donors (NGO Infohouse 2006:6).

4 Available at: www.aparchive.com/metadata/Bosnia-Demo/8b6d5915574c3f71843dc
40ad80d28ef?query=tuzla&current=3&orderBy=Relevance&hits=3&referrer=searc
h&search=%2Fsearch%3Fquery%3Dtuzla%26startd%3D%26endd%3D%26orderBy
%3DRelevance%26from%3D1%26allFilters%3DGeneral%2Bnews%253ASubject%
252CSarajevo%253ALocations%252CAP%2BTELEVISION%253ASource&allFilte
rs=General+news%3ASubject%2CSarajevo%3ALocations%2CAP+TELEVISION%
3ASource&productType=IncludedProducts&page=1&b=0d28ef.

5 Participation declined from 58% of the voting age population in 1998 to 41% in 2002. There is a widespread notion, and some empirical evidence, that abstainers tend to be of liberal orientation (Puhalo and Perišić 2013), and that higher participation would therefore reduce the dominance of the nationalist parties.

6 From 41% to 43% and from 41% to 39%, respectively.

7 SDP barely restored its 1998 share, after dramatic gains in 2000 and even more dramatic losses in 2002. It won the Croatian seat in the tripartite presidency, yet this

Divided they stand 25

success was owed to a recent split that left the nationalist Croat vote divided. NSRzB improved but remained of insignificant size, and did not overcome its confinement to the small constituency of non-nationalist Croat voters.

8 International organisations such as IRI, NDI and the Friedrich Ebert Stiftung had promoted SNSD as a 'moderate' Serb alternative (Nenadović 2012: 21). Yet as Serb-nationalist voters shifted support to SNSD, the party radicalised itself. There are also accounts whereby, in the run-up to the 2006 elections, one NDI consultant *encouraged* SNSD to up the nationalist ante 'to beat their opponents at their own game' (ibid: 34).

9 E.g., by describing combative nationalist rhetoric as a ruse to distract the public from the tacit cooperation of the protagonists when it comes to dividing up economic spoils (Touquet 2012: 109).

10 This concurs with Hulsey's (2010) findings that nationalist parties face *more* opposition in mono-ethnic electoral units; where ethnic dominance is not at issue, the capacity of nationalist rhetoric to force conformity and undergird authoritarian rule decreases.

11 Although not all individuals or organisations in areas that are dominated by nationalist forces necessarily subscribe to such labels, they often have reason to fear for their credibility. Serb or Croat personnel working for Sarajevo-based organisations frequently report encountering *more* hostility than their Bosniak colleagues in areas that are dominated by nationalist co-ethnics, as their work for 'Muslim' organisations is considered traitorous.

12 Such attempts were nevertheless made, often referring to the personal history of CPCD director Fadil Šero in SDP, and his alleged intention to turn GROZD itself into a political party. GROZD campaigners also reported receiving occasional threats when campaigning in Republika Srpska (Touquet 2012: 122).

13 Activists in Banja Luka who initially volunteered for GROZD criticised the participation of former members of the nationalist SNSD, and some withdrew in consequence.

14 NED's 2007 budget included $40,700 for CPCD to conduct monitoring activities as projected by GROZD, available at: www.ned.org/publications/annual-reports/ 2007-annual-report/central-and-eastern-europe/description-of-2007-grant-1.

15 After the electoral defeat of the externally promoted 'Coalition for Change' in 2002, and with the impending draw-down of the OHR, any fundamental change to the status quo appeared increasingly unlikely.

16 Legally, the right to CO already existed; in reality, the option was all but unknown, and the few applications that were filed were not processed. The group recruited thousands of new applicants in the hitherto non-political (or rather, antipolitical) milieu of youth (counter-) culture, staged walk-ins with members of parliamentary committees, etc. (RI Brkan 2011).

17 Before returning to Bosnia in 2004, Mahmutćehajić had acquired a track record in international human rights campaigns (RI Mahmutćehajić 2011).

18 Some of these communications are still accessible on the klix.ba website; for instance, the thread 'Idemo pred skupstinu' (Let's meet at the assembly) started by Mahmutćehajić (screen name stolac92) on 27 December 2005, available at: https:// forum.klix.ba/idemo-pred-skupstinu-t22030s100.html.

19 'We are all Denis' and 'Denis, forgive us' became popular slogans during the protests.

20 On the pelting of the cantonal building, one protester said: 'It is high time to do this. *They* have been throwing stones at *us* for the last 15 years' (UG Zašto Ne 2009).

21 Branković was involved in the construction of the secret tunnel under the Butmir Airport that provided a lifeline for Sarajevo during the siege, but also served war profiteers. Wartime networks propelled him into high positions during the post-war era, which provided ample opportunity for enrichment. He therefore epitomised the new elite that had exploited the war and its aftermath to leverage itself into positions of power and take possession of public property.

26   *Heiko Wimmen*

22 The flat, estimated at around €250,000 in 2007, was bought by the state for 264,000 KM (approx. €140,000) in late May, and sold to Branković for 46,000 KM (€25,000) in early July. Rather than in real money, Brankovic paid using privatisation vouchers, which were trading at around 2% of their face value at the time. Available at: www. cin.ba/en/kupovina-kucice-iz-snova/. For a comprehensive account on the politics of privatisation in BiH, see Donais (2005: 114f).

23 See www.youtube.com/watch?v=tHokwPHDl4s for a report on the events.

24 These sequences were used in a music video produced by Dubioza Kolektiv in the immediate aftermath of the 2008 protests. See www.youtube.com/watch?v=PH0vsRPAWCg.

25 Provoking abuses of power that are then used to compromise the moral legitimacy (or here, to create ridicule) of power holders has been described as 'political jiu-jitsu' by the literature on strategic non-violent action (Sutton 2014).

26 Alternative explanations relate his fall to an internal power struggle in the SDA (Touquet 2012: 151). Yet Branković did not return to politics when the internal balance in the SDA swung back, and his name remains linked to the 2009 scandal (see, for instance, www. mojportal.ba/novost/201439/Nedzad-Brankovic-buduci-direktor-JP-Autoceste-FBiH).

27 For instance, *Zašto Ne* received NED funds to commission Dubioza Kolektiv for public performances and 'to produce a get-out-the-vote theme-song' (www.ned.org/ publications/annual-reports/2010-annual-report/central-and-eastern-europe/2010-grantee-spotlight-cen); the product attacked the ruling elite by invoking the iconic partisan hero Vladimir 'Walter' Perić, and SDP used nearly identical slogans in its electoral campaign (see, for instance, www.klix.ba/vijesti/bih/vratio-se-valter/101001139).

28 Votes for SDP doubled in the contest for the House of Representatives and tripled for the presidency, whereas SBiH lost 2/3 and SDA some 10% of their votes. SDP also emerged as the single largest party in the cantonal parliaments of the Federation, gaining 18 seats whereas SDA lost 19 and SBiH 55. The share of the nationalist Croat and Serb vote remained unaffected.

29 E.g. www.ndi.org/sites/default/files/Public_Opinion_Poll_Bosnia_Herzegovina_1009. pdf.

30 It appears plausible to assume that parallel events in Egypt boosted the response, although Filipović denied any connection. Speculations in Federation media about Egyptian-style unrest in RS may have been a reason for such circumspection, as it provided fuel for accusations that protesters were executing a script directed by hostile external forces (see banjalukain.com/clanak/31584/pokazimo-vladajucoj-eliti-u-rs-u-da-se-glas-naroda-cuje).

31 *Naša Stranka* was established in 2008 by a group of leftist and liberal intellectuals in a bid to create an alternative to the nationalist and (only incompletely reconstructed) post-communist parties dominating the political scene. Its successes, such as they were, have remained largely confined to urbanised areas in the Federation.

32 The news article is available at: http://radovicasokak.blogspot.co.at/2011/03/agencija-srna-protiv-organizatora.html.

33 Filipović emphasised that he himself fully acknowledges the massacre, and that he ended his cooperation with *Oštra Nula* for pragmatic rather than political reasons.

34 The *Mjesna Zajednica* (Local Unit), inherited from the Yugoslav system of self-managing socialism, was recently re-discovered as 'civil society that works' (Belloni 2007). The case described here, and accounts by many activists interviewed for this research, indicate that local consultative structures are instead often turned into tools of parochial control and used to legitimise clientelist resource allocation.

35 See www.banjaluka.com/drustvo/jos-jedan-park-postaje-zrtva-privatnih-investitora/.

36 See www.youtube.com/watch?v=pULDLol7lqk; spontaneous, ostensibly non-political 'walking' through the city (as opposed to partisan political rallies) as a symbolic act of resistance was an important protest technique in Serbia in the 1990s (see Jansen 2001).

37 During the partly violent social protests in February 2014, Inzko displayed a similar tendency by suggesting that EU troops may have to be deployed. After the low-level

Divided they stand 27

violence that occurred during the demonstration in Sarajevo on 13 February 2008, foreign donors of GROZD reportedly threatened their Bosnian partner organisations with the withdrawal of funds if they were to participate in further street action (Touquet 2012: 219f).

38 A term recently adapted from American discourse by Touquet (2012), which denotes a perspective that recognises bonded groups as formative for the identity of individuals, but rejects rigid categorisation and political prescriptions on the basis of such identifications.

39 The student activist quoted in the article, Nikola Dronjak, had co-organised the protests with Filipović in early 2011. See www.balkaninsight.com/en/article/banja-luka-students-defy-police-ban-on-protest.

References

Basta, K. 2013. *Urban Struggles: Activist Citizenship in South East Europe II*. [Online] Available at: www.citsee.eu/blog/urban-struggles-activist-citizenship-south-east-europe-iii.

Belloni, R. 2001. Civil Society and Peacebuilding in Bosnia and Herzegovina. *Journal of Peace Research* 38(2): 163–180.

Belloni, R. 2007. *State Building and International Intervention in Bosnia: After Dayton*. London and New York: Routledge.

Bodruzic, D. 2010. *Civil Society in a Post-Conflict Multiethnic Setting: A Case Study of Bosnia*, Canadian Political Science Association. [online] Available at: www.cpsa-acsp.ca/papers-2010/Bodruzic.pdf.

Chandler, D. 2000. *Bosnia: Faking Democracy After Dayton*. London: Pluto Press.

Chandler, D. 2005. Introduction: Peace Without Politics? *International Peacekeeping* 12(3): 307–321.

Dakić, M. 2012. The Park Is Ours: Civic Awareness and Protests Against Destruction of the Park in Banja Luka. *Koalicija* 143: 12–17.

Donais, T. 2005. *The Political Economy of Peace-Building in Post-Dayton Bosnia*. London: Routledge.

Evenson, K. and V. Marchenko. 2011. *Mid-Term Evaluation of the Civic Advocacy Partnership Project (CAPP II)*. Washington, DC: USAID.

Fagan, A. 2005. Civil Society in Bosnia Ten Years After Dayton. *International Peacekeeping* 12(3): 406–419.

Foley, M.W. 2010. Cautionary Tales: Soft Intervention and Civil Society. In: *Strengthening Peace in Post-Civil War States: Transforming Spoilers Into Stakeholders*, eds. M. Hoddie and C.A. Hartzell. Chicago: University of Chicago Press, pp. 163–188.

Hemmer, B. 2009. *The Democratization of Peace Building: The Political Engagement of Peace Building NGOs in Democratizing Societies*. Irwine: University of California, PhD thesis.

Hulsey, J.W. 2010. Why Did They Vote for Those Guys Again? Challenges and Contradictions in the Promotion of Political Moderation in Post-War Bosnia and Herzegovina. *Democratization* 17(6): 1132–1152.

Jansen, S. 2001. The Streets of Beograd: Urban Space and Protest Identities in Serbia. *Political Geography* 20: 35–55.

Lippmann, P. 2008. *Travel Journal to Bosnia-Herzegovina*. [Online] Available at: http://americansforbosnia.blogspot.co.at/2008/12/journalist-peter-lippman-travel-journal.html.

Lombardo, A. 2011. *'Dosta!'/'Enough!' – Protest, Practices and Representations of Young Social Activists in Contemporary Sarajevo*. Bologna: University of Bologna, MA thesis.

28   Heiko Wimmen

Mujkić, A. 2013. *On the Way to Bosnian Multitude: Review of JMBG Protests of June 2013.* Paper presented at the conference 'Rebellion and Protest from Maribor to Taksim. Social Movements in the Balkans', Graz, 12–14 December 2013.

Nenadović, M. 2012. *Installing Democracy in the Balkans? Analysis of Political Party Assistance in Bosnia-Herzegovina and Kosovo.* Amsterdam: University of Amsterdam, PhD Dissertation.

NGO Infohouse and Foundation Mozaik. 2006. *Non-Governmental Organizations in Bosnia and Herzegovina During the 2006 Pre-Election and Election Period.* Sarajevo: NGO Infohouse.

Ottaway, M. 2003. Promoting Democracy After Conflict: The Difficult Choices. *International Studies Perspectives* 4: 314–322.

Paris, R. 2004. *At War's End: Building Peace After Civil Conflict.* Cambridge: Cambridge University Press.

Perry, V. 2014. *Is Substantial Political Reform in Bosnia and Herzegovina Possible Through the Ballot Box in October 2014?* Sarajevo: Democratization Policy Council.

Puhalo, S. and N. Perišić. 2013. *Apstinenti u Bosni i Hercegovini.* Sarajevo: Friedrich-Ebert-Stiftung.

Putnam, R.D. 1993. *Making Democracy Work: Civic Traditions in Modern Italy.* Princeton: Princeton University Press.

Smillie, I. and K. Evenson. 2003. Sustainable Civil Society or Service Delivery Agencies? The Evolution of Non-Governmental Organizations in Bosnia and Herzegovina. In: *Rethinking International Organizations: Pathology and Promise*, eds. D. Dijkzeul and Y. Beigbeder. New York: Berghahn Books, pp. 287–306.

Štiks, I. 2013. 'We are all in this together': A Civic Awakening in Bosnia-Herzegovina. *Open Democracy.* [Online] Available at: www.opendemocracy.net/igor-%C5%A0tiks/%E2%80%98we-are-all-in-this-together%E2%80%99-civic-awakening-in-bosnia-herzegovina.

Sutton, J. 2014. Explaining Political jiu-jitsu: Institution-Building and the Outcomes of Regime Violence Against Unarmed Protests. *Journal of Peace Research* 51(5): 559–573.

Toè, R. 2013. *Bosnia-Herzegovina and the Failed Revolution of the SDP (2010–2014).* [Online] Available at: www.transconflict.com/2014/11/bosnia-herzegovina-and-the-failed-revolution-of-the-sdp-2010-2014-part-1-241/.

Touquet, H. 2012. *Escaping Ethnopolis: Postethnic Mobilization in Bosnia-Herzegovina.* Leuven: Katholieke Universiteit, PhD thesis.

Touquet, H. and P. Vermeersch. 2008. Bosnia and Herzegovina: Thinking Beyond Institution Building. *Nationalism and Ethnic Politics* 14(2): 266–288.

UG Zašto Ne. 2009. *Demokratija u Prijevodu.* [Online] Available at: www.youtube.com/watch?v=rgmEI3WRC5s.

USAID. 2008. *Evaluation of Civil Society Programs in Bosnia Herzegovina*, Washington, DC: USAID.

Varshney, A. 2001. Ethnic Conflict and Civil Society: India and Beyond. *World Politics* 53(3): 362–398.

Research interviews (RI) quoted (Chronological)

Ševko Bajić, CPCD, August 2010, Sarajevo.
Darko Brkan, Dosta! UG Zašto Ne, August 2010, December 2011, Sarajevo.
Fadil Šero, Naša Stranka, August 2010, Sarajevo.

Divided they stand 29

Dunja Pejić, Naša Stranka, August 2010, December 2011, Banja Luka.

Dejan Ćosić, Oštra Nula, August 2010; June 2013, Banja Luka, Berlin.

Darjan Bilić and Manja Huzbašić, Dosta!/Akcija Građana, September 2010, December 2011, Sarajevo.

Stepan Filipović, student activist, December 2011, Banja Luka.

Denis Gratz, Naša Stranka, December 2011, Sarajevo.

Milan Mrđa, CPCD, December 2011, Sarajevo.

Demir Mahmutćehajić, Dosta! December 2011, Stolac.

Samela Isanović, CCI, December 2011, Sarajevo.

Miodrag Dakić, CZZS, May 2012 (Skype Interview), Banja Luka.

Aldin Arnautović, JMBG activist, November 2013 (Skype Interview, Sarajevo).

Reuf Bajrović, former SDP campaign strategist, November 2013 (Skype Interview, Washington, D.C.).

2 Maribor's social uprising in the European crisis

From antipolitics of people to politicisation of periphery's surplus population

Gal Kirn

Introduction[1]

This chapter takes a closer look at the mass uprisings that took place in winter 2012–2013 in Maribor, a city that in politico-economic terms can be coined and analysed as *periphery*. The working hypothesis is that political outbursts happening on the periphery should not be seen as pure coincidence, but rather a deeper historical sign, which undermines the recurrent myth of Slovenia as a 'success story' of the Balkans. It is noteworthy that Maribor had already been the site of one of the largest workers' mass strikes and protests in 1988, and seen in retrospect, it became a site of the tragic beginning of the end of socialist Yugoslavia. Twenty-five years later, new mass protests emerged in Maribor – notwithstanding their differences in political formations and demands – again triggering a series of consequences, which perhaps even announced the end of a historical sequence of post-socialist transition. Therefore, the chapter performs a double task: in the first part, I outline a historical analysis, which speaks of the disenchantment with post-socialist transition and points to certain negative tendencies of capitalist modernisation, especially in Maribor. In the second part, this ideological and economic analysis is complemented with a political analysis of the irruption of mass protests, where I use Rancière's political theory of dissensus and *demos*. Instead of interpreting the uprisings as a logical, or even necessary, proceeding out of the pauperised conditions of Maribor's social fabric, I show that the events were unexpected and the complete absence of major established powers and agents clearly registers this point. It was only through and after this democratic irruption that the neuralgic point and casual relationship between, on the one hand, the crisis of representative democracy and austerity (neoliberal solution of crisis) and, on the other hand, popular discontent and subjective grievances became evident. The democratic explosion actually opened a space for the emergence of new political groups and parties.

Mythologisation and demythologisation of the Slovenian success story through Maribor

The late 1980s represent a democratic peak in recent Slovenian history and is referred to as the 'spring of democracy' or 'democratic revolution' (Balažić 2004).

The thawing of the 'totalitarian winter' brought a flourishing of democratic civil society, which consisted of a plurality of cultural and political agencies: from environmentalists, peace activists, gay, lesbian and feminist struggles, initiatives from various subcultures, radical art groups, right-wing dissidents and the Catholic Church to reformatory and liberal currents within the League of Socialist Youth. The democratisation process reached its peak momentum after the famous trial against JBTZ (four journalists, one of them being young Janez Janša) before a military tribunal of the Yugoslav People's Army for disclosing state secrets relating to a possible military intervention in Slovenia (Žerdin 1997). The JBTZ affair triggered an immense public outcry, and mass protests spread like a virus across Slovenia. This is retrospectively seen as one of the major tilting points for the independence of Slovenia project. If, previously, diverse groups with very different political agendas were engaged in the process of democratisation,[2] what came in its aftermath was hegemonised by a nationalist project. Here, at least on the institutional level, the League of Communists of Slovenia started playing an important role in moving towards a more nationalist position.[3] The upper hand in the social mobilisation was taken on by the Catholic Church and right-wing intellectuals associated with the journal *Nova Revija*, who translated their theoretical program into a set of political demands united in the call for Slovenia's independence.[4] The new and independent nation-state became the key political subject – the only future for Slovenian nationhood. This process was accompanied by, on the one hand, poetic longings and dreams of having waited 1,000 years for this historical moment, which entailed a whole range of 'reinventing tradition' and historical revisionism, and on the other hand, a skilful marketing-liberal campaign that culminated in the brand 'Slovenija, moja dežela' and separated the good and hard-working Slovenian nation from the rest of Yugoslavia. This shaped the ideological grounds for the nation-building process, which was predicated, *negatively*, against the multinational, federative and socialist Yugoslavia, whereas *positively* it affirmed a secure course of the Slovenian dream into post-socialist transition to a capitalist mode of production in Europe. It was due to the geopolitical situation of Slovenia bordering Western Europe (that did not want to have war immediately on its borders) and the fact that Slovenia was the most ethnically homogenous country in Yugoslavia that there was practically no war there, apart from 10 days of fighting during summer 1991. Furthermore, due to Slovenia's strong existing economic ties with its immediate neighbours, the national economy could – although not without economic troubles – re-direct and solidify trade with Western markets.

During the first part of the 1990s, war ravaged through the post-Yugoslav region, while Slovenia enjoyed its path of success nearing the 'Euro-Atlantic integrations'. Evidently, this path was not without difficulties and paradoxes, which soon undermined the national unity of independence times and the transitional elite. The first major politico-economic decisions on the post-socialist transition regarded how to manage the national economy and what to do with social property. These topics led to a major split in the first democratically elected government (DEMOS and a few other parties). Initially, there was Mencinger's law on workers' takeover of the means of production, a kind of privatisation with

32 *Gal Kirn*

workers' shares, along with Goldman Sachs' plan, which included a wild neoliberal privatisation that was set as a standard in other Eastern European countries (see Ellerman 1991). Instead of choosing one of these options, the new government favoured a middle path that consisted of a *gradual transition* to capitalism with a 'social-democratic' flavour. The government made a rough estimate of 'social' shares in the general social property and the citizens could then, via their certificates, invest their shares into the economy. This operation was constitutive for the companies that would then be launched on the stock exchange (see Mencinger 1994). The individual choice would be very much dependent on knowledge level and some luck in investing in companies that later became successful. Previous accumulation of socialist capital, thousands of invested hours of labour and machinery investments were being gradually privatised and nationalised – given to the economic use that would not be socially controlled. Despite the fierce neoliberal model being temporarily defeated, this process clearly entailed a reintroduction of private property, which was wrongly called 'denationalisation'. On a larger scale, real estate and forests (land) came back into the hands of the Catholic Church and those of formerly aristocratic and wealthy families, whereas the majority of big companies remained in the hands of state managed elites (later called tycoons). This would then mean the return of the privileges, property, land and means of productions to the remnants of aristocratic and bourgeois strata on the one hand, and management over big capital delegated by the government on the other. Workers' participation and the legacy of self-management was quickly forgotten and demonised (see also Kirn 2011). This period saw the advancement of a new economic elite with close ties to the new political class, who would run the largest corporations until the advent of the European Union (EU). This process was accompanied by a slow deregulation of welfare state capacities, which meant that the so-called middle classes lived in relative prosperity and to some extent even improved material conditions. It was here that the 'success story' was born: Slovenia as the *Switzerland of the Balkans*. The ruling class proclaimed its historical mission accomplished after entering both NATO and the EU in mid-2000 with the propaganda slogan 'Home in Europe, safe in NATO'.

However, with the historical advent of the EU and the final exit from the dark Balkans,[5] the protagonists of the success story entered a process of disenchantment. The gradual transition to a more brutal capitalist regime of exploitation meant that class stratification was imminent and in the last 10 years, the level of social insecurity, exclusion and poverty rose. The second round of privatisation not only meant the sale and takeover of state corporations, but also a more radical dismantling of the welfare state, which also resulted in higher levels of unemployment, and other trends that typically accompany neoliberal policies (see Močnik 2003). The reputation and mythology of the Slovenian success story was economically shaken by the crisis from 2008 onwards and politically at the end of 2012, when mass protests spread throughout the country. Social unrest began in November 2012 in the second largest city, Maribor. However, Maribor was struck by the 'transition' previously in the early 1990s and is a paradigmatic case of peripherialisation and de-industrialisation, in short by the negative sides of transitional processes.

Maribor in retrospect: from industrialist past to dreams of de-industrialisation

The gradual transition materialised in the 'uneven development', which means that there are not simply winners and losers of transition, but the process of inequality, gross gaps in wealth, dispossession and disempowerment is the inner core of capitalist recuperation. That being said, Maribor was the other side of the Slovenian 'success story', which cannot be reduced to regional superiority-inferiority, or ascribed to individual or municipal responsibility. The transitory processes on the periphery of Slovenia were brutal from the early 1990s onwards. Within the period of the first five-year plan of deregulation and de-industrialisation, which took place from 1990 to 1995, the everyday life and urban fabric of Maribor went through massive structural changes. Most of the established industries in the times of socialism, including metal (development of cranes, Metalna), Maribor's foundry, production of cars and trucks (TAM), textiles (MTT) and electrometal (Elektrokovina), went bankrupt or were cut drastically (see Slavec 1992; Kirn 2014: 110–112). This was an immediate consequence of the loss of Yugoslav markets and also due to the partial integration of Maribor's industrial pool into the military-industrial complex of the Yugoslav People's Army. A few surviving enterprises were rationalised and massively reduced their economic activity, whereas others were cheaply sold to foreign companies. The unemployment rate in Maribor reached around 25% in the early 1990s and, even worse, around 70% of those fell within the category of structural, i.e. long-term, unemployment. However, industrialisation had already been consigned to the dustbin of history as a response to workers' organisation earlier, and the time of the de-industrialised, redundant army approached. Until then, the 'surplus population' had to survive, and it therefore combined two strategies: it was largely dependent on ever-decreasing social (state) aid and informal networks of charity (Caritas, Red Cross), and it also developed 'survival strategies' around the informal subsistence economy. In the first years after 2000, when the unemployment rate started dropping and the economic situation 'normalised', the 30 largest enterprises employed fewer workers in total than the TAM factory in the 1980s. Accordingly, industrial infrastructure deteriorated and, with it, the whole urban landscape became radically transformed. Maribor became a monument to the past, both to *socialist Yugoslavia*, as it brought together many people from across the former united country, and to *industrialist times* and socio-economic prosperity, which re-invigorated the idea and the *politics of the industrial working class*. The industrialist spectre from the past soon found a companion – the dream of a post-industrialised future.

European Capital of Culture 2012: de-industrialisation with austerity

Every major project holds out a promise and launches a dream. The dream-mission of the European Capital of Culture (ECC) that was launched by the European Commission is not very complex: it consists of commodification of culture and supplying Europe with a new infrastructure of de-industrialised creative

34 *Gal Kirn*

industries. ECC fosters tourism in its region and, most of all, works to re-organise creative potential. As Palmer argues, the ECC has become a major 'catalyst' of urban revitalisation and most interviewed representatives of local organisations have enthusiastically confirmed this notion.[6] In 2012, Maribor finally got its historical opportunity by becoming the European Capital of Culture, and in 2013, the European Capital of Youth. The expectations fostered by becoming the ECC and the previous positive experience of Graz as the ECC fostered a collective dream for a new Maribor.

The reality during and after the project was different, and in retrospect, one can conclude that the most important mission of Maribor's term as the ECC was not accomplished. The project failed to create long-term employment and develop cultural infrastructure in Maribor, although the Urban Furrows programme was a notable exception. What was designed to trigger local and regional creative industries is, at the moment, (still) running to a large degree on self-exploitation and voluntary activism. Many 'creative' young people and their projects were left to themselves, that is, to the market's discipline. ECC did not prevent the rising tide of unemployment, which was nearly 19% at the end of 2012. This failure should not be ascribed simply to the ECC, or the futility of calls for creative industries, but should be contextualised within the global financial and particularly the European economic and political crisis of recent years.

The economic crisis began taking a negative toll in Slovenia in 2008 and previous governments, centre-left or right-wing, have competed in their efforts to upgrade the neoliberal agenda and austerity measures, where 'recommendations' from the European Central Bank (ECB), European Commission and the International Monetary Fund (IMF) (troika) basically meant a tough financial-fiscal discipline and ever more privatisation of the social (re)productive apparatus. The austerity measures adopted in those years included the privatisation of banks (manipulating a public referendum on setting up a 'bad bank' to handle defaulted loans) (Žižek 2013); a special 'holding-expert' institution to sell all domestic capital (especially the profitable ones) to foreign investment firms; massive layoffs and dissolution of collective bargaining agreements in all social sectors; drastic budget cuts for research and universities (in 2012–2013, it fell between 10–20%); cuts in the field of culture (in some subfields, as high as 50%); and pension reduction to as little as 250 euros per month.

As is clear from the adopted austerity measures in Slovenia, they have become the dominant ideological banner of the 'necessary structural reforms', which in reality meant an implementation of the intensification of exploitation and pauperisation of lower/middle classes. Furthermore, the costs of the economic crisis are paid by the general population (e.g. public bailouts of private banks), even though Slovenia registered 13% unemployment according to Eurostat[7] in late 2012, remaining at this level until the end of 2014, with some regions peaking at 20%.[8] Particularly alarming is the drastic relative rise of youth unemployment in Europe, increasing from 15% to 22% in the last months of 2012 and hitting 25% in November 2014. The general rate of economy is stagnating, the BDP has shrunk, and the level of debt rose to more than 80% BDP. The only remedy for the situation – as the mainstream economy teaches – is *privatisation*, which would mean more layoffs, less profits and taxes to be netted into the state BDP and most of all, a veritable social catastrophe, as the networks of small and middle-sized companies would dissolve. The mid-term scenario would mean wheeling towards the Greek example.

The spark of new mass politics, or antipolitics

Within the post-socialist transition, very different individualised forms of 'resistance' that coped with those negative processes ensued. The most common is the apathy and lack of belief in change that has long characterised citizens' attitude to the structural problems that the Maribor region has encountered. One could factor this in with other social phenomena, such as a particularly high suicidal rate and alcoholism, as well as the rise of domestic violence. The disenchantment with the cultural embellishment in the perspective of economic devastation was, in Maribor, accompanied by foreclosures, bankrupt small enterprises and already strained networks of social and familial solidarity. Within these historical circumstances, the local municipality, led by then-Mayor Franc Kangler, introduced a public-private partnership that installed a system of hundreds of radars to measure speed limits. Vezjak (2013) stated that 'more than 2,000 people were issued speeding tickets in only two weeks – in a city of 100,000 inhabitants. There was a sense that residents' household budgets were being targeted'. The sense of clear social injustice grew, while simultaneously the same mayor was implicated in many corruption scandals without any juridical consequences.

People were enraged and in the beginning, a small group of citizens protested in front of the municipality, and a few critical articles were published in the newspapers – nothing spectacular, it seemed. However, in November 2012, thousands of people gathered on the streets. This was a mass democratic irruption that fitted well with what Rancière describes as 'politics of dissensus' and 'rupture'.[9] First, the contingent nature of the politics of rupture means that such ruptures cannot be anticipated from previous historical instances, and second, they cannot simply be reduced to the objective conditions of the situation or explained by economic arguments. If we stick to a purely economic analysis of the situation, the worse it is, the better for progressive politics, and we see that the early 1990s were even worse in terms of statistical index, but no mass protests took place. Thinking and acting in politics of dissensus means to think of politics in its interiority, the moment of radical change that cannot be explained simply by any exterior factor. In this sense, the anger over the instalment of radar systems seems banal, but it was the symptomatic point in which *the objective conditions of poverty were subjectivised* (Žižek 2000).[10] In this moment, numerous citizens started to feel that something was utterly rotten and called for decisive action against objective conditions.

The largest event was coordinated by citizens of Maribor via Facebook and, in the last weeks of November and early December, the main square was occupied by thousands of people. It reached its peak on 26 November 2011, when more

36   Gal Kirn

than 15,000 people gathered and demanded the resignation of both the corrupt mayor and his local municipality. The protest started peacefully and gathered together groups and citizens that came with their kids. The event was violently dispersed by police who used batons, excessive amounts of tear gas, and other repressive methods. This triggered a violent response from groups of young people, pushing into the municipality office, burning trash bins and setting off firecrackers.[11] The images circulated across Slovenia and public rage accumulated, fed also by the cynical responses from the political establishment. Many mass media journalists helped create a critical public sphere, where the protests entered the central stage of attention. What began as an isolated spark in late November 2012 in Maribor spread to other cities and, weeks later, culminated in an 'All-Slovenian Uprising' in Ljubljana accompanied by unprecedented mass protests across the country.[12] By that time, things got out of hand, and revolts evolved into an uprising, a mass democratic irruption of frustrations and confrontation with the existing power.

There were few occasions in the history since Slovenian independence in which masses took to the streets, protesting against Demos government (trade unions against privatisation, women on anti-abortion legislation), and in mid-2000, there were a few general strikes organised by trade unions against the Janša government that wanted to implement neoliberal reforms.[13] This was an orchestrated political action that contributed to the autonomy of trade unions vis-à-vis the state, but it largely remained within a conservative position of protecting what was in the process of being destroyed (the welfare state and industrial labour force) and within the political space of the liberal state and its organised political apparatus. However, this was the first time something so immense and also violent, and not organised by any institutionalised agent, took place. In late 2012, trade unions and other political parties were caught by surprise, or remained silent about the uprising. It was as if all the major cities saw a veritable democratic eruption and spontaneous protests from below without any solid political platform. Just a few months earlier, Slovenia seemed to be a relative stable democracy of the Balkans, a successful new member state of the EU and Eurozone, but now, people were waking up from the fairytale of a painless transition to find themselves engulfed in a real social catastrophe, or as Tomšič (2013) coined it, we woke up in the worst nightmare.

Theoretical note on political subjectivity: from people to surplus population

Instead of using the official-formal channels or strategies of the dominant established institutions (petitions, pressure groups, parties, trade unions, civil initiative), the mass protests – 'All-Slovenian Uprisings' – brought out, in Rancière's terms, a radical 'dissensus' at the core of the society and its order of 'police'. The uprising was not interested in making a compromise with the political class, but rather launched a rigorous critique of the foundations of liberal democracy and success: the (capitalist) state and its representative apparatuses. The central

Maribor's social uprising in the European crisis   37

message that mass uprisings uttered radically challenged the very meaning of democracy and could be read along the lines of Rancière:

> Democracy is not, to begin with, a form of State. It is, in the first place, the reality of the power of the people that can never coincide with the form of a State. There will always be tension between democracy as the exercise of a shared power of thinking and acting, and the State, whose very principle is to appropriate this power.[14]

What had previously been the recognised and established 'distribution of the sensible' of liberal democracy, with its logic of counting voices and parts of society to manage the population and adapt to the capitalist subsumption, was now disturbed by the political force of social uprising. The state apparatuses attempted to treat those involved as criminals and minimise their appeal by promoting a conspiracy theory about the recrudescence of old communists; however, such cynical remarks only made the movement stronger. Those on the streets did not agree to follow the formal procedure of being citizen-subjects who wait to perform a ritual every four years and choose what has already been chosen for them, voting for people who are partially responsible for the existing situation. They participated in a political process that brought together many people who had never had any political experiences. Despite the differences and heterogeneity of the mass uprisings, people were united around the political slogans: 'It is enough! It is over with him/them!' [*Gotov je! Gotovi so!*]; 'They are all crooks!' [*Lopovi!*]. These statements express a central paradox of the uprising, which is common to most recent movements on the periphery. On the one hand, one could firmly claim that these uprisings are the greatest mass and political events on the periphery since the 1980s, but on the other hand, we should bear in mind the very strong 'antipolitical' tone that can be recognised in the demands, desires and interpretations of many participants in the protests.[15] The rejection of corrupt individuals and the whole political class could well signify an 'escape' from or rejection of the dominant order of the police, thus emphasising protesters' desire for an angelic position of not wanting to dirty their hands with politics. On rare occasions, this radical position functions as the departure point for a more systemic critique of the political representation and reproductive mechanism of the entire political class that implicated in the transitional process. With demands for the overthrow and resignation of all leading figures and questioning of the functioning of the established (democratic) institutions, the dissensus grew with every manifestation. It was by this uncompromised political split that a process of democratic action by 'the people' started. This split and heterogeneity can be further analysed through the social structure of protest participants consisting of a variety and plurality of social groups and individuals with different political affiliations and from different generations, young and old, workers and students, LGBT activists, feminists, partisan veterans, precarious workers, ecologists, anarchists and socialists. More relevant than the concrete social positions and habitus of participants is their actual political recomposition and diverse political positions.

38　*Gal Kirn*

Taking these lessons seriously means that the political concept of 'the people' cannot be defined as a homogenous majority of those engaged in protests, or that they all follow a unanimous consensus on political demands. Rather, I see the people as the demos in Rancièrean terms, as a political figure of dissensus, of those excluded, invisible and exploited, who take politics out of the hands of experts, professional politicians, and opinion leaders. Based on their own experience of acting and thinking, they at first only rejected the order of the 'police' in an antipolitical refusal. However, in the subsequent phase of the uprisings, different groups began formulating diverse demands, which I claim can be seen as an important mark in the constitution of 'people'. The people, in this sense, cannot but preserve their heterogeneity and constitute a 'partial, politically constructed universality' (Laclau 2005: 240). The people as a political category and practical entity is only formed through struggles full of splits and differences, both against those in political power and internally within the social uprising. One can easily see how diverse and barely reconcilable positions may exist: from liberal-moralism ('we need new good people to uphold the rule of law'[16]) and nationalism ('for a better Slovenia, we need to bring forward sincere Slovenians; politicians have betrayed the national cause') to strong tendencies in support of social transformation (demand for democratic socialism and anarchist demands for change in everyday life).

This diversity, on the one hand, united people in the struggle against the political class; on the other hand, it provided intellectual tools to help them understand the deeper structural crisis of our time: the crisis of the global and particularly the European capitalist system and the peripheral role that Slovenia assumes in it. Apart from the negative speeches against the corruption of governmental and other officials, most notably, against the mayor of Maribor (Franc Kangler) and the prime minister (Janez Janša), participants in the uprising organised an alternative program through a series of performances, cultural events and new popular councils, committees and initiatives that took seriously the search for the broadest possible democratic platform. These included the Committee for Direct Democracy, the Coordinating Committee for a Cultural Slovenia, and the General Assembly of the All-Slovenian Uprising and Protestival, to name a few.

But is the concept of 'the people' still adequate or operative enough to describe new uprisings and transformations on the horizon? Or should we speak of movements, masses or even the formation of a new proletariat? Leaving aside a longer theoretical discussion, the text here embraces the Rancièrian category of 'people', which unbinds itself both from the existing codification within parliamentary democracy (legal) and from the notion of empirical majority (statistical counting in surveys). Instead, a politics of demos brings the split within people, between those that allegedly represent and those that are represented, or even excluded, into the core of politics. Moreover, such 'people' who do not want to simply be subjugated to the established political forms always present an imminent threat to that order. In this respect, people cannot be identified with the national substance that fuses nation and people.[17] Again, in the post-Yugoslav conjuncture and civil wars, the concept of 'people' was thoroughly hegemonised by the concept of 'nation', in particular working through the linguistic-semantic confusion of

Maribor's social uprising in the European crisis 39

the term *narod*, which means both nation and people.[18] For historical revisionists, and against the former stress on the Yugoslav multinational solidarity, the whole history was to be re-evaluated through the lenses of nations (Slovenian, Croatian, Bosnian, Serbian).[19] In contradistinction to this trending affirmation of 'nation', which came with the disavowal of 'people', I mobilise the conceptual history of 'people' that can be tied especially to the revolutionary experiences of the People's Liberation Struggle (PLS) during WWII.[20] Contrary to the nostalgic recuperation of partisan struggle into Slovenian state sovereignty that would only affirm its 'national' component – the way in which the partisan struggle performed the political recognition of the Slovenian nation – the PLS worked on a broader platform that was based on antifascist solidarity and social revolution.[21] Furthermore, instead of affirming merely 'nation' as political subjectivity of the struggle, it is more precise to speak of the emergence of 'revolutionary people' as central political subjectivity. This not only brings into attention the multinational character of the partisan struggle, but also emphasises its radical difference towards the other political paradigm that was bound to the model of ethnical cleansing in those territories, be it fascist occupation regimes or local collaborationist groups. PLS, conversely, built antifascist solidarity among different Yugoslav and non-Yugoslav nations, which in the second phase of the war, after the capitulation of Italy and the declaration of the AVNOJ revolutionary government, started taking the shape of a new federative political entity with strong socialist undertones. Moreover, in the post-war years, the conception of the people was given a political twist and revised to the 'working people', which clearly referenced the 'revolutionary people', as a kind of specific political subjectivity in socialist Yugoslavia that built on popular and national liberation.

This is the historical perspective, a kind of alternative genealogy of *people* that is worth defending today once taking into account the outbursts of popular and democratic energy that were in radical dissensus with the established order. As mentioned previously, I situate this political rethinking of 'people', which reveals novelties brought by the uprisings, within a more general frame of economic analysis. In other words, the Rancièrian frame is complemented by Marxian lenses through radicalisation of the category of people. The Marxian political theory mostly refers to 'proletariat' as the central category, which emanates from the politicisation of the working class and its organisation into a revolutionary party, and for many radical political theorists today, such as Badiou, Rancière and Balibar, seem now inoperative. However, there are a few other ways to introduce the Marxian frame: one would be to connect the concept of people to the framework of 'intersectionality' – where and how the 'people' connect to other categories, such as class, gender, and race (Balibar and Wallerstein 1991). This approach I leave for another time because I believe that in the current predicament of crisis, another Marxian conceptual take is more fruitful. What used to be the fragmented and invisible, even dissolved, bonds of a working class moulded as a mass of (self-)employees with diverse working contracts and conditions is now replaced by a working class increasingly conscious of sharing the same predicament: dispossession, privatisation, intensified exploitation and most of all unemployment, which made millions of people across Europe redundant. This is why I suggest

40   *Gal Kirn*

complementing the category of 'people' with the category of 'surplus population'. Already for Marx, the 'economic' exclusion of certain layers of the population was internal for the functioning of the system of capitalist accumulation. In *Capital*, he would define 'surplus population' as 'industrial reserve army':

> But the greater this reserve army in proportion to the active labour army, the greater is the mass of a consolidated surplus population, whose misery is in inverse ratio to its torment of labour. The more extensive, finally, the lazarus-layers of the working class, and the industrial reserve army, the greater is official pauperism. This is the absolute general law of capitalist accumulation.
>
> (Marx and Engels 1975–2005: 638)

The sharpened economic crisis, which has long ago abandoned its strict 'financial' frame of sovereign debt crisis,[22] resulted in a real social catastrophe on the periphery. One face of the crisis, which could be seen as the entering into yet another phase of 'primitive capital accumulation', is its brutal logic of redundancy. In short, if we take into account the unemployment rates on the periphery, we see them oscillate between 15–25% of 'registered' unemployed, and up to 55% among youth populations (Spain, Greece). This leaves a large part of the population on the periphery redundant. However, one ought to revise Marxian insight because a large portion will never return to industrial production. It is not only that the 'surplus population' is a structural characteristic of capitalist accumulation, in the last decades of de-industrialisation, 'industrial reserve army' should also be renamed 'de-industrialised reserve army'. The ongoing process of 'pauperisation' and 'proletarisation' is further strengthened by the dismantling of social services and infrastructures. In this situation, there is no unequivocal answer from the side of the dispossessed, which we cannot simply term a passive mob, or *Lumpenproletariat*. The mass of those dispossessed search undoubtedly for individual survival strategies, which through the years has evolved into emigration abroad or to the countryside, as well as the parallel collective institution of local exchange of food and other social services. However, I am more interested in the political answer of 'surplus population', which either runs into more right-wing populist composition (anti-immigrant movements, rise of extreme right parties) or a more left-wing political response. The former completely obfuscates class antagonism by displacing the socio-economic problems onto the hatred of immigrants, returning to traditionalist and ethnical models of political community; conversely, the left hegemonic movement tackles the structural issues of the capitalist crisis and founds its political stance in affirmation of universal rights: social justice and equality. Both processes – the extreme right-wing and the new left recomposition – could be understood as 'politicisation' of all those excluded, and made redundant by the current crisis.

Evidently, the articulation of new popular political forms (people's assemblies) and the level of their organisation regarding class and emancipation varies throughout the countries of the European periphery. There is no single formula that would sum the diverse protests and uprisings from 2009 onwards; however, one can at least name two common political aspects: first, one can speak about the politics of masses, which were for quite a substantial time organised outside the established institutions, and second, the protests share an 'antipolitical' mood, which is expressed in the refusal of all official modes of politics and political parties. As mentioned, there are different tendencies and the conjunctural analysis would show that some uprisings tend towards right-wing populism, especially those historically connected with a strong anti-communist tradition (in the East[23]), or those in the core countries; whereas others in the periphery are generally more open to the leftist alternative. Despite the looming historical question of Rosa Luxembourg, if the future is one of socialism and barbarity, analysis and political action should aim to find the extent to which these new groups and movements are able to continue building new organisational forms and affirmative political platforms, which, in a Gramscian way, expand mass intellectuality and political forms in a new hegemonic bloc. Despite the many politico-theoretical questions that deal with the people, the masses, the (sub)proletariat, and Left parties, which should be further elaborated and debated, some of these can be responded to (only) by the political work of the people within a new socialist-oriented hegemonic bloc. Evidently, even if there are some strong emancipatory traces throughout the European periphery, there is no guarantee that the political tendency within the people will necessarily go in the direction of socialism.

The end of mass protests in Slovenia: after the overthrow of the government, the rise of new parties

If we return to the Slovenian context, what started in November and December 2012 continued well into 2013. The political demands of resignation of the corrupted elite were to some degree realised: the mayor of Maribor resigned, and the protests took a more anti-austerity stance. First, trade unions joined the tide of protests and organised (23 January 2013) a massive general strike with 20,000 workers on the streets of 14 cities across Slovenia. March 2013 brought a victory for those active in the uprising. Central political figures and some other functionaries resigned due to mounting pressures in March 2013. Most notably, Janez Janša resigned from his position as prime minister (replaced by the more moderate centrist government led by Alenka Bratušek from the party of Zoran Janković, mayor of Ljubljana), and Zoran Janković, the leader of the Positive Slovenia Party, resigned from the presidency of his party. This seemed to be a historical victory for the uprising, with tough austerity measures bringing to life a new sense of solidarity and popular emancipation. However, by the time of this victory, new political forms had not yet been created; furthermore, they did not form a historical bloc with a coherent political program that would challenge the new government and crisis situation. After April 2013, popular enthusiasm and interest in building institutions from below came to a halt. Some individuals who took part in the protests called for a no-compromise struggle against official politics, whereas others urged waiting for new governmental policies that were supposed to take a different course. The new government consisted of old parties

42 *Gal Kirn*

and, although it did tone down the social Darwinist discourse, the general direction remained the same: the austerity measures and privatisation processes blissfully continued, further indebting Slovenian economy. Once the biggest political power, Pozitivna Slovenia gradually lost legitimacy and was split into two parts. It seemed the protesters' energy had introduced some chaos within the dynamic of the ruling political class; however, they have mostly just dealt the cards anew. The protests were wrongly concentrated merely on the overthrow of individual figures and the years-long obsession with Janša and fear of right-wing authoritarianism became major impediments to real emancipatory politics. When the mayor of Maribor, France Kangler, and Prime Minister Janez Janša were deposed from political power, the majority of the movement gradually disappeared from the public's attention, and only the most engaged groups remained active on a local basis.

It was only a year later in early 2014 that some agents of the uprisings started forming new political parties: the Society for Justice and Solidarity, the 'All-Slovenian Uprising', and the Network for Direct Democracy founded the *Solidarity Party*; another important 'Initiative for Democratic Socialism' (IDS) launched an alternative development program for Slovenia. They founded their own party in March 2014, joined forces with two other marginal parties – Party for Ecosocialism (TRS) and Party of Democratic Labour (DSD) – and founded a coalition called *United Left* (Združena Levica, ZL), which was premised after the Greek model of SYRIZA as a radical left platform of parties and movements. United Left especially advocated a clear left-oriented program based on principles of democratic socialism, workers' self-management, building of cooperatives and participatory budget.[24] To a certain degree, United Left succeeded in radicalising and further articulating political demands of uprisings, but more importantly, if most of these political demands seemed either nostalgic or totalitarian prior to uprisings, they were gradually becoming a part of the mainstream media and political discussions. Apart from Solidarity and ZL, a third political party was formed, called Party of Miro Cerar (SMC). Led by a successful and morally responsible lawyer, this party seemed to embody the spontaneous desire and prevalent antipolitical demand of the uprisings: SMC promised to end the corruption and (old) ideological struggles – not being part of the old political games – while advocating for the technocratic effective governance that would lead Slovenia out of the crisis with no clear program.

Within a span of five months in 2014, European, local and national elections all took place. The major winner of the most important elections in July was SMC, which won almost 35% of the votes, whereas the United Left (ZL) received only 6%, equal to that of the Social Democrats. The new parties – SMC and ZL – entering into the parliament clearly indicated that a mandate for a new orientation of politics was given to 'new faces'. However, new faces are not enough to change the deeper logic of social processes – 'new politics' was also needed. As the new coalition government was formed, it consisted of centre-left forces – SMC, Social Democrats and Desus (Party of Pensioners) – and from its start it was oriented on the same approach to political economy and sovereign debt as all previous

Maribor's social uprising in the European crisis   43

governments: it continued with the austerity measures that were undermining the collective contracts with trade unions and employees, and, most notably, it continued selling the state companies that generated the most profit and were of strategic infrastructural interest, such as airports and airlines, big industry, and telecommunications. In the last months of 2014, popular support for SMC and the government hit low levels, and Janez Janša, a former prime minister, was released early from prison due to political pressures on the judicial system. The great comeback into the parliament re-affirmed the role of martyrdom and now his party, SDS, polls at the top. However, the real line of discontent is not only the return of old faces and repetition of old politics, but the persistent and continual structural cause for future protests: the recipe of austerity and privatisation is again becoming the major front around which the political struggle within, and even more, outside the parliament is organised. In this respect, with a large degree of certainty, one can predict the emergence of future protests.

Conclusion: politics of periphery and surplus population for a different and social Europe

This chapter illuminated the way in which the uprising on the periphery of Slovenia, in Maribor, 25 years after the end of socialism triggered a wave of mass protests that demythologised the successful transition and material basis of the old political class. After the overthrow of a few political figures, some political initiatives continued with the work in local communities, such as Maribor's Initiative for City Council, although in terms of emancipatory politics reinventing party politics, I would emphasise the work of United Left. If Maribor's struggle illuminates the ways in which the periphery can become the very centre of politically engaged thought and revolutionary action, then the case of United Left shows the way in which the socialist alternative can become a viable strategy in an environment where any left signifier has been for a long time connected to a totalitarian or nostalgic frame – in other words, banned from official politics. That being said, it is important to recognise that the Slovenian uprising is only one part of the mosaic of struggles on the periphery of the EU, including in Greece, Spain, Portugal, Ireland, Italy, Bulgaria and Romania, as well as beyond, in Bosnia and Turkey. These struggles bring to light the underlying structural inequalities within the EU: *the periphery rises and re-invents both a popular democracy and socially oriented politics that articulates the masses of the redundant, that is, the 'surplus population'.* For the periphery to form a new hegemonic bloc, its historical mission consists of moving beyond (self-)isolation and orienting political demands towards the centre: for instance, how to democratise the European institutions and regulate financial capital, and how to balance socio-economic relations between North and South. This is not only to be answered by the periphery, but should be considered by anyone who wishes to continue the collective socially oriented project of Europe. Despite certain theoretical reservations on the party politics – how can a party not be completely immersed into state sovereignty, which pacifies revolutionary energies of uprisings – the conjunctural analysis shows that the

44 Gal Kirn

neoliberal project in the EU advocates the dismantling of the state and its social apparatuses (except the repressive apparatus). In this respect, discovering how to sustain the political mobilisation and connect the local struggles and protests of the peripheries with the tide of new left parties is crucial. It seems that after years of historical defeats, the left government has again become a historical possibility. What started in early 2015 with SYRIZA's promise might well continue in Spain (Podemos) and Ireland (Sinn Fein and the left alternative) in the struggle for renovation and an alternative Europe. To conclude with Machiavelli: *the sea has opened.*

Notes

1 This contribution is a revised version of the article 'Slovenia's Social Uprisings in the European Crisis: Maribor as Periphery from 1988 to 2012' (Kirn 2014); the previous version focuses on Maribor by comparing two historical events of mass protest, whereas this article focuses on recent events and transformation with an update on the latest consequences of the mass protests. Available at: http://stasisjournal.net/images/kirn_eng.pdf.

2 There exist multiple accounts on the late 1980s, from the reformed communist, liberal position to the Nova Revija, right-wing conservative position connected to the Catholic Church. For a more objective historical account with a liberal touch, see the work of Repe (1992); for a feminist perspective, see Jalušič (2002); for a left-liberal perspective, see Mastnak (1987). Although a more progressive left-oriented interpretation of the events of the 1980s remains to be written, some important notes were taken by Močnik (2010).

3 This culminated in the event in January 1990, when Slovenian delegation left the 14th (extraordinary) Congress of the League of Communists of Yugoslavia. For more on the historical background of this event and the road to the collapse, see Centrih (2015).

4 The 57th edition of *Nova Revija* in 1987 was a draft for a national program; this national memorandum was written at the same time as the memorandum from the Serbian Academy of Sciences and Arts by their nationalist counterparts in Serbia. For more on intellectual history and the rise of nationalism, see the excellent study of Dragović-Soso (2002); for media and the literature history of the nationalist rise, see Wachtel (2002).

5 Močnik (1999) incisively showed how the exclusive alternative Europe or Balkans rested on the racist culturalist differentiation of West (progress) and East (regression, war) and was the binding ideology of the whole ruling class.

6 Palmer's study of 2004 showed positive results for the majority of the interviewed cities (see http://ec.europa.eu/culture/key-documents/european-capitals-of-culture_en.htm).

7 See: http://epp.eurostat.ec.europa.eu/cache/ITY_PUBLIC/3-31102012-BP/EN/3-3110 2012-BP-EN.PDF.

8 See Slovenian statistical office report from January 2015, available at: www.stat.si/eng/novica_prikazi.aspx?ID=6773.

9 I rely on the concept of politics developed by Jacques Rancière in his seminal book *Disagreement* (1999).

10 Žižek has on several occasions spoken of this moment in the context of Hegel's 'concrete universality' and political subjectivisation, which is at work in a similar vein in the strategic moment of class 'in itself' becoming class 'for itself' in Marxian political theory.

11 The images of riots, broken windows, tear gas and police repression also documented unprecedented political violence on the streets. Even in the late 1980s, mass protests

Maribor's social uprising in the European crisis 45

had occurred practically without violence. Police made many arrests and several of the youngsters received imprisonment and financial fines.

12 For a video report from 21 December 2012, see www.youtube.com/watch?v=UTU lI6UUqVA.

13 Most trade unions united against successive governmental attempts to either extend the welfare state's privatisation and change legislation that protected workers' rights or impose a flat tax rate. On the relevance of trade unions for rethinking alternative politics, see also Močnik and Lukič (2011).

14 Taken from the interview: http://hiredknaves.wordpress.com/2012/01/21/jacques-ranciere-interview-democracy-is-not-t/.

15 For more on the antipolitical current of protests, see Ivancheva's (2013) analysis of Bulgarian protests.

16 The moralistic critique was already popular in the Occupy protests, in which the whole dynamic of the capitalist crisis was reduced to an antagonism between 1% and 99%, and only certain representatives of financial speculation (in that case, bankers; in social uprisings, politicians) were seen as corrupt individuals, the source of all evil. Some interpretations even pointed to the unfinished revolutions of 1989, which now are viewed as demonstrating a backward Eastern European mentality and lack of political culture and democratic institutions. This appears to be a mix of orientalism and conspiracy theory and succeeds in keeping people blind to the more structural nature of social relations and the logic of the capital's functioning.

17 See also Balibar (2002). This does not mean that the parliament cannot become a space of democratic, radical or even revolutionary politics; however, the established ruling parties have by and large been discredited and the public mistrust and low confidence level in parliamentary institutions has been an acute problem in most European countries. With political sovereignty 'externalised' to the European Commission, ECB and IMF, most people feel extremely alienated from any kind of imagined community.

18 The Slovenian language allows for differentiation between people (*ljudstvo*) and nation (*narod*), although the term 'narod' is sometimes used interchangeably for both meanings depending on the situation. For a specific development of the terms nation and nationality in the Yugoslav context, see Banac (1984: 23–27). Banac embraces the thesis that if it is true that nationalism is a modern phenomenon, it does not mean that certain national affiliations and a certain national consciousness did not exist prior to the late 19th century. However, this thesis overemphasises nationalist ideology as a kind of eternal ahistorical formation. Karl Deutsch (1996) defines nationality as follows: the people that are on their way to achieving political, economic and cultural autonomy. During WWII, different terms were used in the partisan struggle, with the exception of the French-derived version of 'nation' (*nacija*), which was left out due to the pejorative unitaristic connotation from the Kingdom of Yugoslavia ('integrative Yugoslavism'). For details, see Kirn (2015).

19 More on critique of historical revisionism after 1989 in Buden (2009); on the specificities in the post-Yugoslav context, see the introductory chapter in Kirn (2012).

20 Komelj (2009) authored what is believed to be the most important study on the status of partisan art. Spanning 600 pages, it is crucial for understanding the deep rupture that took place both in politics and culture.

21 I discussed social revolution and national liberation in detail in chapter 6 of my dissertation (Kirn 2012).

22 The understanding of this crisis in terms of 'primitive accumulation' and the apparatus of capture was excellently showed by Walker (2014).

23 Obviously, there is what Balibar (2008) called a strong 'fear of masses'. The masses are feared both by the official ruling class and by anti-authoritarian progressive orientations, which – also from historical examples – rightfully detect pro-fascist elements among them. However, instead of disinvesting from the masses and not dirtying hands

46 Gal Kirn

with politics, an emancipatory politics has to enter these difficult struggles and keep both feet on the ground.
24 Lategano (2014) wrote a more detailed article on the rise of socialist alternative, available at: www.internationalviewpoint.org/spip.php?article3696.

References

Balibar, É. 2002. *Politics and Other Scene*. London: Verso.
Balibar, É. 2008. *Masses, Classes, Ideas: Studies on Politics and Philosophy Before and after Marx*. London: Routledge.
Balibar, E. and I. Wallerstein. 1991. *Race, Nation, Class: Ambiguous Identities*. London: Verso.
Balažić, M. 2004. *Slovenska Demokratična Revolucija*. Ljubljana: Liberalna Akademija.
Banac, I. 1984. *The National Question in Yugoslavia*. Ithaca: Cornell University Press.
Buden, B. 2009. *Zone des Untergangs*. Frankfurt am Main: Suhrkamp.
Centrih, L. 2015. *The Road to Collapse: The Demise of the League of Communists of Yugoslavia*. Belgrade: RLS. [Online] Available at: www.rosalux.rs/userfiles/files/Lev_Centrih_Published.pdf.
Deutsch, K. 1996. *Nationalism and Social Communication*. Cambridge: Cambridge University Press.
Dragović-Soso, J. 2002. *Saviours of the Nation? Serbia's Intellectual Opposition and the Revival of Nationalism*. Montreal: McGill-Queen's University Press.
Ellerman, D. 1991. Dve poti privatizacije. *Mladina*, September 10.
Ivancheva, M. 2013. The Bulgarian Winter of Protests. *Open Democracy*, 15 March. [Online] Available at: www.opendemocracy.net/mariya-ivancheva/bulgarian-winter-of-protests.
Jalušič, V. 2002. *Kako smo hodile v feministično gimnazijo*. Ljubljana: založba/*cf.
Kirn, G. 2011. Nacrt tranzicije u kapitalističkoj nacionalnoj državi kao projekat liberalno proljeća, odnosno killing us softly na slovenački način. In: *Kroz Tranziciju*, eds. Z. Gajić and Ž. Popović. Novi Sad: Ako, pp. 21–43.
Kirn, G. 2012. *Conceptualization of Reproduction and Politics in the Work of Louis Althusser: Case of Socialist Yugoslavia*. Nova Gorica: University of Nova Gorica, Dissertation thesis.
Kirn, G. 2014. Slovenia's Social Uprisings in the European Crisis: Maribor as Periphery From 1988 to 2012. *Stasis Journal* 2(1): 106–129.
Kirn, G. 2015. *Partizanski prelomi in protislovja tržnega socializma*. Ljubljana: založba Sophija.
Komelj, M. 2009. *Kako misliti partizansko umetnost?* Ljubljana: založba/*cf.
Laclau, E. 2005. *On Populist Reason*. London and New York: Verso.
Lategano, J. 2014. Crisis and Class-Struggle in Slovenia: The Growing Momentum of Socialist Politics. *Lefteast*, November 14. [Online] Available at: www.criticatac.ro/lefteast/crisis-and-class-struggle-in-slovenia-the-growing-momentum-of-socialist-politics/.
Marx, K. and F. Engels. 1975–2005. *Marx and Engels Collected Works* (MECW). New York: International Publishers.
Mastnak, T. 1987. Totalitarizem od spodaj. *Družboslovne razprave* 4(5): 91–98.
Mencinger, J. 1994. Lastninske iluzije. *Javnost* 1(1–2): 95–103.
Močnik, R. 1999. *3 teorije: ideologija, nacija, institucija*. Ljubljana: Založba/*cf.
Močnik, R. 2003. Social Change in the Balkans. *Eurozine*, March 20. [Online] Available at: www.eurozine.com/articles/2003-03-20-mocnik-en.html.
Močnik, R. 2010. Nismo krivi, ali smo odgovorni. *Up and Undergorund* 17/18: 139–156.

Repe, B. 1992. *Liberalizem v Sloveniji*. Ljubljana: Borec.

Slavec, A. 1992. *Industrija Maribora*. Ljubljana: FF.

Tomšič, S. 2013. The People Returns: A Footnote to Protests in Slovenia. *Critical and Legal Thinking*, January 16. [Online] Available at: http://criticallegalthinking.com/2013/01/16/the-people-returns-a-footnote-to-protests-in-slovenia/.

Vezjak, B. 2013. Slovenia's Uprising. *Eurozine*, January 10. [Online] Available at: www.eurozine.com/slovenias-uprising/.

Wachtel, A. 2002. *Making a Nation, Breaking a Nation: Literature and Cultural Politics in Yugoslavia*. Stanford: Stanford University Press.

Walker, G. 2014. Primitive Accumulation and the State Form: National Debt as an Apparatus of Capture. *Viewpointmag*, October 29. [Online] Available at: https://viewpointmag.com/2014/10/29/primitive-accumulation-and-the-state-form-national-debt-as-an-apparatus-of-capture/.

Žerdin, A. 1997. *Generali brez kape*. Ljubljana: Založba Krtina.

Žižek, S. 2000. *Contingency, Hegemony, Universality: Contemporary Dialogues on the Left*. London: Verso.

Žižek, S. 2013. The West's Crisis Is One of Democracy as Much as Finance. *The Guardian*, January 16. [Online] Available at: www.theguardian.com/commentisfree/2013/jan/16/west-crisis-democracy-finance-spirit-dictators.

3 The 'stronger state' and counter-democracy

Bulgarian street protests, 2012–2013, in the accounts of participants

Valentina Gueorguieva

Introduction

The last decade has born witness to a proliferation of social movements in Bulgaria. What began in 2006 as a small action of a group of friends aiming to protect their favourite wild beach – the 'Save Irakli' campaign – evolved into a fully fledged social movement in defence of nature. Moreover, it gave impulse to other groups, who organised in defence of a variety of causes. The peak of active engagement in self-organised protests came in 2012–2013, when mass demonstrations flooded the streets of Bulgaria's largest cities, voicing demands for citizen participation and the restricted influence of privileged (financial) lobbies on political decision-making. Although Southern European protesters and the global Occupy movement questioned austerity policies and neoliberalism as the doctrine of minimal state intervention, the Bulgarian case with its demands for a stronger state, political responsibility and citizens' control featured a certain degree of local specificity. Protesters demanded participation, but at the same time embraced a vertical organisation of their own movement, demanded the resignation of the government and engaged in the opposition parties' struggles for power. They demanded citizens' control and the protection of public goods, but entrusted these to the same bureaucratic apparatus of the state that they identified as corrupted and ineffective.

Studies of recent social movements around the world have outlined their new rhizomatic form (Della Porta 2015: 17) or describe their organisational patterns as following the logic of aggregation (Juris 2012). This distinguishes them from the previous wave of counter-globalisation protests defined as the 'network of networks' (Juris 2008), as well as from the post-May 1968 movements known as 'new social movements' (Touraine 2013) or movements for identity (Castells 2010), fighting for the post-material values of the new middle class (Offe 1985; Pichardo 1997). Numerous established social scientists and political theorists have recently published a growing number of research monographs devoted to social movements (Badiou 2011; Castells 2012; Gerbaudo 2012; Žižek 2012; Della Porta 2013; Touraine 2013). At the same time, more intense and varied forms of collective action are being developed, with a corresponding proliferation

The 'stronger state' and counter-democracy   49

of protests. Some of these are sustainable social movements; others are single-issue protests or spontaneous reactions of discontent over a particular policy. Both varieties can be seen in Bulgaria in 2012–2013. Some were directed against governmental power and engaged in power struggles; others raised specific demands and did not aspire to take power. To make sense of all these varieties, the term 'contentious politics' is preferred, encompassing 'public performances, inherited forms of collective action (repertoires) and invented new ones', helping protesters to advance their claims (Tilly and Tarrow 2015: 7).

Because the movements in question experimented with forms of collective action and political expression, they do not have an elaborated and coherent programme or blueprint for their involvement in the political process. At the core of their emerging programmes and organisations lay the participants' understandings of democracy, of public interest or the state. By focusing on the accounts provided by ordinary citizens and activists, this chapter aims to show how they conceptualised the impact of their actions and their visions of change. The methodology approach includes in-depth interviews and anthropological observation. The data were collected between 2009 and 2014. The data corpus consists of 35 transcribed in-depth interviews with activists and protesters held during latent periods of protest, when no mobilisation was scheduled. In the following analysis, a special focus is placed on the accounts of the participants in the environmental movement, as well as the founders of the Protest Network – the only organisation formed after the summer protests that survives to the moment of writing (Anon 2013). After a short chronology of events and a description of the protest repertoire, the second part focuses on the conceptions of the *state*, the *public good* and *citizens' control*. By analysing these three categories, the text reconstructs the 'action frames', or 'schemata of interpretation that enable individuals to locate, perceive, identify and label occurrences within their life space and the world at large' (Snow et al. 1986: 464; see also Della Porta 2013: 143). Such action frames may become injustice frames and legitimate resistance (Snow et al. 1986: 466).

Street protests in Bulgaria 2012–2013: a chronology of events

Bulgaria did not remain isolated from the global wave of protest movements in 2011. Although the country was affected by the financial crisis and austerity policies were implemented by the government of Prime Minister Boyko Borisov and Deputy Prime Minister and Minister of Finance Simeon Djankov (2009–2013), no popular movements seemed to form in opposition to these policies. Nevertheless, the Arab Spring, more importantly the anti-austerity protests in neighbouring Greece from 2010–2012, and the international Occupy movement were discussed in activist circles, and became an inspiration for some small collective actions.[1] The impact of the international Occupy movement in Bulgaria could be seen in October and November 2011, when public assemblies were held every week in a central Sofia park located between the parliament and the University of Sofia. Participants discussed alternatives to the existing political agenda, which they defined as a 'vicious alliance of the economic with the political, of corporative

50 *Valentina Gueorguieva*

interests with political parties' (Gueorguieva 2012a: 74). These rather minor gatherings of about a hundred participants did not widely spread the ideas of the global Occupy movement. 'The movement for direct democracy', as the activists preferred to call it, remained marginal in Bulgaria.

The massive demonstrations of 2012 and 2013 were provoked by different causes. The beginning of 2012 saw the uprising of a popular campaign against scientific testing and commercial use fracking for the extraction of shale gas.[2] The movement was active in the winter months of 2011–2012 in Sofia, Varna and the other major cities of Bulgaria, where a series of marches were staged. The most important demonstration was on 14 January 2012, when between 2,000–5,000 people marched on the streets of 12 cities across Bulgaria. The next date of massive mobilisation was 11 February 2012, the international day against ACTA.[3] According to various sources, on the streets of Sofia alone, there were between 6,000–10,000 protesters. Demonstrations were held in 18 other cities of Bulgaria. In June 2012, some 2,000–3,000 protesters gathered in a flash mob and blocked a main intersection in Sofia, known as *Orlov Most* [The Eagle's Bridge]. By means of this action, the protesters stood in opposition to the passing by parliament of a new law that endangered forests and natural reserves. The legal act in question, according to the activists, was conceived to serve the interests of large big investors in the field of mountain tourism and ski facilities.

The forms of collective action in 2012 and 2013 reproduce the repertoire of contentious politics of the previous two decades. There are two main forms: demonstration, and the blockade of key intersections. The most frequently used form of protest during 2012 and 2013 was the street march. In the early 1990s and especially in winter 1997 – when the last major anti-government rally was held – street demonstrations were organised and led by the oppositional parties, whereas in 2012 and 2013, the coordination of collective actions was performed by small groups of ordinary citizens rejecting any political affiliation. The activists themselves often named this form a 'spontaneous' demonstration, meaning they were not part of an official organisation (be it a non-governmental organisation [NGO], trade union or political party), nor did they have the ambition to continue with collective action after the mobilisation. They claimed they simply launched the call for mobilisation on social networking sites, and never knew how many participants to expect. Their tactic was to summon people for action at a previously announced place and – if enough people showed up at the 'spontaneous gathering' – they would start a demonstration with slogans and banners brought by participants. Sometimes artistic performances may take place when smaller numbers of participants are engaged in the action. The advantage of artistic performances is they attract more attention, both from media and bystanders. When the numbers are significant, protesters start a march and direct their collective efforts towards the siege of respective institutions (ministries, the parliament, the headquarters of political parties), demonstrating the massive support they have received.

Another form of contentious action in 2012 and 2013 was the blocking of traffic. Orlov Most became the preferred place for gathering in summer 2012, during the protest against the Forestry Act. Orlov Most is a major road junction in central

The 'stronger state' and counter-democracy   51

Sofia. It is this space on the bridge – usually occupied by cars and public transport vehicles – that the protesters reclaimed and 'occupied'. They formed live chains or sat on the roadway until they were forced to leave by the police. The first blocking of Orlov Most took place in 2007 during the campaign for the protection of the nature reserve 'Strandja'. In 2007 and 2012, the blockades lasted only for about an hour or two. It was an act of reclaiming the public space, but instead of erecting tents and building the whole temporary infrastructure of a camp (like in Tahrir, Puerta del Sol, Syntagma or Zucotti Park), in Sofia, the action consisted of blocking traffic.

In 2013, there were three large waves of protests in Bulgaria: those from February–March (the so-called February protests, or winter protests); daily demonstrations during the summer months (the #ДАНСwithme movement); and the student occupations that started on 23 October from Sofia University and spread to 11 other universities. The winter protests were defined by their participants as protests against monopolies – monopolies on the distribution of public infrastructure (electricity, central heating, water), but most importantly on distribution networks for electricity. The central motive was the unaffordable bills for electricity received during the winter months. In February and March 2013 in Sofia, Varna, Plovdiv and other cities, tens of thousands of protesters gathered in the streets. Varna was the most active city during the winter protests, reaching 50,000 on certain dates.[4] The protests were ignited by the economic difficulties of the population of the coastal city, whose major income depends on the tourism industry during the summer months.

During the same period and earlier in January 2013, another cause was defended in a parallel series of protests: the protection of natural reserves in the mountains and the seaside. The environmental cause was championed especially in Sofia, with significantly fewer participants. The actions took place every Tuesday and Thursday during January and February, provoked by a government act allowing for more constructions and ski facilities in the mountain of Pirin. During the winter 2013 protests, Orlov Most was blocked during the evenings by small groups of protestors. The greater part of protestors gathered in front of the Ministry of Economy and started a march on the central streets of Sofia. In most cases a minivan was present, with the leaders of the protest speaking from the top of the vehicle through a megaphone. The largest actions were the Sunday marches along Tzar Osvoboditel Boulevard, connecting Orlov Most with the square in front of the parliament and the buildings of the Presidency and the Council of Ministers. These marches occurred every Sunday from 24 February to mid-March. Similar demonstrations were organised in other big cities, the most active city being Varna.

On 20 February 2013, Plamen Goranov, an environmentalist and former activist of the anti-fracking movement, set himself on fire in front of the municipality in Varna. He demanded the resignation of the mayor and the community council of Varna, who were suspected to be under the strong influence of a group of local businessmen (known as TIM) related to organised crime in the past (see more in Hristova and Krastev 2014). Five more men immolated themselves during

52 *Valentina Gueorguieva*

February–March 2013. On the same day, in Sofia, Prime Minister Boyko Borisov resigned a couple of months ahead of the end of his term. This was in response to the violence exercised by police troops against the protesters in Sofia during the previous night, 19 February 2013. A small number of people were lightly wounded. Early parliamentary elections were scheduled for 12 May 2013. Regardless of the resignation, the demonstrations continued in masses until mid-March, the most important of them on the Sundays of 24 February and 3 March 2013. After 10 March 2013, the numbers of participants started to decrease. The early elections on 12 May 2013 were won by Boyko Borisov's party, but it did not achieve the required majority of 121 Members of Parliament (MPs) (out of 240 MPs in the Bulgarian parliament) and was not willing to form a government in coalition. This led to a further deepening of the political crisis. The Bulgarian Socialist Party (BSP) formed a cabinet of experts with Plamen Oresharski as prime minister (former minister of finance in the cabinet of Serguey Stanishev [BSP], 2005–2009). New small protests coincided with the appointment of the government of Plamen Oresharski on 28 May and 2 June 2013, but the second big wave of protests did not start until 14 June. It became known under the hashtag #ДАНСwithme.[5] The protest continued on a daily basis until the beginning of August, when the parliament dissolved for a vacation of one month. The incident that re-ignited the anger of the masses was the appointment of a media mogul, Delyan Peevski, suspected of having links with criminal circles, as director of the State Agency for National Security. Under pressure from the street protests, the incumbents withdrew the nomination and Peevski left the 42nd Parliament on 18 June 2013. But the protesters did not withdraw from the streets of Sofia. With the progress of collective actions, their demands increased in number: they now asked for the resignation of the government, changes in the electoral code, criminalisation of the presence of 'elements of oligarchy' in the current government, and 'the dismantling of the State based on the plutocratic model' (Kharlamov 2013: 1).

During the summer 2013 protests, the demonstrations took the same two forms: the blocking of Orlov Most and marches on the central streets of Sofia. The greater part of the protesters joined the street marches, passing in front of the headquarters of all the big political parties. The same route of almost 7km was repeated every evening. They expressed their anger against the political elites, and at the same time blocked the traffic in the central part of Sofia for hours. There were no visible leaders in the crowd. Orlov Most was blocked every evening for a period of two months, and remained closed during the whole evening. Protesters reclaimed the street and performed various actions on the spot: artistic performances, sports games and leisure activities, games for families with children, informal gatherings, and an assembly – a form of debate and an instrument for making movement for direct democracy, attracting from 10 to 50 participants.

There was no violence during the street protests from 2012 and 2013, and no public or private property was destroyed. Clashes with the police occurred only three times during the whole period of two years: on the evening of 19 February 2013; during the night of 23 to 24 July 2013, when protesters formed a

The 'stronger state' and counter-democracy   53

blockade around the parliament and would not let the MPs leave the building; and in the early afternoon of 12 November 2013, when the same action was performed by students. On 23 October 2013, a group of students from Sofia University occupied its central building, demanding the resignation of the government of Plamen Oresharski and the dissolution of the 42nd Parliament. The wave of occupations spread out to other universities in Sofia, Plovdiv and Veliko Turnovo, and gained the support of their professors and the citizenry. Two popular marches took place in Sofia on 1 and 10 November 2013, with students and their professors leading manifestations of almost 10,000 participants. The students adopted the same form of collective action as the anti-government rallies of the 1990s and the previous two big waves of protest of the same year – the demonstration. They aspired to massive support and visibility in the public space and embraced the same anti-government rhetoric, demanding the resignation of Oresharski and the dissolution of parliament.

The actions of the students re-ignited a spark in the #ДАНСwithme protests, with a couple more massive demonstrations in November and December 2013. By the end of January 2014, the occupations in all the universities had lost energy and support, and the headquarters of Sofia University announced the end of the occupation. The goal – the resignation of the government of Plamen Oresharski – was not achieved. The protest activities of #ДАНСwithme were slowly fading away. In early summer 2014, the government announced its plans to resign and dissolve the 42nd Parliament on 6 August 2014. Early parliamentary elections were scheduled for 5 October 2014, and won by the political party GERB. Its leader, Boyko Borisov, formed his second government and was inaugurated as prime minister on 7 November 2014.

During the period of this research, contentious politics in Bulgaria varied in their form of organisation as well as in repertoire. Whereas the mobilisations from 2012 were the result of the actions of self-organised groups that dissolved as soon as the action was completed, and no leaders or protest organisations emerged from these actions, the winter protests had leaders and the summer protests had the Protest Network. Some protesters were part of a sustainable social movement (the environmental movement), whereas others conceived their actions as single-issue protests or brisk reactions of discontent over a particular policy. This latter strategy is seen as an exercise of citizens' control over the decisions of power. In what follows, these two varieties of 'frames of action' are presented.

'We are the state' or the protection of public good

The emergence of the green movement in Bulgaria was marked by the symbolic actions of the group 'Save Irakli', which started in March 2006. 'A group of friends', as they refer to themselves, were concerned about the prospect of massive construction works on their favourite wild beach. The area of Irakli was one of the last remaining localities untouched by the overdeveloped tourist sector on the Bulgarian Black Sea coast. The problem of excessive construction and the

54 *Valentina Gueorguieva*

devastation of nature in the coastal areas, as well as deforestation in the mountains near the ski resorts, was largely felt among the population and the actions of the 'group of friends' received popular support. However, the roots of the 'spontaneous' green movement for the protection of nature in Bulgaria can be traced further back to the beginning of this century. The first actions for the protection of natural reserves took place in the mountain of Pirin, in 1999 or 2000, according to the accounts of activists (interview with Z., green activist, held in Sofia, 5 February 2013; interview with Z.M., visual artist, held in Sofia, 15 March 2013). They remember how a rumour was spread regarding the illegal felling of trees in the proximity of the ski resort Bansko, and they immediately mobilised to take action. The green activists quickly realised that their cause was not just an isolated case, but a more general problem of the privatisation of public goods, of corruption and inefficient administration. The peak of activities was between 2006 and 2008 with 'Save Irakli', and the campaigns 'Save Strandja' (after the name of a mountain and national park in the southeastern part of Bulgaria) and 'Citizens for Rila' (named after the highest mountain). Thereafter, a series of environmental campaigns were modelled after the actions of this 'group of friends' and took the form of 'spontaneous demonstrations'.

Later, they formed coalitions with other activists from differing social and political backgrounds. For the campaign against the deregulation of genetically modified organisms (GMOs) in 2010, the environmentalists joined efforts with the virtual community of the web forum 'BG-mamma' (which focuses on motherhood and other social issues). In 2011, when the government granted permission to a large foreign corporation to perform tests and work on the industrial exploitation of shale gas using fracking technology in the north-eastern part of Bulgaria, an even larger coalition of self-organised citizen groups was formed. The campaign lasted more than five months, until a moratorium was passed by the parliament in January 2012. The next campaign was for Vitosha, the mountain closest to the capital, Sofia, which culminated in the June 2012 protests. It came as a surprise to the long-standing supporters of the environmental movement to see how, on 14 June 2012, a rather marginal campaign of the group 'For Vitosha', whose first actions had already taken place in February 2012, generated massive support. It was a great success, and it was this event that had the broadest response. The actions of the environmentalists during winter 2013 for the protection of the sea coast and the natural reserve in Pirin were a continuation of the previous campaigns of the citizens-environmentalists: they took the same form, had the same motives and demands, and the same familiar participants could be seen in the crowd.

Throughout these campaigns, the citizens-environmentalists movement demonstrates continuity and a coherence of demands from 2006 until today. After the actions of 'Save Irakli', a group of interested young people was formed who shared more than just concern for the protection of nature: they shared a cause, a lifestyle, a set of leisure activities, often spending time together in the mountains and vacations on deserted beaches. By their own accounts, they can be identified

The *'stronger state' and counter-democracy*   55

as a group even by their visual appearance. Speaking with self-awareness, they admit that they have evolved into some kind of a sub-cultural style.

> My father noticed that. He saw one of my friend activists on TV, and he exclaimed: "Look, she even has the same pants like you! You are like a sect!" And he is right, we do have the same beliefs, even the same lifestyle and dress code, we do the same things, it's more like a subculture.
>
> (interview with Z.M., visual artist, held in Sofia, 27 March 2013)

The citizens-environmentalists movement can be framed in the logic of the protection of public goods. This logic is best defined in the words of the activist who initiated 'Save Irakli', Nadezhda Maksimova:

> All our protests are for justice, for a better sustainable development of our country, for the rule of law. Because what we do in Bulgaria is to allow people with money, the so-called investors, to do whatever they want, to treat our country as if it were their patrimony [*bashtiniya*[6]]. Their private interest is above all, which is absolutely incorrect. Despite their accusations to the environmental organisations – that we are some kind of communists, still when there are public goods they have to be managed by the public, in common. This is why we insist that we need a stronger state that would be in charge with the public interest, and would defend the public interest against private interests.
>
> (interview, held in Sofia, 25 March 2013)

This passage introduces an understanding of nature as a public good. I prefer here the term 'public good' to translate the Bulgarian expression *obshti blaga*. This may also be translated as 'commons', but because in the language of the respondent it is coupled with expressions like 'the rule of law' and the need for a 'stronger state' protecting the 'public interest', I have chosen 'public good' as closer to her understanding of this concept. Further in the interview, she clarifies that a solution to the problem is to be sought through strict regulation of public property on behalf of the state, and not by managing it as 'commons', by entrusting the natural resources to the community.

The conflict, as seen by the activists, is between the protection of nature and the development of tourism. The 'enemy' is identified as 'the investors': large- and small-scale business in the field of tourism. Just as the landscape of the seaside was changed by the profiles of immense resort complexes and tightly neighbouring family hotels in the coastal towns, the development of ski resorts with their infrastructure and sport facilities has led to deforestation in the nearby mountain slopes. In both cases, the pursuit of profit maximisation in the business of tourism has led to massive construction works, accompanied by water pollution and logging to build ski lifts and open more space for ski slopes. To the logic of profit maximisation and economic growth, the environmentalists oppose the

56   *Valentina Gueorguieva*

post-material values of sustainable development, of a more responsible attitude towards the environment.

> Most people are used to seeing nature as a resource. Especially in Bulgaria. They only think about how to take advantage of it. The very idea of sustainable development is completely absent here. All they want is to construct more [hotels], to take everything they can from nature, and to keep on profiting from it as long as they can. And if it's gone, uh, well, we'll think about this later.
>
> (interview with P.D., held in Sofia, 10 February 2014)

In the conflict between nature and tourism, the loser is nature. Instead of being used as a resource, nature needs special protection. Its preservation from industry (in this particular case, tourism) should be subjected to special regulations. Special strategies have to be designed for its preservation by environmental organisations. The concern about nature needs to be brought into the day-to-day practices of ordinary people. The growth of tourism is perceived by respondents as shortsighted, as a wrong and irresponsible approach towards nature. They believe that in the conflict between tourism and nature, the state can serve as arbiter, for it is only the state institutions that can impose regulations on business to protect nature.

Yet the state has almost completely deregulated private property and encouraged private initiative in developing small-scale or larger investments in tourism. For cases in which the property of land is public, the legal instrument used by the Bulgarian state is the concession – a set of legal rights given to a private company for a certain period of time for the economic use of the land and its resources. Concessions on specific areas – beaches, forests, parts of natural reserves – were granted to economic agents operating in the field of tourism during the last two decades. The process was subjected to fairly weak oversight on the part of the state institutions, which led to growing cases of abuses and violations of the terms of concessions restricting public access to the areas, and deteriorating the environment.

The solution to this problem, according to the green activists, was a stronger state. The state – they believed – is too weak or malfunctioning, and has a tendency to withdraw from the responsibility of preserving natural reserves. The state discharges itself of the obligation to protect public interest using the instrument of concessions. The result is that public goods are no longer accessible to all of us, but treated as a resource to be explored by the investor in his pursuit of profit. This, in turn, underlies a more general problem, which is – according to the activists' formulations – that the state does not belong to its citizens. It does not act in favour of the public interest or express their will. Instead of protecting public goods against the abuses of the investors, the state allies with the investors and their economic interests and turns its back on the public interest.

Hence, the slogan of the June 2012 blockade: 'We are the State'. We – the citizens of Bulgaria – need to remind the government that the state belongs to us,

The 'stronger state' and counter-democracy   57

and that the elected representatives are in power to serve the public interest. This slogan was also used in the winter 2013 actions, and worn by ordinary citizens in the form of a self-made paper crown. By claiming 'We are the State', protesters adopt the classical understanding of the state as 'res publica est res populi' (after the formulation of Cicero): the public affairs are the matter of the people. This was coupled with a different understanding of the state, seen from its negative side – protesters see the state as the instrument of power that was expropriated by its sovereign ('the people') and is now in possession of 'the oligarchs'.

> Well, according to me, the enemy is that other state that is hiding behind the state. Somehow the enemy are the big fish in the economy. Those people for whom the state works. Some very rich bankers, who possess two ski resorts, for example. Some famous names from the resort business at the seaside. People for whom the laws are being written. Somehow, of course, the enemy is also the legislative power that works that way – whether it be the parliament or a ministry [. . .] The fact that they prefer to serve in favour of a very wealthy man, who has great influence, instead of [serving] all those who voted for them.
>
> (interview with Y.P., held in Sofia, 30 March 2013)

The 'other state' is a metaphor, also used by other respondents, to designate the illicit connections between politics and corporate interests, a metaphor for lobbyism or 'the backstage games' of politicians and their 'rich friends'. In other formulations, the same idea is exemplified by 'the model of the backstage', 'the oligarchy', or even a list of 150 oligarchs who rule Bulgaria. That 'other state' can be criticised and ridiculed by the image of an octopus that the protesters in the #ДАНСwithme movements used for their Facebook profile pictures. In their interpretation, it refers to the criminal organisations or the mafia, the inheritors of the old socialist *nomenklatura*, or the network of agents of the former state security service. This negative conception of the 'other state' legitimises resistance and manifests itself in the demand to take the state back into 'our' hands.

The feelings that the state is too weak and does not represent the public interest became even stronger during the 2013 protests. No doubt, they intensified with the failure of Oresharski's government to convince the citizens that it was interested in public service, and not an ostensible cover for the oligarchy. As writer and activist Ivan Dimitrov said:

> [We need to] stand together against those who apparently ruin this state. Because this is a ruined state. In fact the place we live in is not even a state.
>
> (interview, held in Sofia, 27 November 2014)

Therefore, resistance is understood as the fight for the state itself. Nevertheless, by claiming that they need the state returned to their hands, protesters do not to aspire to win power or be in charge of government. Their quest is not to be the

58 *Valentina Gueorguieva*

next incumbents, but to gain control over public institutions and make sure these institutions work in favour of the public interest.

Both the positive and the negative visions of the state reduce it to an instrument of power. In the negative vision, the state serves 'the big investors' and is used by them to maximise profit. In the positive vision, the state is an instrument to impose regulations on private interests, to protect nature or implement other policies that we, the people, desire. It is curious to see that protesters do not see the state as some kind of community (the 'imagined community' of the nation, for example), nor as a territory or organisation that holds the legitimate exercise of violence. It is not an entity, nor an autonomous actor, but rather a set of institutions that operate in some other agents' goals and interests (be it the rich people or the protesters and their claims). In this instrumentalised vision of the state, it becomes the target of the resistance movement.

Citizens take control

Every mass protest in the series from 2012 and 2013 began as a negative reaction against a particular act of government. Protesters defined their actions as spontaneous reactions of discontent, and demanded to deter a particular government decision, legal act, or appointment to an office. The protesters conceive of the street protests as an instrument of control by the citizens over the decisions of power-holders. This form of street protest uses the logic of negation – they are an opposition against something, an expression of disapproval. Collective actions staged in the public space are understood by the participants as manifestations of their radical disapproval: they present their actions as spontaneous reactions of indignation, aroused in ordinary citizens by policies judged as intolerable.

As a rule, activists engaging in some form of reactive mobilisations reject any association with a pre-existing structure, be it a citizens' organisation, NGO, trade union or political party. Such demonstrations are, so to speak, organised without organisation through the 'ridiculously easy group forming' made possible by digital media, to use the expression of Clay Shirky (2008: 155). The claim is that a genuine reaction of discontent or indignation is enough to summon masses of ordinary citizens to the streets. The energy of protest actions is nurtured by such moral reactions as anger, exasperation, a sense of powerlessness, and relentless opposition. Unlike the citizen-environmentalist movement, these protest actions cannot be seen as a continuous chain of events, growing stronger one after the other. Rather, they are isolated cases of dispersed discontent, or what is usually called single-issue mobilisations. Participants dissolve with the end of collective actions; they do not try to design a campaign or found an organisation because they do not aspire to have sustainable organisations.

According to their understanding, by participating in manifestations, people may have an impact over the decisions of government and thus exercise control. Such influence, they claim, cannot be achieved through the traditional, old-style party politics, which has proven to be inefficient, corrupted or simply inadequate to their tasks. It was mistrust in 'the political system' that has led the citizens

The *'stronger state' and counter-democracy*   59

to seek new ways of expressing discontent, of exercising control, of citizen empowerment.

The events from 2012 and 2013 can be interpreted according to the same line of thinking: in June 2012, it was a protest against the new Forestry Act, and in June 2013, against the nomination of Delyan Peevski as head of the State Agency for National Security. The winter 2013 protests were also a form of negative contestation, provoked by a particular case –inflated winter electricity bills. In 2012 and 2013, the slogans from previous years of protests reappeared: 'You do not represent us!' (worn by protesters during demonstrations in June 2012); 'We do not want replacement [of the political party in power], we want real change!' (February–March 2013); 'I do not want GERB back, I want a future!' (June 2013). What unites the participants in these 'spontaneous' mobilisations is not a collective interest, nor a collective identity like in the movement of citizen-environmentalists. They do not maintain links during latent periods when there is no mobilisation. They are united by their negative reaction, a strong and urgent opposition to power. The opposition was articulated in the form of emotional or moral reaction: 'This is unpardonable' or 'This cannot be tolerated'; 'They [the politicians] cannot do whatever they want!'; 'I just had to do something' or 'Enough!', 'This cannot go on like this!' (slogans and interviews with participants in 2013).

For some, the summer 2013 protests were 'the desperate cry of a lost hope' that the so-called transition would bring social change and a better life (interview with I.M., protester, held in Sofia, 24 November 2014). Protestors defined their motivations to join the actions as stemming from indignation, as a reaction to the arrogance of the ruling class. They had the feeling that nothing had changed, not only during the current year of political crisis, but for the last 25 years of democratic transition.

'It is all the same, I can't get rid of the feeling, that one and the same thing has been happening for 25 years; these are all the same people, a product of one and the same workshop'[7]; 'it was only a replacement' (interview with I.M.).

For another participant, mass protest is a way to show the ruling elites that 'there are certain things the society cannot tolerate' (interview with K.V., protester, held in Sofia, 17 November 2014). He defined the acts of politicians in power as arrogant and unacceptable. He was convinced that on both sides of the political spectrum – the party of Boyko Borisov and their opponents in the Bulgarian Socialist Party – the connections with corporate interests and oligarchic lobbies is very strong. He identified the biggest problem of the Bulgarian government as 'the coalescence of political parties, the state rule, with business circles and some criminal formations at the bottom of all this'. The role of the people, therefore, is to demonstrate that this will not be tolerated. Various wordings were used by respondents to explain the idea that the mass protests are an instrument of citizens' control over the decisions of power.

> There is this saying that the price of democracy is to be vigilant.[8] This means to me to be on the street. [. . .] When, in Bulgaria, society can control the government, then life will be better in this country.
>
> (interview with H., green activist, held in Sofia, 14 January 2010)

60 *Valentina Gueorguieva*

It is a common saying among green activists that they act as a fire brigade. Whenever a vigilant citizen discovers an abuse of power, or corruption, or illegal construction works, he sounds the alarm and the engaged citizen-environmentalists are on the streets. With the time and experience of spontaneous protests, the same mechanism is put into practice for the single-issue causes and reactive mobilisations, up to the anti-government rallies in 2013. After the alarm is given, the manifestation takes place, and – if it is successful – the legal act or government decision that provoked it is deterred. The assumption is that citizens can therefore control the decisions of the incumbents by exercising a veto power. This logic of the immediate reaction of discontent is, therefore, essential to the democratic process because it is a necessary corrective to political decision-making, and can be a motor for the development of contemporary democracies suffering from a crisis of representative democracy. Reactive mobilisations, seen from this angle, are a form of what Pierre Rosanvallon (2008) describes as 'counter-democracy'.

Counter-democracy is the positive work of distrust that aims 'to make sure that elected officials keep their promises and to find ways of maintaining pressure on the government to serve the common good' (Rosanvallon 2008: 8). This principle of the constructive work of mistrust is manifested particularly in post-totalitarian societies, as the author states. Another historical example is the post-revolutionary period in France, when the principle of surveillance was established as a complementary form of sovereignty. 'Perpetually vigilant, the people were to oversee the work of the government. This diligent oversight was celebrated as the main remedy for dysfunctional institutions and in particular as the cure for what might be called "representative entropy"' (Rosanvallon 2008: 13). The analogy between contemporary Bulgaria and post-totalitarian states, or even with the post-revolutionary period in France, is no doubt too schematic. There are important differences. But we are actually experiencing both problems referred to in this fragment – the malfunctioning of institutions and a distorted link of political representation. We may call this second problem representative entropy, or a crisis of representative democracy, or as protesters themselves paraphrase it, the state does not belong to the citizens, and citizens are trying to regain control over the state (after the slogans used in June 2012 and winter 2013).

When protesters adopt the logic of citizens' control to frame their actions, they believe that the sovereignty of the people is manifested through constant reaction against the decisions of government. Citizens' control can take the form of 'eternal vigilance', pressure exercised through disclosure or leaks, and judicial review. But the form of citizens' control that is most commonly used is to deter or impede a particular decision until the authorities revoke its implementation. This is the power of the 'negative sovereignty', or a form of veto exercised by the citizens. Technically, it is the most effective means. 'Blocking government action yielded tangible, visible results. Success in blocking the passage of an undesired bill was plain for everyone to see [. . .] The power of the people is a veto power' (Rosanvallon 2008: 14, 15). If by means of protest actions, a bill is withdrawn or a planned act is revoked, this completely satisfies the demand of the protestors. They have the satisfaction of preventing the implementation of an undesirable

The 'stronger state' and counter-democracy   61

policy; they won a victory. Therefore, it is not surprising that counter-democracy often takes a negative form. The people, as a sovereign, exercise a veto on a government decision. This form of exercising collective will has tangible results and easily satisfies the need for citizens' control. The two most prominent examples are the repeal of the Forestry Act from 2012 and the withdrawal of Peevski's nomination in 2013. But these were small victories. The real question was what to do next? Shall they continue with citizens' control and reactive mobilisations and act as the fire brigade or could they find more sustainable solutions? How could they build more reliable institutions and bridge the gap between citizens and their political representatives?

One solution, proposed by the protesters of the summer 2013 wave, was the foundation of an organisation – the Protest Network (PN) – as a way to coordinate collective action, and later as a place for debate and decisions about strategies and concrete actions. The first meetings of PN were in mid-July, and were very informal. The task was to organise street art performances for the next couple of days (according to the account of Ivan Dimitrov, one of the co-founders; interview from 27 November 2014). The formative idea was also to be the unit that expresses the will of the protesters. The structure of the network was horizontal – there were no leaders. Debates were very active online (via Facebook) and soon reached the important questions of who we are and what are our demands. We questioned whether we have demands in common, as we come from different movements and protest backgrounds, even different ideologies. Discussions were ardent and consensus was very difficult to achieve. The process was emotional and time-consuming. Some activists withdrew from the debates. The others formed a minimal consensus around the demand for resignation. For Ivan Dimitrov, the adoption of this overarching rhetoric of '*Ostavka!*' [Resignation] was detrimental for the movement because it lost specificity: the search for specific solutions became secondary.

> Yes, the protest operates in the negative logic, to stop something that you do not agree with, but it is at the same time positive [. . .] Because you see how things can be done in a better way, you can find the right way to do it, the fair way to do it. From this point of view, the summer protests were a failure to a certain extent. Because they adopted this rhetoric [of the resignation] and lost their concrete character.
>
> (interview with Ivan Dimitrov, held in Sofia, 27 November 2014)

During the previous actions of the environmentalists, protesters engaged actively in searching for positive solutions to particular issues. At that point, their efforts were directed towards convincing the responsible institutions to implement these concrete solutions, via various strategies (pressure groups, flash mobs, negotiations, demonstrations). This trend was visible in the environmental movement, in the actions of the Green Advocates, for example. During the last wave of protests, such positive solutions were no longer sought. All energy was devoted to overthrowing the government. When Peevski's nomination was received on

62 *Valentina Gueorguieva*

18 June 2013, the protest demonstrations did not withdraw from the streets of Sofia. The feelings of indignation were still very strong, and a reformulation of protest demands was worked out by one part of the protesters, in collaboration with a newly formed coalition of opposition parties – the Reformist Bloc. They demanded the resignation of the government, dissolution of the parliament and early elections. By raising these claims, they changed the stake of collective actions – from a form of citizens' control over the incumbents, it became an anti-government rally.

Inside the Protest Network, still defined as 'an instrument and an environment for citizens' control' (according to its Proclamation), the debates over the adoption of 'the rhetoric of resignation' were ardent. As time went on, and after some activists withdrew, the structure of PN became more centralised. Divergent understandings of some core issues, like citizen participation and the working of democracy, led to disagreements between the initiators and supporters of the political party GERB, who joined the network and started to act according to their party affiliation. The participants soon realised they had no common grounds. The process of decision-making was very slow and became even more problematic.

> Finally, it became easy to slip into some kind of centralised form of taking decisions. It was the circle around some figures – the group of the initiators – that took the decisions.
> (interview with G.L., held in Sofia, 14 November 2014)

The transformation of the Protest Network from a unit of coordination to an organised structure of member groups with some elements of centralisation in the process of decision-making was not unproblematic. This transformation led to the disappointment of some participants, who left PN. From an organisation expressing the popular will, whose function was to be a corrective of the government, 'some kind of a mirror for the political class' (interview with G.L.), it eventually evolved into a centralised federation of members, united under the 'minimal consensus of the resignation' (interviews with I.D. and K.V.). It lost a large number of participants and supporters, and found itself at a loss regarding how to define citizens' control.

Conclusion

To sum up, the participants in the protest movements in Bulgaria from 2012 and 2013 take their collective actions to be a manifestation of the 'sovereignty of the people'. The negative exercise of sovereignty is the citizens' control, or the power of the people to impose a veto on certain decisions of power that they judge inadmissible. The positive exercise of sovereignty is to reclaim the state, as exemplified by the slogan 'We are the state!' If the core problem is identified by the majority of protestors as the vicious alliance between the political parties and oligarchic elites, which leads to a weakening of the state, the search for solutions can move in the direction of a 'stronger state'. But the insistence for a strong

The 'stronger state' and counter-democracy   63

state should not be confused with the strong, centralised, populist or authoritarian rule of one figure, or a group, or the political elites in general. The populist or authoritarian version of 'the stronger state' is propitious to the same vicious alliance of political and economic elites. The demands for stronger and well-functioning state institutions, which operate in defence of the public interest, go hand in hand with the demands for citizens' control over the decision of power, or counter-democracy. The positive claim for a 'stronger state' cannot be dissociated from the negative sovereignty of the veto. The necessary corrective function – called counter-democracy – is essential for the development of a stronger system of representative democracy. The positive and the negative stance of the protest demands need to be taken together: the protection of the public good together with persistent and effective control on behalf of the citizens. The stronger state can be achieved through and find a corrective in counter-democracy. The two fundamental problems – the malfunctioning of the institutions and the gap between the citizenry and the state (representative entropy) – can find solutions in more forms of citizen participation, in self-organisation and different procedures of taking decisions from below.

The infusion of the protest organisations like PN and the student occupation with representatives of party structures and the adoption of the common demand for resignation resulted in reformulating the protest movement as a variant of old-style party politics, as a form of power struggle. When the former prime minister, Boyko Borisov, returned to office in coalition with the Reformist Bloc, this was seen, from the protesters' point of view, as 'one last chance' (interview with K.V.) for democratic rights. Other activists expressed disappointment that their actions did not result in social changes in the desired direction. From the point of view of the development of social movements in Bulgaria, after 2013, wider networks of collaboration between different 'networks of trust' were created. At the same time, there is a persistent negative feeling that these networks are subjected to the influence of oppositional political parties and the interests they represent.

Notes

1 Global events were covered in mainstream media, and received more attention in alternative channels like *Indymedia Bulgaria* (http://bulgaria.indymedia.org/), *Bezlogo* (literally 'No Logo', an alternative channel named after Naomi Klein's 2000 book, http://bezlogo.com/), and *Saprotiva* (literally 'Resistance', http://saportiva.org). Two Facebook groups named 'Occupy Bulgaria' channelled the discussions. See more in Gueorguieva (2012b).
2 Hydraulic fracking is used to extract oil and gas from shale plays, creating fractures in the rock structure by pressurised liquids. The technology is highly controversial. Its opponents underline the risks of ground and surface water contamination, as well as the deterioration of soil. It can also increase seismic activity. In Bulgaria, identified reserves of shale gas are in the north-eastern part of the country, where the major economic activity is agriculture. This area is called 'the granary of Bulgaria' for its fertile soil and the production of wheat and other cereals.
3 The Anti-Counterfeiting Trade Agreement (ACTA) was a multinational treaty prepared during 2011 for enforcing the protection of intellectual property rights. The proposed

64 Valentina Gueorguieva

regulations on counterfeit goods, including generic medicines, and on copyright infringement on the Internet were judged as a threat to civil liberties. An international campaign against the treaty was initiated in the member states of the EU, with an international day of action on 11 February 2012. On 4 July 2012, the European Parliament rejected the document.

4 For reference, the population of Varna is approximately 350,000. The capital, Sofia, has about 1,250,000 inhabitants.

5 'ДАНС' is an acronym that stands for the name of the State Agency for National Security in Bulgarian; in Cyrillic, it is spelled the same as the English word 'dance'.

6 The Bulgarian word *bashtiniya* has a pronounced negative connotation.

7 By 'the workshop', the respondent refers to the structures of the former state security services.

8 This expression is used by more than one participant. It is probably an adaptation of the quote 'The price of liberty is eternal vigilance', attributed to Thomas Jefferson.

References

Anon. 2013. *Proclamation.* [Online] Available at: www.protestnamreja.bg/about-us/.

Badiou, A. 2011. *Le réveil de l'histoire.* Paris: Lignes.

Castells, M. 2010. *The Power of Identity.* Oxford: Wiley and Blackwell Publishers.

Castells, M. 2012. *Networks of Outrage and Hope: Social Movements in the Internet Age.* Cambridge: Polity Press.

Della Porta, D. 2013. *Can Democracy Be Saved? Participation, Deliberation, and Social Movements.* Cambridge: Polity Press.

Della Porta, D. 2015. *Social Movements in Times of Austerity.* Cambridge: Polity Press.

Gerbaudo, P. 2012. *Tweets and the Streets: Social Media and contemporary Activism.* London: Pluto Press.

Gueorguieva, V. 2012a. Distorted Representation and Active Citizenship. Digital Media and Spontaneous Street Demonstrations in Bulgaria (2006–2010). *Südosteuropa* 60(1): 53–77.

Gueorguieva, V. 2012b. Indymedia et le mouvement pour la démocratie directe en Bulgarie, automne 2011. In: *E-Citoyennetés*, ed. A. Krasteva. Paris: L'Harmattan, pp. 185–202.

Hristova, T. and S. Krastev. 2014. *Zlatnata yabalka Varna i triglaviat TIM'/ 'Varna as the Golden Apple and TIM, the Three-Headed Dragon.* [Online] Available at: www.seminar-bg. eu/spisanie-seminar-bg/broy10b/item/419-zlatnata-yabalka-i-trigrlaviyat-tim.html.

Juris, J.S. 2008. *Networking Futures: The Movements Against Corporate Globalization.* Durham: Duke University Press.

Juris, J.S. 2012. Reflections on #Occupy Everywhere: Social Media, Public Space and Emerging Logic of Aggregation. *American Ethnologist* 39(2): 259–279.

Kharlamov, I. 2013. Vague de protestations en Bulgarie. *La Voix de la Russie* [Online]. Available at: http://french.ruvr.ru/2013_07_24/La-vague-des-protestations-en-Bulgarie-7762/?slide-1.

Offe, C. 1985. New Social Movements: Challenging the Boundaries of Institutional Politics. *Social Research* 52(4): 817–868.

Pichardo, N. 1997. New Social Movements: A Critical Review. *Annual Review of Sociology* 23: 411–430.

Rosanvallon, P. 2008. *Counter-Democracy: Politics in an Age of Distrust.* Cambridge: Cambridge University Press.

Shirky, C. 2008. *Here Comes Everybody: How Change Happens When People Come Together*. New York: Penguin.

Snow, D.A., E.B. Rochford and S.K. Wordon. (1986). Frame Alignment Process, Micromobilization, and Movement Participation. *American Sociological Review* 51(4): 464–481.

Tilly, C. and S. Tarrow. 2015. *Contentious Politics: Second Edition, Revised and Updated*. New York: Oxford University Press.

Touraine, A. 2013. *La fin des sociétés*. Paris: Seuil.

Žižek, S. 2012. *The Year of Dreaming Dangerously*. London: Verso.

4 The spaces of social mobilisation in Greece

Kostis Plevris

Introduction[1]

During the last decade, Greece has been the scene of the development of a series of social movements, spontaneous and organised, violent and non-violent, escaping 'traditional' repertoires and not. These emerged primarily as a public response to the economic crisis, although many of them did not explicitly refer to it, but rather targeted many of its outcomes. Thus, demonstrations against austerity or the leasing of public assets, but also against the restraint of domestic liberties, against oppression and fascist currents in society, may constitute the greatest social confrontation with the effects of the crisis in the recent period. In this chapter, we refer to the principal moments of the Greek social struggle up to early 2015. However, we do not tackle them literally, descriptively or typologically because this method of approaching social reality results in static schemes, failing to interpret the laws of human social activity. Such categories exist here prior to their species: they do not have real existence, rather they are formal, and hence not meaningful (Ilyenkov 1960). Instead, we interpret social processes in constant motion and in interconnection with the whole of social reality. Of course, the scope of such an attempt is vast and cannot fit in a single chapter, or even the work of a single researcher. What we attempt to describe is that these social mobilisations had a strong spatial analogue concerning the way they were expressed and developed, but also restrained. Space was not a simple 'attribute' following them; matter, and therefore human activity, cannot exist outside time and space, while both are the objective forms of being (Engels 1963; Lenin 1972). Space and time appear as distinct categories only for philosophical thought; however, they should not be conceived as separable for the sciences that study them (Alayev 1986). So, the development of human society unfolds in space and time together, and that is why both are not a mere conceptual product, but a constitutive element of the world around us.

The process of understanding how space is produced is therefore connected to the comprehension of social procedures themselves – in our case, social mobilisations. Hence, scientific thinking regarding this object should never downgrade space to a simple carrier of social activity, in which places are mentioned only as dead property in the background of a certain act, passed over in favour of

The spaces of social mobilisation in Greece   67

information such as the number of participants, their demands, age structure and so on. On the other hand, scientific thinking should also avoid an apotheosis of space, treating it as the cradle and shell that hosts anything in regard to social life; for example, regardless of their often vital role, squats, LGBT clubs, green spaces and so on should not be considered to comprise all the prerequisites necessary for social movements to appear. Such ways of thinking approach space as fragmented from the rest of social interconnections, assuming an autonomous role that de facto deprives them of any effort to interpret social procedures globally. Of course, a scientific context that respects the link of collective claims with spatial questions, without losing contact with reality, already exists; there is no need to re-invent the wheel here. We simply apply it to the Greek reality and attempt to enrich it with new facts from the objective world around us. Thus, by using cases from Greek social movements, we attempt to show that the study of space is emerging as a necessary condition for our schemes to agree with reality.

Social movements and space: examples from the Greek scene

It is empirically tangible that social claims and rivalries have been further developed in those cases in which space had always played an important role. In December 2008, following the assassination of a 15-year-old boy named Alexis Grigoropoulos by a police guard at Exarheia city district – with symbolical connotations and activist networks that could set up the material preconditions for the development of social confrontations – there began a nearly month-long period of intense clashes with police and multiple mobilisation repertoires, in which several latent social claims came forth. In May and June 2011 at Syntagma, one of the main squares of Athens, just in front of the Parliamentary House – a spatial antithesis that could symbolically express social rivalry, but also an imaginary historical continuation of social mobilisation that dates back to the adoption of the first constitution in 1843 – the largest popular assembly in Greek post-war history took place, also bringing issues of broader social claims to the fore. Early in 2015, when the EU and the IMF were struggling to impose the continuation of austerity measures on the new SYRIZA government, people once again gathered in the same central squares. In July 2015, when a referendum was announced regarding the acceptance of the EU austerity agenda, it was again the central squares of all the major cities that hosted mobilisations by both sides, as well as the one struggle that would demonstrate the largest social breadth. A few months earlier, in December 2014, a countrywide mobilisation took place for the benefit of a hunger-strike prisoner, Nikos Romanos, whose democratic rights had been violated by the state. The protesters occupied administrative buildings and used tens of squats throughout Greece to spread the striker's claims, which were ultimately satisfied. Regarding the antifascist struggle, which has been intense since 2012 when a Neo-Nazi party entered the parliament, there has also been an upgraded role that social actors retained for space: the battle against fascism did not take place solely in the central political scene, but rather local activism was considered to be of enormous importance. It is true that the struggle was fiercer in certain popular

68 Kostis Plevris

neighbourhoods of Athens; this was mostly connected to a higher residential density of immigrants and being the traditional neighbourhoods of the industrial labour-class, but they were also home to symbolic places where the World War II anti-Nazi struggle took place. In one of those areas, in the Keratsini municipality north-west of Piraeus, a member of the Neo-Nazi Golden Dawn party assassinated the activist and rap singer Pavlos Fissas in September 2013. What followed was a reaction by the antifascist movement that considered it highly important to take back the neighbourhood's streets from any far-right activity. Moreover, earlier the same year, in January 2013, tens of thousands of militants defended multiple squats across Greece against a scheduled attempt by the police to take them over. These squats were considered to be of major importance for the spread of social movements in the neighbourhoods, the promotion of 'alternative' channels of music, information, art and so on, as well as the blockade of fascist infiltration.

Inversely, when the SYRIZA government adopted the austerity measures agenda, social mobilisations also receded in space. Those that endured were mostly spaces built-up based on more advanced social claims, but in any case, space lost its rival content and forms, and returned to an institutional normality.

We have already described how space has assumed a more nodal role in recent years, in terms of its radical rival production by the protesters. But signs of this production were already visible some years ago. For example, during the student movement of 2007 and, similarly, in 2003, when Greece held the European presidency, participants moved spontaneously to occupy 'red zones' forbidden by the police, trying to contest institutional centrality and impose, with their bodies, their own centralities. Particularly for the youth, the occupations of schools and universities were nearly always part of their efforts and no victory has been recorded that did not use such spatial forms of mobilisation. During the period of preparation for the Olympic Games, when ideological aggression, national 'reconciliation' and class aggression were very intense, there was a continuous presence by some social groups, so as not to leave the leasing and control of space unhindered. In addition, the LGBT pride festival has, for a decade, consciously or unconsciously targeted social space: people parade in central Athens and kiss each other inside an enemy space to assert their right to do so everywhere and on all days of the year.

Meanwhile, new places are being formed as a crystallisation of social struggles and, in turn, they also affect social movements elsewhere, such as the strong resistance of the citizens of Keratea, a municipality of east Attica, to the installation of a landfill in their vicinity in 2011, or the case of Skouries, a village in Northern Greece situated near a gold extraction field that has in recent years led its own struggle against investors. Both have become exemplary representational spaces for social movements across Greece, and are now often invoked to be 'baptised' in a radical context, adopting the characteristics of a long-term, vicious and non-mediated social struggle. Such is the case of Elliniko, previously the civil airport of Athens, now a real-estate target by local and international financial houses, and the movements against the private fencing of many beaches and natural resorts across the country.

The spaces of social mobilisation in Greece   69

These are only some of the cases that witness the interconnection of the spatial form to the social process (in this case, mobilisations). This very relation is extended from the material and symbolic links to the collective or individual imaginary of the social subjects. Whoever was part of the previous social movements, whenever s/he frequents these places or even hears their names, s/he will, by association, feel expectation or disappointment, intensity or anxiety, passion or fear. Thus, even the imagination is not a-spatial.

Space is not given, but is being produced

We start from the following hypothesis that we further develop based on Greece's case: people construct their space in the context of how they construct their history, with possibilities and limits. Therefore, space is a product of the interaction of nature and society; Lefebvre's (2003) argument, that space never exists in itself but always refers to something else, a form seeking for an object to express its content, holds an exceptional rigour. Built-up and generally all spatial forms reflect upon social mobilisations the way they have been produced, namely through human labour in a certain social system. These forms often pose obstacles to mobilisations because they are not compatible with the subversive content of the latter. Other times, these forms condense new content, connected to the demands of the protesters, thus showing again the close connection of (subversive) human activity with space. In any case, space is produced uniquely in each era and within specific social relations, i.e. *historically*.

As space is by no means alien to the conceptual system of its contemporary society, it is distorted by the manner in which we contemplate it. Ideology is determinative here, as it 'achieves consistency only by intervening in social space and its production' (Lefebvre 1991: 41). This is one of the main problems regarding the interpretation of social mobilisations. In any case, regardless of whether the conceptual schemes of researchers may accurately reflect reality or not, space's objectivity is independent from those that study it. However, the failure to understand social relations as objective spatial relations necessarily leads to a deficiency in interpreting the world around us; this poses significant problems for those who want to change things through movements. In most cases, admittedly, the public understand the constitutive objectivity of space faster and better than researchers: they tend to raise barricades during their uprisings after a certain level of development to change the space they occupy, distorting the symbols of power and creating their own to symbolise their struggle using names from the places where they fight, and so on. However, this empirical ascertainment does not downgrade the necessity of *scientifically* understanding our world. This is what Marx (1970) was referring to, namely the necessity of thought to impel reality, and reality thought.

Space is therefore not a hyper-historical form, rather it is social reality in itself, *historically specific* in each era, standing *objectively* aside from how we conceive it, and enabling the *interconnection* of human activity because it is a product of human labour. But if space – in our case, the space of mobilisations – changes, what happens to older spatial forms? This is important to note, as contemporary

70 Kostis Plevris

capitalist spatial forms do not only falsely appear as linear products of a single history – they also appear as the only existing reality that has erased any trace of previous modes of social organisation. Nevertheless, the latter are not always lost; rather, those that are *necessary* for subsequent social development (and this includes not only capital, but also popular acts) are inscribed – although dominated – inside the urban palimpsest (*palímpsestos*, literally scraped again), in a way defining current relations.

Let us note how human history unfolds in time and space through some cases referring to different Greek places. We proceed to such a study because we want to see how contemporary space has been produced, as this also determined the 'scene' of the development of mobilisations. First, how did cities grow in late Greek history and who did they host? Studying the space of Athenian popular neighbourhoods, we have to consider the effects of the Greek Civil War of 1946–1949 and the subsequent paramilitary terrorism that followed. These cannot be conceptualised without taking into account the 800,000 displacements during the following internal migration period towards the cities. The provincial space, of which those people were deprived, was at the same time the space of provincial relations that they transferred to the urban centres; the repressive economic space of the cities was concurrently a space freed from the village's gendarme physical violence; the vast urban space, in comparison with that of the village, was simultaneously the space of their limits. But it is not only about cities; the contemporary situation of a relatively conservative Greek provincial periphery[2] cannot be realised outside this primary population displacement if we do not take into account that it was the most progressive and younger persons that migrated. Equally, the contemporary situation of the urban centres cannot be realised outside these gradual ideological consolidations that the displaced had gradually to accept, but, at the same time, cannot be interpreted outside the islets of a different social organisation that the same people installed. Behind the intense spatial romanticism of 'the basil and the quicklime', there is a hidden allegory of the representation of the everyday toil of 'the Saturday dusk that, again, has gone', the hope for emancipation 'that will not be late and will come to you during the dawn' and the oppression from 'ruthless regimes' that blot out the poor mother and forced one of her sons to leave 'because he was the son of Antonis'.[3] Cities have become a place of escape for the defeated, a space of a certain sociability, but also a space of social integration, namely of capital reproduction. It would be worthwhile here to note that the positioning of the popular and refugee dwellings inside the urban agglomeration and the constitution of their particular urban life had both a high correlation with the votes cast for the EDA party (United Democratic Left) before the military junta, and the Communist Party afterwards (Leontidou 2006). Nowadays, the demise of these social networks, as it coincides with high unemployment and different forms of social pathogenesis, leads to a political affiliation – as observed since the June 2012 general elections and again during the 2014 local elections and 2015 general election – still preserving an inherited left-wing ideological relevance, but also introducing diametrically opposed, even

The spaces of social mobilisation in Greece 71

Neo-Nazi, choices.[4] As we have foretold, recorded experiences in space affect reality in a multifarious way.

Second, do we find non-institutional methods of organising the built-up space? Observing the way that popular unplanned dwellings with no legal building permit were built in the municipalities of Perama and Drapetsona, at the western fringe of the Athenian agglomeration, during the internal migration period of the 1960s and 1970s, we can find in their spatial forms those social relationships that are connected to mutual aid and a situation of urgency; the construction had to be completed 'within a night' to evade the control of the town planning services and police. Moreover, the spatial contingency permitted the participation of the whole neighbourhood in the construction of a single house, until the next neighbour was to start building. One can spot similar repertoires in N. Koundouros's movie *A Magic City* (1954), an artistic piece depicting Athenian post-war reality. Here, as well, the city allowed the development of certain social relationships: mutual aid, friendship, comradeship, illegal love, surveillance and resistance against the elites. Of course, these relations are historical products of their social context; they could not flourish within the modern private apartment of the flats-for-land period.[5] Neither could the 'Magic City' flourish inside the evaporating and always alien 'spectacular city', where commodity production defined nearly everything – popular ethic and aesthetics included. It also could not fit in the typical spatial nomenclature of the authorities: these districts were something more than just poles of another 'functional urban zone', or statistical administrative units, or parts of the 'suburban belt'.

Third, what happened in those cases in which the urban palimpsest was violently erased, where dominant relations violently uprooted all past spatial relations and almost nothing reminds us of this past? Here, a present spatial and temporal vacuum may be recognised in the contemporary interpretations of the city. The latter cannot assert itself integrally, but only in a deficient way. Perhaps the best example here is Thessaloniki, the second largest city in Greece. After the fire of 1917, it was re-planned by the French architect Ernest Hébrard, based on an open-plan scheme that introduced 'historicist monumentality', inspired by the principles of functionalism and the garden-city movement (Komninos 1986). This new pattern equally guaranteed the circulation of commodities (including labour power). The new city was built where Jewish neighbourhoods had been organised around *tsarsis* (market roads) and religious spaces. The occupation of the Jewish graveyard by the new buildings of Aristotle University has completed this sentiment of loss of orientation in a city where, today, nationalism contributes to a generous surplus extraction from the dominated. Furthermore, nationalism has always been a refuge for those who wanted to solve the anxiety of a collective imaginary, namely that they live in an ex-intercultural city that was not exactly 'liberated' by the Greek army during the Balkan wars.

Yet the production of space is not always a fully developed imposition of forces. Particularly in the Greek case, we have to bear in mind the role of the production of consent through urban space as most decisive, in certain times, for the

72 Kostis Plevris

shaping of the accumulation process, as well as of the conscience of its citizens. After World War II, the explosive ambiance that was being formed, and persisted even after the great oppression that followed the communists' defeat, had to be defused to 'normalise' patterns of everyday life. Therefore, space had to be produced with the extended participation of Greek citizens, with land to be considered a social right, based on a petty-ownership that the state 'owed' to its citizens. Thus, private property in dwellings gained a certain role in the reproduction of the social system, namely a value in social conscience, something that remains today. Ultimately, it was established that each individual's right to own land had to be fulfilled through state responsibility, even by violating legitimacy and, of course, against the natural environment (Oikonomou 2010).[6] Here, the production of a space was being developed in parallel with the demise of concurrent forms of spatial (social) organisation. Of course, the oppressive presence of the state was never absent in the planning of urban space, but rather was always combined with this procedure of consent-production. To make things clear, we do not claim that it must be taken for granted that property acquisition leads inevitably to the demise of alternative ways of organising society; a case to the contrary is that of the Greek refugees of the Lausanne 1922 population exchange, who occupied peripheral zones in the city of Athens and achieved a right to homeownership and popular control of space through formal and informal channels (Leontidou 2001). However, the neighbourhood sentiment of mutual help, collective mobilisation and class-politics was quite different from the very space that emerged through dwelling's commodification.

What we have attempted to note here is that the space where Greek social mobilisations have taken place, and continue to do so, has been the culminating product of its past social relations. This posits the scientific lens through which it must be contemplated: capitalism fragments social activity, its forms and contents to measure and exchange them. Commodified space should be accepted as the foundation upon which all mobilisations take place, but also what they inherently want to upset. Of course, each era carries to the next those spatial relations that are necessary for further social development, under the dominant social relations. In those cases in which past relations were violently eradicated, the vacuum must be filled in another way. This is not always a success, considering capital circulation; popular everyday patterns, as long as they do not contest the dominant relations, may serve them through their civil society. In any case, social mobilisations may benefit both from the legacy of the past – remnants of another social organisation – and from the unstable way that spatial (social) relations are erected. On the other hand, as social movements do not emerge from nowhere, they also carry negative elements of the past: unresolved tensions, expectations, fears and illusions. 'The dead seize the living', as Marx (1976: 91) wrote. People who have been defeated during guerrilla warfare and chased throughout their lives may carry this mixed sentiment of personal pride, ethics, as well as desire for social peace. What they may have passed on to their own children is the necessity to fight along with certain chagrin. A person raised with national myths regarding his/her nation and city expects social solutions to be solved through means that

The spaces of social mobilisation in Greece 73

reproduce and proliferate the divisions of the oppressed. Furthermore, a person who, before the crisis, was engaged in petty transactions with the state – be they shadowy or transparent – and still expects the state's deputies to solve problems shares different interpretations of reality and other visions for social change. Of course, the disappointment of his/her expectations may be a source of anger, but it is still uncertain where this anger will be directed: in recent years, we have seen plenty of examples of this anger being channelled towards voting for fascist parties, even if for a short time those people may have participated in mobilisations, such as in the 'Movement of the Squares' of 2011.

Mobilisations attempting to restore unity

We have considered enough cases to assume that space is formed historically, in its widest sense: history is constructed socially, and past considerations, even if dominated, weigh upon the present. Indeed, as social struggle is the motor of historical change, we should consider that mobilisations define their space, not only as they change its material substance, but also by filling it with new social content: material and representative. Similarly, Harvey (2012) insists that collective struggle does not only concern what is taking place in space, but also the very space itself. This genesis of a new space, from the minor changes that a notable people's assembly may impose to the general ones that a revolution may bring about, should be the basis upon which all spatial relations are examined. We have demonstrated that these should be considered to be historical, interconnected and objective.

Mobilisations attempt to restore the unity of the social Being. Not through cultural, ideographic and ethical terms – therefore ideological, partial and distorted – but through praxis, namely (subversive) human activity. If developed, this opens up the possibility for appropriating space: the city now reinvents the community on a higher level, restoring fragmentation (Lefebvre 2003). Even before a general change of society, mobilisations attempt, to different extents, to build places where the organisation of social activities between people or between people and nature is exempt from the category of the 'commodity'. This detachment from the cumulative and fetishist content of the commodity form is to be found where aspects of the people's everyday lives become self-organised. Some tangible facts of this are social projects that offer propositions on how knowledge has to circulate (neighbourhood 'anti'-lectures, theoretical 'anti'-universities), nutrition (collective kitchens), entertainment (rap crews, non-commercial concerts), health (social clinics), solidarity (neighbourhood meeting points) and information (blogs, posters). These partial experiences appear as if they contained the whole of another society because they are regulated by use value. Meanwhile, they also represent the projection of a total organisation of everyday life, although they are still vulnerable because they are not generalised. The rupture with normality indicates that a social change integrally implicates a different everyday life *in space*, and not just a linear social readjustment. This new space – elements of which we might foresee in contemporary mobilisations – is different in every

74   Kostis Plevris

aspect: the way we live in it, we conceive it and its physical dimensions. It is different from the relative distances of circulation, the absolute distances of property and the relational distances of 'economic perspectives' (Harvey 2005). It hosts equally new experiences that cannot be dictated by the current facts of anxiety and constructed desire (Harvey 2005). Aspects of this space appeared clearly and qualitatively when social mobilisations tended to assert themselves on a daily basis, as was the case in Syntagma Square during May and June 2011 and the December 2008 revolt.

It was then that protesters attempted to rebuild their surrounding space in its sensory aspects: tents, colours, graffiti, barricades and so on. These initiatives had both a creative and destructive dimension: people were raising their new space upon one that should be destroyed. In addition, it was then that protesters *conceived* space differently: the new circular planning groups facilitated the conduct of assemblies, respected difference by not imposing hierarchies in the spatial layout, and changed the formal 'use' of the buildings into the needs of the insurgents. Take, for example, the National Opera House ('Ethniki Lyriki Skini') that functioned as a meeting point for new artists, dropping the formal and 'specialist' way that art was supposed to address itself publicly; or that of the occupied National Workers' Confederation, which functioned as a meeting point for the unemployed and under-employed, a status of employment that the formal confederation neglects to cope with in many cases. Finally, it was then that the way we live in space had changed. Everyday anxiety was dropped, and subjugation to the police officer and the boss were dropped too. Racism and nationalism within the space also took a step back (and whenever this was not fully pursued by the protesters, as in some cases during the 2011 'Squares movement', this poisoned the future development of movements, appearing as radical extreme-rightism). It was then that a new way to imprint things in memory through collective experiences in space came to the fore: memory (*mnimi* in Greek) and not monument (*mnimeion* in Greek) (Giannitsiotis 2010), as the real human experience and not its alienated mediation.[7]

Conclusion

One notable aspect of the social mobilisations that have taken place in Greece since December 2008 is the reassertion of the right of each mobilisation to a distinct and particular space. These spatial claims culminated after 2008, diffused in society and evolved to certain awareness that social struggle is grounded in space and, in turn, only a particular space enables social struggle to flourish. This may be a space that is produced by its users themselves. Likewise, the occupation of working places, even ministries (as in October 2011), became almost a spontaneous act when activists were confident of themselves. In many cases, workers who saw their firms preparing to leave the country occupied them to put pressure on their administrations. There is also one instance of a factory put under workers' control (VIO.ME.), and the struggle of the workers in public television, who maintained a great part of infrastructure and equipment under their own control

The spaces of social mobilisation in Greece   75

and broadcasted a full programme, even though the previous government had sacked them. During their protest, they regularly called for people and artists to participate in various actions in local television departments. In addition, many public places were not simply occupied, but functioned under assemblies' rules. This was not only an attempt to gain the support of other citizens, but, in many cases, the overcoming of the role of 'the specialist'.

On a neighbourhood level, what we have witnessed in recent years is the control of space as a reflection of political forces. The emergence of the Neo-Nazi groups of the Golden Dawn party was closely connected to a particular neighbourhood of the Athens municipality, the Saint-Panteleimon. There, Neo-Nazis had not only been gathering for several years before their appearance in the central political scene, but were also erecting a new space in symbolical and quantitative terms: they were building the representation of an urban cavern to assert their spatial sovereignty and consolidate their fascist techniques of patronage and lethal bullying in the everyday life of the neighbourhood, mainly against immigrants, while building up the image of the phallic organisation of a military group. What is more, they established themselves in the area by using forms of spatial organisation that had previously belonged to progressive politics, such as neighbourhood committees. Social mobilisations have learned much from this: five years ago, when this process began, there were few voices calling for radical opposition to it, but today, activists are mature enough to engage in battle on a local level in various ways. Within these neighbourhoods, it is indirectly recognised that even political graffiti or a motto on the walls itself constitutes a space. Writing on walls or erasing rival mottos has been recognised as important for political action itself because it represents a method for asserting or mirroring relations of domination and installing a podium of communication. Of course, this is only an elementary anti-fascist action: anti-fascist movements also call for multiple other actions, from mobilisations that demand the shutting of fascists' local offices to night patrols of 'antifa' militia.

Aside from the strictly antifascist struggle, many mobilisations target the dominant uses of space: a freely chosen sexual orientation can occur only in places where gestures and gazes do not assert the heterosexual use of space. Similarly, the emancipation of women is at the same time an emancipation of the female body in space; a place of military reaction or aggressive and salacious communication, or a provincial place of supervision, all constitute a hierarchical and phallic place.

Yet these remain incomplete if the mobilised activists do not form themselves into a political subject and do not attempt to assert themselves generally on an urban level. Once the part of the oppressors, fragmented space produced under late capitalism must find a centre to keep its fragments together. For this reason, political power acts as a performance; that is, it reasserts its conditions of hegemony and domination on a daily basis. This was made apparent during the first days of the December 2008 revolt, when institutionalised 'normality' lost its performative attribute and broad state hegemony was substituted by the defending of a minimum of governmental buildings by the whole police force. On the other

76 *Kostis Plevris*

hand, it was made equally apparent that centralisation is needed from the other side for mobilisations to socially assert themselves permanently, which must be found aside from the sum of the events of confrontation. Additionally, after the electoral victory of SYRIZA, it was made evident that no centralisation, in the name of the people, would be suitable: even before their coming to power, such parties drove social resistance to assimilate a partial social experience. Mobilisations were treated here as predefined social manifestations. Violence, the duration, aims, repertoires, places and means of protest were all inscribed within a social contract that dictated how social rivalry should be evolved; therefore, these manifestations remained inside an immediate, alienated reality. Of course, after its election, SYRIZA also openly attacked multiple social mobilisations and their spatial analogues.

On the other hand, as social mobilisations in Greece have consistently shown, the possible transformations of everyday life emerging from the activity of social movements imply a total rupture with today's space. This refers to the space of rationalism that contains and delimits social action in states, cities and neighbourhoods, as well as the space of irrationality that forces people to seek their everyday life in alienated places, deprived of a house and decent living conditions, at the very time that unevenly distributed social wealth has reached globally unprecedented levels. This rupture is related to new concurrent spaces that are being born, which contest the non-permeable, hierarchical limits of social organisation: from the enclosures of private property to the frontiers of the motherland, from the 'holy family' to the 'salvation nation' and from 'personal consumption' to 'gross national product'. We witness that the organisation of everyday life is inspired by social movements and produces new spatial experiences that although remain partial and incomplete, stand in tension with the space born from the commodity form. Namely, they rest in concurrence with the national, racial, sexual and class space of institutionalised normality, which always remains a monumental space (Athanasiou 2010), either in its rational or its irrational, spectacular, form.

Notes

1 This paper was presented in the series 'Southeast European Dialogues', organised by the University of Graz, Austria, in December 2013 and was revised one year later for publication, shortly before Greece's general elections of 25 January 2015 and the electoral victory of SYRIZA. In the time since, many things have changed that require fully developed empirical research to understand; indeed, new research should be conducted on how social mobilisations have also receded in space following the election of a party that promised to its voters that it would undertake the expression of social claims in an institutional way. So, we inform the reader that this paper is mostly intended to cover a period of social struggles that ended shortly after the general elections of January 2015.
2 Take, for example, the notable retardation of the Greek periphery regarding electoral change. In the June 2012 elections, the ruling right-wing party 'New Democracy' acquired a national 29.66%, but only 25.7% in the urban centres, whereas SYRIZA received 26.89% nationally and 29.8% in the urban centres. Similarly, the Communist Party of Greece had 4.5% nationally and 4.9% in urban centres. The Neo-Nazi 'Golden Dawn' party reached 6.92% nationally, almost evenly distributed among the urban

The spaces of social mobilisation in Greece   77

centres (Vernardakis 2012). Only in the general elections of January 2015, when the social polarisation had culminated after five years of heavy austerity, did the periphery adapt: it was then that SYRIZA abruptly took 37.5% in the periphery, up from 22.2% in 2012, even surpassing the vote that it received in the urban centres (35.6%) (Mavris 2015).

3 Lyrics from Greek popular songs, which record everyday life, namely 'Saturday Night' (*To Savvatovrado*) by Tasos Leivaditis, 'Have a Little Patience' (*Kane ligaki ypomoni*) by Vassilis Tsitsanis and 'Ruthless Regimes' (*Apones Exousies*) by Mihalis Kakogiannis.

4 Concerning 'geographical polarisation', Vernardakis (2012) indicates that, in the elections of June 2012, in neighbourhoods with many wage-labourers, SYRIZA received 35–37% and the CPG received 5.5–8.5%, both quite above their national average, whereas the ruling right-wing New Democracy party received a low 16.5–19%. Meanwhile, the Neo-Nazi Golden Dawn acquired 7.8–12.5%, quite above its national average. Regarding the January 2015 elections, Mavris (2015) notes that 'class-based votes came back': in wage-labour neighbourhoods, SYRIZA received 43–45%, whereas the New Democracy won under 20%; in the affluent suburbs, the former got less than 15% and the latter over 55%.

5 The flats-for-land, or the *antiparohi* system, is an arrangement between the owner of the land and the developer, whereby the former offers his plot while being compensated with apartments in lieu of payment.

6 Let us point out a new law that was voted for in 2011 (law 4014/2011) for the state to raise money that enabled the legalisation of every illegal construction, except very few cases. For the legislator, the number of incompatible floors, surface, distance from adjacent buildings or natural reserves, aesthetic form and so on did not matter. Everything was transformed into a 'fetishized' coefficient and, finally, into a certain sum of money. A certain practice, used in older times by the Greek's state clientele network to legalise residential buildings without a permit, has evolved nowadays to a legal act, with a guaranteed social consensus.

7 Theo Angelopoulos, in his film *Megalexandros* (1980), stressed how memory, even revolutionary memory, when defeated, becomes an alienated monument that 'enters the cities'. The struggle for the lived city is the struggle for the right to the city, the struggle for memory itself and, eventually, a struggle for the real against the alienated.

References

Alayev, E.B. 1986. *Social and Economic Geography: An Essay in Conceptual-Terminological Systematisation*. Moscow: Progress Publishers.

Athanasiou, A. 2010. Black in the Square: Mapping Forbidden Memory. In: *Contested Places in the City: Spatial Approaches of Culture*, eds. G. Giannitsiotis and K. Giannakopoulos. Athens: Alexandreia, pp. 227–266 [in Greek].

Engels, F. 1963. *Anti-Duhring*. Athens: Anagnostidis [in Greek].

Giannitsiotis, G. 2010. Aris Velouhiotis Returns to Lamis: Spatial Conflicts Around a Memorial Space. In: *Contested Places in the City: Spatial Approaches of Culture*, eds. K. Giannakopoulos and G. Giannitsiotis. Athens: Alexandreia, pp. 267–314 [in Greek].

Harvey, D. 2005. *Spaces of Neoliberalization: Towards a Theory of Uneven Geographical Development: Hettner-Lecture 2004 With David Harvey*. Stuttgart: Franz Steiner Verlag.

Harvey, D. 2012. *Rebel Cities*. London: Verso.

Ilyenkov, E. 1960. *Dialectics of the Abstract & the Concrete in Marx's Capital*. [Online] Available at: www.marxists.org/archive/ilyenkov/works/abstract/.

Komninos, N. 1986. *Theory of Urbanity*. Athens: Sigxrona Themata [in Greek].

Lefebvre, H. 1991. *The Production of Space*. Oxford: Blackwell.

78 *Kostis Plevris*

Lefebvre, H. 2003. *The Urban Revolution*. Minneapolis: University of Minnesota Press.

Lenin, V.I. 1972. Philosophical Notebooks. In: *Collected Works*, ed. V.I. Lenin. Moscow: Progress Publishers.

Leontidou, L. 2001. *Cities of Silence: Working-Class Space in Athens and Piraeus, 1909–1940*. Athens: ETVA.

Leontidou, L. 2006. *The Mediterranean City in Transition: Social Change and Urban Development*. Cambridge: Cambridge University Press.

Marx, K. 1970. *Critique of Hegel's 'Philosophy of right'*. Athens: Anagnostidis [in Greek].

Marx, K. 1976. *Capital: A Critique of Political Economy Vol. 1*. (B. Fowkes, Trans.). New York: Penguin Books.

Mavris, Y. 2015. *The Social Forces of the Anti-Memorandum Alliances*. [Online] Available at: www.mavris.gr/4610/antimemorandum-social-coalition.

Oikonomou, L. (2010). Plots of Land by Installments: The Production of Space in the Periphery of Athens (1950–1960). In: *Contested Places in the City: Spatial Approaches of Culture*, eds. K. Giannakopoulos and G. Giannitsiotis. Athens: Alexandreia, pp. 77–116 [in Greek].

Vernardakis, C. (2012). The Elections of 17th June and the New Trends Concerning the Electoral System. *Avgi Newspaper*, June 24 [in Greek].

5 At the crossroads of cultural and ideological exchange – behind the visual communications of 2012–2013 Slovene protests

Ksenija Berk

Introduction

Winter 2012–2013 was a turbulent time in Slovenia, a small country, which generally goes unnoticed on the European political stage. However, in November 2012, protests demanding resignations of the corrupt power elites began in Maribor, Slovenia's second largest city, and soon spread across the country. Protesters called for the resignation of the government, several leaders and managers of local municipalities, as well as representatives of the Catholic Church. Thousands of people in Slovenia joined the street protests against the corrupt elites, and created diverse and unique visual communications of street protests. Posters, flags, banners, puppets, masks and artworks contributed significantly to the rich legacy of international protest culture. Slovene protests have strong connections to the nation's past, manifesting in various visual symbols, predominantly from earlier revolutions, and from the period of socialism when Slovenia was one of six republics in the former Yugoslavia. With this tradition in mind, I have focused on each visual element, which appeared in significant numbers in the 2012–2013 protests, in its historical context to give the reader a hand to decode the social and symbolic meaning of visual culture of the Slovene protests. To analyse a rich visual repertoire, I have drawn from a wide range of sources and adopted a range of interdisciplinary methodological perspectives from contemporary aesthetics, political theory, visual culture, history of art and design, and performative studies.

A brief outline of the events leading up to the protests

Various sources of protest statistics show us that in 2012–2013, there were more than 40 protests across all the major Slovene cities, with more than 150,000 participants. This may not seem like a large number until one considers that the population of Slovenia is barely 2 million, which means that overall, more than 5% of the population took to the streets. Protests were diverse, with different groups united by different initiatives, including the Maribor uprisings, the All-Slovenian People's Uprisings and Protestivals, and protests organised by the Slovenian cultural workers against government cuts in cultural funding. It is important to realise that the Slovene uprisings were much more than anti-austerity protests, and to

80 *Ksenija Berk*

understand what it is that differentiates them from other similar protests around Southeastern Europe and the Balkans. The people of Slovenia have not protested on the streets against the government in such high numbers for more than 20 years. The recent protests have more in common with the early 1990s, when a Slovene referendum almost unanimously agreed to leave the political arrangement of the former Yugoslavia, than with similar contemporary protests in the region. The popular ideology spread by politicians for the past 20 years that Slovenia will become a second Switzerland (regardless of the vague meaning of the words) has vanished into thin air with the advent of the global economic crisis. Several companies and most of Slovenia's heavy industry have recently failed financially, and large numbers of people have lost their jobs, becoming permanently unemployed. At this point, it became clear that the period of transition from a planned economy to a market economy was not, in reality, thought through. Excluding the negative connotations of the Yugoslavian planned economy, it has become clear that Slovene politicians have not actually developed a strategy for the future of the young democracy after Slovenia's exit, and the dissolution of the political formation of the former Yugoslavia.

Bearing these factors in mind, the Slovene protests should not really come as a surprise. It was only a matter of time before people would go onto the streets again in protest against the politics that brought the country from a prosperous transitional state to one crippled by corruption (see STA and T.M. 2014). The only thing that is surprising in this story is why the people of Slovenia have closed their eyes for so long, waiting for more than two decades to rebel. The protesters' intention was not only to rebel against government austerity politics, which have rapidly and without prior consultation begun to cut into existing social benefits. They also wished to reinterpret and change those social conditions. This brings us to questions concerning the nature of the human condition as discussed by Arendt (1999), and the categories of labour, work and action. The latter category in particular can never truly manifest through a predictable, deterministic series of consequences. Hence, the subject, by acting, is placed within a complicated web of relationships, which cannot be predicted beforehand. As mentioned in the introduction, the Slovene protests began in November 2012 in Maribor, which was once a flourishing industrial city in Yugoslavian times, but is now facing a destiny similar to Detroit. The *Gotof je!* [He is Finished!] theme first appeared as a constitutive part of protests against the former mayor of Maribor, Franc Kangler, but soon expanded into an emblematic slogan of the Slovene uprisings. He was involved in several scandals, which led to a number of criminal investigations.

The trigger that finally incited people to action and engaged them in organising street protests was the new fixed radar system initiated by the mayor on all major traffic arteries to and from the city centre to monitor and fine drivers who were travelling above the speed limits. In less than a month, over 25,000 people, representing 20% of the Maribor population, were issued mostly minor speeding tickets. The crucial problem was not the radar system itself, but the way in which the company Iskra Sistemi, which provided 46 radars in 2012, was selected. The

At the crossroads of cultural and ideological exchange 81

process of public procurement was non-transparent and highly suspicious, leading to an unusual public-private partnership between the company and the municipality of Maribor. Kangler soon faced accusations in regard to the financing of the project and alleged irregularities within the contract. High fines caused much distress and anger among the people and some tried to express their dissatisfaction by vandalising the speed radar cameras, with equipment being set on fire or demolished during the night. The street protests followed. Faced with pressure from the media and the people, Kangler then pardoned all drivers who had been accused of minor traffic offences. Due to the corruption allegations, pre-trial processes, and criminal charges made against him, the citizens of Maribor demanded his resignation. He stepped down on 6 December 2012, with his mandate lasting until 31 December 2012. An additional trigger that brought people onto the streets was a report by the Commission for the Prevention of Corruption. This accused both the former prime minister, Janez Janša, and the leader of the largest right-wing opposition party and Ljubljana mayor, Zoran Janković, of corrupt behaviour (Stojanovic 2013).

Gotof je! protest posters hit the streets

From Maribor, the protests quickly spread to other Slovenian cities, with *Gotof je!* becoming the unifying slogan of dissent across the country, condemning the corrupt elites. Each city had its own stories of corruption connecting the local/municipal with the global/state levels. Local dialectal variations on the *Gotof je!* slogan appeared across Slovenia. One of the most distinctive visual elements was a cluster of so-called *Gotof je!* posters, which became a leading symbol of the Slovene protests during winter 2012–2013. These were the first in a long succession of *Gotof je!* protest posters that were closely attuned to people's claims and emotions, and influenced every poster that followed in that visual category. They portrayed the former mayor of Maribor, Franc Kangler, in black and white graphics with a black frame, and a stencilled or solarised photographic portrait denoting the mayor's basic facial features. The *Gotof je!* call became the trademark of anti-corruption protests across the country. The emotional slogan, which initially functioned as the poster's caption, became a call to rebel against the representatives who were involved in corruption scandals. These posters were quickly and easily embraced and adopted across Slovenia due to their accessible graphic vocabulary and powerful slogan, which were easily translated into other dialects. The use of a local dialect instead of a literary language is an important element of the bottom-up strategy of dissent, a protest voice that comes directly from the people. Their success was due to a favourable balance of elements, or in the words of poster specialist Margaret Timmers (1998: 7): 'They can have a broad popular appeal, and yet specifically target the individual who is alert to decode their deeper meaning'.

As the protests began to spread from Maribor to other cities, and evolved into the All-Slovenian People's Uprisings, new faces from the corruption scandals quickly found their way onto the posters. They ranged from members of the

82 *Ksenija Berk*

political elite and managers to representatives of the ecclesiastical elites – more specifically, individuals involved in the financial scandal of the Catholic Church in Slovenia. It left the Maribor Archdiocese with an 800 million euro deficit (mainly as a result of financial mismanagement and imprudent investments) and resulted in bankruptcy (Barker 2014). The scandal echoed all the way to the Vatican chambers of Pope Francis, and on 31 July 2013, he accepted the resignation of both the Ljubljana (Anton Stres) and Maribor (Marjan Turnšek) archbishops as unsuitable for their office. The portraits of corrupt officials were initially displayed on single sheets of paper to be later combined with several others into an emblematic image of the Slovene corrupt body of politics. This method of creating a composite portraiture and combining different 'criminal types', as is done in police criminal profiling, is in itself a very powerful political statement. The visual language spoke to all protesters, regardless of the differences in their political opinions, and managed to access all levels of Slovene society by revealing hidden connections between corrupt politicians and managers. The poster message, however, is not easily comprehensible from the position of an outside observer, who would not be familiar with the complex connections between various events that finally brought people onto the streets. Nevertheless, the strong visual coherence and unified message concerning local politicians was a significant characteristic of posters that emerged in similar protests around the region at this time. The simple black and white design, as so often in the history of protests, proved to be the easiest and most cost-effective imagery for immediate mass distribution. By communicating a brief, compressed insight into the complex problem of corrupt behaviour between members of Slovene power elites, the posters raised awareness among the citizens. They offered them an opportunity to communicate their demands in public spaces by combining simplified designs with widespread dissemination.

Cultural historian Peter Burke (2001) described posters as reflections of their time and place, but even more as extensions of the social contexts in which they were produced. *Gotof je!* posters expressed the perspective of Slovene citizens, presenting their side of the story, while at the same time revealing subtle contextual layers that are not obvious in the rhetoric of the protests. The posters reflect contemporary Slovene society, and represent a rich repertoire of claims by civil society whilst simultaneously acquiring power from the political ideas represented. Similar examples have appeared at various historic times across the world, covering a wide range of protest types – from the most extremist political ideas to pacifism, from war recruitment and propaganda to awareness campaigns on human rights, political freedom, free speech, discrimination and elections. We have several important historical examples of political poster genres flourishing at specific times, including World War I and II propaganda, and the French civil unrest of 1968. Slovene *Gotof je!* protest posters can be understood as the recent offspring of this long chain. Regardless of their message, they functioned as a form of visual telegram addressed to the power elites, and have fulfilled their primary function of mass communication.

Reminiscence of the glorious revolutionary past

Slovene protests have strong connections to the nation's past, manifesting in various visual symbols, such as the Slovene flag from the time of the former Yugoslavia, a symbol of the highest Slovene mountain *Triglav* (also a symbol of the Liberation Front in WWII), a red star, and the image of liberated *Verigar* (the man in chains). The latter motif was one of the most intriguing on the streets of Ljubljana, showing an image of a man who breaks the chains of his slavery, surrounded by the glorious radiance of sunshine in the background. The aureole of sun rays, the circle of light that encircles the body of the male figure, can be attributed to man's supreme powers (Ferguson 1966) and martyrdom (Ladner 1996), and the figure of the almost naked man wearing a *perizoma*, or loincloth, suggests analogies with depictions of Jesus in Christian art in more than one point. The *Verigar* motif symbolically marks the period of October 1918, when the Austro-Hungarian Empire collapsed and brought political freedom to the Slovene nation.

On 29 October 1918, a union of the national sovereign State of Slovenes, Croats and Serbs was formed, amalgamating the territories of the southern Slavic nations, which on 1 December 1918 became the Kingdom of Serbs. The establishment of a new political entity seemed to be an occasion sufficiently worthy to celebrate with a new postage stamp. According to Znidarčič's (2013) biographical notes, the newly appointed government asked Slovene painter and illustrator Ivan Vavpotič (1877–1943) to design a postage stamp to commemorate the occasion. He proposed several alternatives, and the authorities decided upon the motif of *Verigar*, which was printed in Ljubljana and Vienna at the end of 1918. On the stamp, we can see two different inscriptions of the name of the new State: at the top, it is written in Serbian, in Cyrillic script; at the bottom, it is written in Slovene and Croatian, in Latin script. Yet when the stamp was finally printed, issued and began to circulate, the State SHS, where it was initially designed, no longer existed. Nevertheless, the authorities wilfully ignored the fact and the stamp was put into mass circulation in the succeeding Kingdom of Serbs, Croats and Slovenes. Bearing in mind the primary functions of a postage stamp are indexical and commemorative – pointing to the country of origin and remembrance of an important state-related event (Scott 1995: 7) – the use of the *Verigar* stamp is a phenomenon in itself. The motif is remarkably important in Slovene history for its historicity and symbolism, which is deeply connected to the process of establishing an independent state. The expressive wealth of this motif appeared whenever the people experienced a time of great disturbance, confusion and uncertainty, particularly during the emergence of new political entities, as occurred during the dissolution of Yugoslavia in 1991 when the Slovenes finally established a democratic nation-state, as well as during the protests of 2012–2013. Although this particular visual style is out of favour, re-appropriation of the motif indicates that the vision of a free and independent state has not lost its appeal. It held strong emotional appeal during the Slovene protests, when people went into the streets to express their dissatisfaction with the current political conditions, which failed

84 *Ksenija Berk*

to resonate with the notion of a democratic state. In that light, we can interpret the emblematic power of *Verigar* as symbolically transgressing the political category of state, while stressing the freedom from oppression of the Slovene nation.

The flag and the red star

Flags are a ubiquitous symbol of any protest, and in this the Slovene protests were no exception. There were two different categories of flags used in the protest marches. The first category represented various sections of civil society who participated in the protests, such as the black and red flags of the anarchists, the flag of the International Workers' Movement, rainbow flags of queer communities, and a white flag with a black fist (migrating from the Serbian *Otpor* movement). The second category included national flags such as the official, contemporary Slovene flag, and the former flags of Slovenia and Yugoslavia with a distinct red star from the socialist period before the dissolution of Yugoslavia. In a country where the menace of past events weighs heavily, and where it often appears as though the nation has begun to lose faith in the ideas it had at the time of Non-Aligned Yugoslavia, it should not come as a surprise that the memory of a socialist past is still strong today.

The protests have certainly made clear the painful reality that ideas expounded by the Slovene politicians of transforming Slovenia into a second Switzerland were merely elaborate ideological propaganda. The spectres of totalitarianism, nationalism and all kinds of discrimination are still very much on the political agenda. Therefore, the ubiquitous symbols of the past regime, from the Yugoslavian federal flag, and the flag of the Slovene republic from the same period, quickly found their way into contemporary protests. The colours of the Yugoslavian flag – blue, white and red – were adopted from the tricolour flag of the SHS Kingdom (1918). During WWII, the partisans added a red star to the centre of the white area, marking the leading role of the Communist Party in the antifascist and anti-Nazi resistance. Later, it became the official flag of the Democratic Federal Yugoslavia (1943–1946). On 31 January 1946, the gold fimbriation was introduced to the red star, allegedly by the president, Josip Broz Tito, and the specific proportions of the flag design were adopted in the first constitution of the Federal People's Republic of Yugoslavia. The design of the flag did not change until the disintegration of Yugoslavia in 1991, when Slovenia and the other former Yugoslavian republics agreed upon a new flag. The colours of the new Slovene flag were identical to the socialist version of the flag: white at the top, blue in the middle and red at the bottom. The centrally positioned red star was replaced with the new Slovene coat of arms in the upper left corner, designed by artist Marko Pogačnik, displaying three gold stars on a blue background with two white waves in the upper left corner. Although this was not the only appearance of the five-pointed red star during contemporary protests, for the clarity of this paper, I postpone that discussion and return to it later.

Carrying the official flags from the period of the former Yugoslavia was seen as a way of sustaining a Yugo-nostalgia. This can be understood in the way

At the crossroads of cultural and ideological exchange   85

suggested by anthropologist Dominic Boyer (2012: 18) in considering Johannes Hofer's 1688 medical dissertation, in which he defined nostalgia as a type of homesickness, a desire to return to the place of origin. A longing for the dissolute Socialist Federation was particularly strong due to the anti-capitalist and anti-neoliberal tendencies of younger generations, most of whom were born after 1991. A further group of strong supporters could be found amongst the surviving old partisans, former members of the Communist Party, sympathisers and nostalgias (Ugrešić 2007) of the old socialist regime, and ordinary people who had lost faith in Slovenia's new political system. Boyer suggests that in our 'post-medical' era of nostalgia, we are rarely confronted with the 'corporeal' or 'territorialised' notion of grief as it occurs in the search for a country or home, but instead with a 'socio-temporal yearning for a different stage or quality of life (as Kant put it, for our youth)' (Boyer 2012: 18). Nevertheless, the presence of 'Yugo-nostalgia' at Slovene protests signifies the possibility of a direct manifestation of the people's political desire. A call to return to state socialism can be explained as a desire to recapture what life once was in the former Yugoslavia. This type of nostalgia, which Boyer (2012) examined in a case study of the former East and West German people, could be interpreted as 'coping behaviour'. A sort of

> defence mechanism for people who have lived half their lives in a state-imposed stasis only to have all those certainties, true and false, swept away in the second half of their lives by the uncomfortable forces and of course "realities", of life in a market-centred society.
>
> (Boyer 2012: 19)

Socialism revised

Nostalgia is, however, also an indexical practice, a mode of inhabiting the lived world through defining oneself in it. We have witnessed a further appearance of the red star in protest posters, albeit in a more contemporary context, but still in connection with the history of the workers' movements and the Socialist International (SI). In this particular example, the so-called 'nostalgias' are members of the younger generation who have explicitly turned to socialist and Marxist ideas. The return of Marxist ideas (Farris 2015) was not evident only in the Slovene protests. It can be continuously detected since 1968 and with greater strength in 2009 with the first wave of the international banking crisis and the crisis of neoliberal capitalism. Bearing in mind that Slovenia shared a socialist past with the other republics in the Socialist Federal Republic of Yugoslavia (SFRY), it was but a matter of time before Marxist and socialist ideas appeared again on the streets during times of protest. These ideas are evoking interest and attention particularly in younger generations who do not carry the burden of a communist past, and can thus re-read Marxist theories in a new light. Many of them have discovered a liberating potential in Marxist theories, especially during the protests against neoliberal politics.

86 Ksenija Berk

As a result of contemporary approaches to Marxist theories, a series of striking bright red posters with white slogans and a star were paraded during the Third All-Slovene People's Uprising on 8 February 2013. Their appearance was visually striking against the grey winter cityscape. This application of bright red evoked all the emotional appeals that the colour brings to mind: passion, revolution, socialism, communism, revolt and the visual memory of historical avant-gardes. Easily discernible from a distance with slogans such as 'For democratic Socialism, against the dictatorship of Capital', 'What is robbing a bank, compared to establishing a (bad) bank?', and 'Workers of all countries unite!', the posters brought back memories of the socialist past when they were used to communicate state ideology to the citizens. However, posters alluding to socialism were not reminiscent of Tito's Yugoslavia alone. They also awakened revolutionary concepts similar to those of post-WWI Europe, when the quest for a new social order motivated people from many different professions, including artists El Lissitsky and Alexander Rodchenko, to creatively combine socialist and communist ideas.

The slogan alluding to robbing and establishing banks was triggered by the government's austerity measures and debt restructuring in the Slovene banking sector. In 2010, just after the banking crisis spread globally, the balance sheets of Slovene banks were decimated. As a consequence, the Slovene Central Bank decided to increase the capital requirements for banks, and in 2012, the Slovene Government established the Bank Asset Management Company (BAMC), also known as 'the bad bank' (Furlan 2014). The anti-banking slogan did not originate with the Slovene protests, as it is a paraphrase of a legendary line from Bertold Brecht's *Threepenny Opera*. Towards the end of the opera, the character Mackie Messer (Mack the Knife) asks: *'What is robbing a bank, compared to establishing a bank?'* (Brecht 1998: 267). The revelatory moment of those posters depends on the viewer's depth of knowledge in the Slovene language, the political ideas of Bertold Brecht, and the influence of Marxist ideas on Brecht's work. Lawrin Armstrong (2007: 41) suggested that Brecht was most likely familiar with this form of ethical critique through reading Marx's *Capital*, although the idea could not be inscribed directly to Marx. According to Armstrong (2007: 41), this type of ethical critique can be traced back to Aristotle and his *Politics and Ethics*, in which he condemned profit on loans as an unnatural and asocial use of money. Not unexpectedly, members of the new Initiative for Democratic Socialism (IDS) supported these ideas. Inspired by Occupy Wall Street, the IDS first established its collective leadership structure (without a single leader) after the protests of 2014, and in November of that year, elected Luka Mesec onto the IDS council. It did not take long for a new left-wing electoral alliance, the United Left (ZL), to form. It is an amalgamation of the Democratic Labour Party (DSD), Party for Sustainable Development of Slovenia (TRS), and the IDS. The United Left supports the concept of a socialist model for Europe as an alternative to neoliberalism. After becoming active in the protests, they managed to get elected to parliament with 4.7% of all votes in the 2014 elections. The establishment of this new left-wing political party, and the expansion of the new European Left, was supported by the attendance of the Greek SYRIZA party leader and acting Prime Minister

Alexis Tsipras at the founding congress (Korsika 2014) of the United Left on 8 March 2014.

The red posters of the IDS worked in a twofold manner: as an open critique of government decisions, particularly the establishment of 'the bad bank', and as a vehicle for communicating political ideas and achieving greater recognition. The visual language of symbols and slogans in their posters was clearly expressive of the newly articulated political goals in Slovene civil society. Although the posters were designed in a typical modernist style, they demonstrated that the dormant potential of Slovene civil society had been awakened. They offered a site for reflection on the political situation, and an autonomous space for commentary and engagement. This resurgence of socialist ideas is not a return to the plan politics of the former Yugoslavia, but is more related to pertinent ideas around worker participation in business leadership, and contemporary attempts at reviving workers' self-management strategy. The trend in Slovenia of rising inequality, poverty, political instability and corruption, and the repeated disruption of general elections before the end of government mandates, are adversely affecting the lives and futures of the Slovene nation. In view of the current economic and political crisis in Slovenia, a large number of protesters have clearly expressed their dissatisfaction with neoliberal capitalism, which fails to serve the interests of the vast majority of people, and is both economically and environmentally unsustainable.

Protesting with celebrity works of art

The history of art is saturated with examples of the ways in which art and politics overlap. Theorist and activist Gerald Raunig (2007: 16) explains that transgressing the boundaries of 'art into the social and political field' is not an invention of the early 20th century, but has been present throughout history, suggesting that we should try to understand the crossings of art and politics as trans-historical patterns. Sometimes these crossings have resulted in the development of new ideas, and stirred social and political movements. At other times, they have become absorbed by, or included in, the propaganda. On a smaller scale, there were two specific examples of artistic visual interventions in the Slovene protests that, for various reasons, are worthy of further attention: one was in Maribor, and the other in Ljubljana. First, these protests demonstrated the specific conditions under which art enters the sphere of everyday politics in Slovenia. Second, they suggest that these kinds of artistic interventions reveal what is going on in society itself, and are not limited to revealing the radical new perspectives under which the culture is engaging with critical issues. The protests in Maribor brought us the appropriation and adaptation of the Campbell's soup motif, originally created by famous pop-artist Andy Warhol. While in Ljubljana, we witnessed the artistic 'extensions' of postmodernist and retro-avantgarde art by the notorious Slovene art group IRWIN. Both poster examples – the Maribor adaptation and Ljubljana extension – entered the street protests with rather complex symbolic messages. This type of complex visual coding is not easily comprehensible to those for whom art and its history, or more specifically, the history of modernist

88   *Ksenija Berk*

and postmodernist art, are alien. During my research of the various protests across Europe, especially in the larger Balkan region, I could not find any evidence elsewhere of this appearance of famous modernist works of art in protest visuals. The Maribor example is somewhat specific, both in its execution and in the appropriation of Warhol's work, whose aesthetic conceptions have nothing in common with the theme of protests.

The poster in question appropriated the notorious image of Campbell's soup cans created by Andy Warhol in the early 1960s. When art critic G.R. Swenson asked Warhol in 1963 why he painted soup cans, the artist replied, 'I used to drink it, I used to have the same lunch every day, for twenty years' (Comenas 2010). On the poster, three identical soup cans are illustrated in the typical manner of Warhol's multiplication of images, and each can bears the image of one high-ranking employee from the Slovene Ministry of Education. The red colour of the soup cans calls attention to the portraits of the three politicians. The creators of these posters did not pay much attention to designing a unique poster, but have sought instead for a high-impact image. They have successfully avoided a critical message, and the populist and fetishist imagery from Warhol serves merely as an 'empty' carrier for the message, which is inevitably lost during translation. As described by Craine (1998: 86), Warhol focused mainly on the 'quantitative aspects of mass consumer goods', which have nothing in common with the claims of Maribor protesters. Images of the Campbell's soup cans served as a vehicle for transmitting the protesters' message in such a way that we become aware of the existence of public taste. Warhol's appropriated images stood out from the other visual material that appeared on the streets of the Slovene protests and served more as an ornament for the marching crowd, a 'poster fetish' as Guffey (2015: 215) candidly wrote. The adapted motif of Campbell's soup was not transformed sufficiently to take on new meanings, but has, unfortunately, created just another form of protest image fetishism. Warhol's Campbell's soup posters have been circulating widely on numerous occasions, and were exploited for various purposes, but activist groups have never used them as an element of dissent for its explicit connections to art fetishism.

The second example, from the streets of Ljubljana, is a typical sample of the formal vocabulary of the previously established artwork for the purpose of making a political statement at the street protests. Bright red square posters with a red circle and the slogan *It is time for a new state!* were carried by the members of the IRWIN art group. They belong to the *Neue Slowenische Kunst* (NSK), the notorious retro-avantgarde platform from the 1980s and 1990s that over the past 30 years has developed into one of the most exported institutions of Slovene culture. The NSK platform has been subject to changes in membership throughout its history, and today consists of the music group Laibach, art group IRWIN, design group *Novi Kolektivizem*, and the Department of Pure and Applied Philosophy. The NSK are familiar with the world of politics, especially those from the time of the former SFRY, when in 1987, the group *Novi Kolektivizem* was responsible for one of Slovenia's biggest 'visual art' scandals. They fraudulently presented the image of Nazi artist Richard Klein, with small adaptations, as the

At the crossroads of cultural and ideological exchange   89

official poster for the Relay of Youth event celebrating Tito's birthday. Although all groups of the NSK platform work independently in the area between ideology and art, they share the same principles of action, and powerful propaganda-like imagery. According to their version of the story, they wanted to express solidarity with the particular gesture of the protest.

As on many previous occasions, they decided to use provocative posters that were created originally as part of a new art project by the NSK collective, called *Time for the New State*. This project was developed from the NSK's State in Time (IRWIN 2014: 7) concept, which started in 1992, a project of the state without physical territory, which includes specially designed passports for which anyone can apply. The group were interviewed on many occasions by the Slovene media, and described the posters used in the Ljubljana protests as part of an earlier project developed in Lagos (Nigeria) in 2010 for the occasion of a visit to the largest group of NSK passport holders. One thing they discovered in Lagos were advertising posters with the captions 'Time for a New State' and 'Some say you can find happiness there'. According to their testimony, nobody in Lagos knew at the time what kind of idea the posters were advertising, but that did not stop people using the same words to express their desire to become an NSK citizen. Later, the NSK used the same poster as part of an art project in Moscow, Leipzig and London. Similarly, in Ljubljana, they did not try to conceal their artistic strategies of using advertising and appropriating political events – in this case, the All-Slovene People's Uprisings. Rooted as they are in unquestioned retro-avantgarde artistic practices, which emerged in the territory of the former Yugoslavia in the 1980s, their ideas of political art do not fully transcend their pop-up strategy in contemporary political events. The IRWIN group has called for a New State, and has successfully developed the illusion of challenging the political status quo. Despite this, one cannot ignore their ever-present propaganda strategies, which successfully corroborate the existence of their well-maintained art institution, often supported by the Slovene Ministry of Culture.

This position offers new perspectives and calls for a reassessment of the relationships between artistic practices and their immediate interventions in political events. However, on most occasions, and as was evident in the two examples analysed from the Slovene protests, artistic interventions serve more as vehicles for self-promotion, rather than contributing to the general oeuvre of protest movements. Extracted from the original environment and naively appropriated for protest actions (Bishop 2012), they become devoid of any artistic function, whilst at the same time failing to deliver the desired message in the broader protest landscape. Posters of this type are nice to look at, but unfortunately, their message is invested with so many layers of meaning that it becomes too complicated to deconstruct during the protests. When posters are extracted from their original context, whether it is cultural, social or political, their message very soon becomes misleading and dubious (Groys 2008: 27). Those posters should not be understood as a kind of nostalgia, although we could accept the unlikely possibility that some protesters may have appeared more attuned to the milieu of high modernism. We should understand them as a sign of the paradox

90   *Ksenija Berk*

of being trapped in a specific situation, and as an example of aesthetic populism in protest graphics.

Zombies strike back or the resurrection of political performance

As we saw in the preceding paragraphs, on 21 December 2012, the first All-Slovenian People's Uprising took place in Ljubljana and other major cities. Several protesters sung revolutionary songs, including the Socialist International (SI), and protested peacefully with assorted posters, banners and flags displaying a central red star, reminiscent of the time of the former Yugoslavia. The protests did not deviate from the typical notion of protest movements in the region. It was the reaction of the leader of the Slovenian Democratic Party (SDS) and elected Prime Minister Janez Janša who agitated the debate and fuelled the subsequent protests. Janša, obviously irritated by the rebelling citizens, tweeted the same day that the protests were not instigated by Slovene citizens, but by an uprising of communist zombies: '#resistance? Communist International, rhetoric of civil war, totalitarian symbols? The rising up of Zombies not the rising of a nation' (see M.R. 2012). This was a surprising tone of communication for a country claiming to have a democratic constitution. The citizens did not take the comment lightly and its effects echoed far beyond Slovenia's borders. As a consequence, powerful reactions against the accusation followed at the second All-Slovenian People's Uprising on 11 January 2013. Many people expressed their determination to assert their democratic right of protest against the government directly to the prime minister and his supporters. For that reason, they decided to protest in a way that mirrored Janša's comment, through a creative strategy of design. As philosopher Samo Tomšič (2013) noted in one of his commentaries, they were 'the mirror of the grotesque political elites, lacking every trace of democratic sovereignty, the actual void in the political body'. Within just a few days, protesters created numerous varieties of zombie masks, developing an unexpected yet highly effective strategy of dissent. Nonetheless, we should exercise prudence and avoid mistaking what Rockhill (2014: 54) described as the identification of political effects with political action. As he aptly pointed out in his book *Radical History*, the works of art should not be defined as the 'instrumental production of political action', but 'should allow space as well for reconfiguration of the networks of cultural hegemony' (Rockhill 2014: 54).

We can identify three major types of zombie masks in the Slovene protests, challenging the circumscribed space of national politics with dramatic content. In the first group, we find large, white paper masks, which may share some common origins with a version of the Guy Fawkes mask of the Anonymous hacktivists. Slovene masks were bigger, less expressive, and intended to be held in front of the face, or mounted onto some type of carrier. Their effect lay in the power of multiplication, creating a large, homogeneous group of marching protesters. Their performance, as with those of other types, was choreographed, and created a gestural dialogue with other 'zombie' characters, as well as with other protesters who were not wearing masks. The second group were comprised of zombie face-painted masks. The faces of protesters were camouflaged with white and grey face paint and lips were coloured black, creating the 'authentic' zombie look. Heads were covered in white elasticated netting with cut-out holes for facial orifices. By painting the body to represent the non-dead yet non-alive, the zombies were creating a visible expression of the political situation that had been triggered by the prime minister's comments. The third group of zombies was the most diverse and most theatrical. It consisted of huge white caricatured puppet-skeletons, made of papier-mâché. The giant puppet mechanics enabled the person carrying it to mount it onto their shoulders and navigate their spatial movements. Some of the giant skeletons were wrapped in white organza, which lightly floated when moving, creating a flair of drama. Nunley and McCarty (1999: 15) explain that mask-wearing is 'the most ancient means of changing identity and assuming a new persona'. Additionally, they tell us that 'masking helps reconstruct social memory' (Nunley and McCarty 1999: 17), which is of particular importance during times of crisis and turmoil. With that knowledge, we can understand why masks were so popular in the Slovene protests. The diverse zombie characters served first as mirrors to government intolerance of the protests, and second as ironic manifestations of the political body.

Zombies in the context of the Slovene protest did not portray a particular character. Dramatic as these grotesque masks were, it is obvious they were intended to release the pressure of repressed political frustrations at the collective level. What is of particular importance here is that they were as much a matter of politics as style. Their aesthetic and political relevance was sufficiently explicit to be quite broadly understood, and not merely from the perspective of the insider. Across the spectrum, one can pinpoint a fascinating combination of activist and citizen political views working together. As part of the Protestivals[1] (artistic section of street protests), they brought to attention the notion of civil society and the coexistence of differing alternatives: 'It is connecting people through their cultural expression, via musical performances, physical theatre, puppets, poetry, as well as giving a voice to the protesters themselves, thus creating a unique people's forum' (Novak 2013). Zombies acted twofold: as a strong political message to the prime minister and as a form of political art emerging from the protests. They also served as an unwelcome reminder of the excessive exercise of political power. The appearance or intervention of zombie characters at social protests was not an invention of the Slovene protests, although they were particular in many respects. These types of visual objects from protest culture occupy a special position in protest research, as they can be examined and paralleled to similar objects in other similar protests occurring at about the same time in different parts of the region and globally. Mouffe (2007) implies in *Artistic Activism and Agonistic Spaces* that performances have become key tools of protest.

Many on the left saw this performance as part of the collective struggle towards a more democratic politics, and against the government takeover of media discourse and the diminishing of freedom of the press. Many on the right saw it as a trivial, merely provocative action. Nevertheless, the people's protests managed to

92   *Ksenija Berk*

upset many on the political right who openly ridiculed the zombie actions in the mass media, as well as in parliamentary debates. On 8 February 2013, apparently on impulse, the right-wing pro-government Assembly for the Republic organised counter-protests in support of the government at Congress Square in Ljubljana. In this emotionally charged environment and with much anticipation from the supporting crowd, Janša transmitted his controversial speech. He was not physically present among his supporters, as was usually the case when making public speeches, because he was in Brussels attending an EU budget summit. This did not prevent him from being tele-present, as his speech was streamed to his supporters in the centre of Ljubljana on the big screen. The prime minister's speech was by far one of his most controversial since he began in politics, expounding a thinly veiled analogy between the methods of his opponents and those of the Nazis at the beginning of the Holocaust, with the 'left fascism'(Žužek 2013, Čefarin 2013). Only a few hours later, the third All-Slovenian People's Uprising began at various locations around the city, condemning the speech of the prime minister, and calling even more forcefully for political change. The two opposing events had been deliberately planned for the same date but at different venues and times. However, the anti-governmental third All-Slovenian People's Uprising had been announced weeks before the gathering of the Assembly for the Republics. By choosing the same date, the Assembly had attempted to discredit the protesters with their opposing provocations, but undoubtedly failed.

In attempting to sum up, we could ask what the zombies as political phenomena represent. First, they managed to revive a form of political performance familiar to us from the European protest movements of the 1960s, and arouse an otherwise dormant political scene by activating citizens' participation into what Edinger (2015) while referring to Bishop (2006) describes as the 'collective dimension of social experience'. After Janez Janša's unsuccessful attempts to bring the anti-government protests into disrepute by explicitly identifying protesters as 'communist zombies', the conjunction of revolutionary thought and social movements grew even more powerful. The zombies were the most visible and unconventional amongst the large number of groups using irony and parody to protest against oppression. They were an embodiment of the irregularities associated with the pathological dysfunctionality of governing politics, uniting the physical bodies of protesters across the divisions of class in a forceful body of politics with its own standards of action.

After the protests were over. . .

What makes visual material, or visual communications of contemporary Slovene protests, so interesting is not so much their ironic and naturalistic commentary on social reality, but rather their aesthetic strategy to successfully intertwine the spectator's mentality with complex image discourse for a political cause. The strength of these materials lies in the successful connections between various semantic levels to form a single unified message: bring corrupt politicians to a certain act – resignation. These strategies work by way of juxtaposing complex

At the crossroads of cultural and ideological exchange   93

layers of symbolic meaning, so that every visual material was at the same time a constitutive part of the protest movement. Many of the images and symbols analysed here document and transcribe into history by various aesthetic means a range of creative strategies that were juxtaposed by people upon the state apparatuses. I hope they remind the readers of those who were involved in the protests, be it activists or ordinary people, or those who only followed the events via news coverage, of the richness and deep symbolism of Slovene protests, in which people were communicating much more than just dissatisfaction with authorities. If I make parallels with the theories of cultural historian Peter Burke (2001: 9), I have tried to place visual material of Slovene protests, or the 'testimony of images', into different contexts that have succeeded to make 'visible an abstract concept' of dissent and brought forth the 'rich cultural history of the nation'. But at the end of the day, the reason I so meticulously tried to pin down even the tiniest specificities of Slovene visual culture of the 2012–2013 protests is, first and foremost, that they are not lost or forgotten from historical treatments of events.

Note

1 Protestivals were organised by a large variety of social movements and initiatives. To name just a few: the General Assembly of the All-Slovenian People's Uprising, Committee for Social Justice and Solidarity, Coordination Committee of Slovenian Culture, Committee for Direct Democracy, Movement of the Responsible, Today is a New Day, Federation for Anarchist Organisation (FAO), Workers and Punks' University (WPU), student association Iskra, Invisible Workers of the World (IWW), Association of Free Trade Unions of Slovenia, Pirate Party, and Party for Sustainable Development.

References

Arendt, H. 1999. *The Human Condition*. Chicago: University of Chicago Press.
Armstrong, L. 2007. Law, Ethics and Economy: Gerard of Siena and Giovanni d'Andrea on Usury. In: *Money, Markets and Trade in Late Medieval Europe: Essays in Honour of John H.A. Munro*, eds. L. Armstrong, I. Elbl, and M.M. Elbl. Leiden: Brill, pp. 41–58.
Barker, A. 2014. Church Finances: Holy Disorder. *The Financial Times*. [Online] Available at: www.ft.com/cms/s/0/7ce00cc6-7def-11e3-95dd   00144feabdc0.html#axzz4HaBzr1PI.
Bishop, C. 2006. Introduction: Viewers as Producers. In: *Participation: Documents of Contemporary Art*, ed. C. Bishop. London: Whitechapel Ventures Limited, pp. 10–17.
Bishop, C. 2012. *Artificial Hells: Participatory Art and the Politics of Spectatorship*. London: Verso.
Boyer, D. 2012. From Algos to Autonomos: Nostalgic Eastern Europe as Postimperial Mania. In: Post-Communist Nostalgia, eds. M. Todorova and Z. Gille. Oxford: Berghahn Books, pp. 17–29.
Brecht, B. 1998. *Ausgewählte Werke*. Frankfurt am Mein: Suhrkamp.
Burke, P. 2001. *Eyewitnessing: The Uses of Images as Historical Evidence*. London: Reaktion Books.
Čefarin, A. Kje je premier Janša našel navdih za petkov govor o levih fašistih? [Where has PM Janša Found an Inspiration for Friday's Speech on Left Fascists?] *Dnevnik*. [Online] Available at: https://www.dnevnik.si/1042576023.

94   Ksenija Berk

Comenas, G. 2010. *The Origin of Andy Warhol's Soup Cans or the Synthesis of Nothingness*. [Online] Available at: www.warholstars.org/andy_warhol_soup_can.html.

Craine, R. 1998. Form and Ideology: Warhol's Techniques from Blotted Line to Film. In: *The Work of Andy Warhol*, ed. G. Garrels. Seattle: Bay Press, pp. 70–93.

Edinger, C.I. 2015. Cool Anthropology. *Anthtropology News*. [Online] Available at: https://anthrosource.onlinelibrary.wiley.com/doi/abs/10.1111/j.1556-3502.2015.560501.x.

Farris, S.R., ed. 2015. *Returns of Marxism: Marxist Theory in Time of Crisis*. London: IMG Publications.

Ferguson, G. 1966. *Signs and Symbols in Christian Art*. Oxford: Oxford University Press.

Furlan, S. 2014. What Is To Be Done With the Bad Bank? *LeftEast*, April 15. [Online] Available at: www.criticatac.ro/lefteast/slovenia_bad_bank/.

Glatz, C. 2013. Slovenian Archbishops Resign Because of Ties to Financial Collapse. *Catholic News Service*. [Online] Available at: http://www.catholicnews.com/services/englishnews/2013/slovenian-archbishops-resign-because-of-ties-to-financial-collapse.cfm.

Groys, B. 2008. *Art Power*. Cambridge, MA: MIT Press.

Guffey, E.E. 2015. *Posters: A Global History*. London: Reaktion Books.

IRWIN. 2014. NSK State in Time. In: *State in Time*, ed. IRWIN. Wivenhoe, New York, Port Watson: Minor Compositions; Novo Mesto: Dolenjski muzej, pp. 7–13.

Korsika, A. 2014. Founding Congress of the Initiative for Democratic Socialism. *Transform!europe* [Online] Available at: www.transform-network.net/en/blog/article/founding-congress-of-the-initiative-for-democratic-socialism.

Ladner, G.B. 1996. *God, Cosmos and Humankind: The World of Early Christian Symbolism*. Berkeley: University of California Press.

M.R. 2012. SDS na Twitterju: Vstaja zombijev, ne pa vstaja naroda [SDS on Twitter: The Uprising of Zombies, not the Uprising of a Nation]. *24ur.com*. [Online] Available at: www.24ur.com/novice/slovenija/janseva-stranka-ne-vidi-protestnikov-temvec-zombije.html.

Mouffe, C. 2007. Artistic Activism and Agonistic Spaces. *Art&Research: A Journal of Ideas, Contexts and Methods*. [Online] Available at: www.artandresearch.org.uk/v1n2/mouffe.html.

Novak, M. 2013. Slovenia Rises in Artful 'protestivals'. *Waging Nonviolence*, March 21. [Online] Available at: http://wagingnonviolence.org/author/marjetanovak/.

Nunley, J.W. and C. McCarty. 1999. Introduction. In: *Masks: Faces of Culture*, eds. J.W. Nunley, J. Emigh and L.K. Ferries. St Louis: St Louis City Art Museum, pp. 15–21.

Raunig, G. 2007. *Art and Revolution: Transversal Activism in the Long Twentieth Century*. New York: Semiotext(e).

Rockhill, G. 2014. *Radical History & the Politics of Art*. New York: Columbia University Press.

Scott, D. 1995. *European Stamp Design: A Semiotic Approach to Designing Messages*. London: Academy Editions.

STA and T.M. 2014. Slovenia Up 4 Spots in Corruption Perceptions Index. *Slovenia Times*. [Online] Available at: www.sloveniatimes.com/slovenia-up-4-spots-in-corruption-perceptions-index.

Stojanovic, D. 2013. Slovenia's Prime Minister Accused of Corruption. *The San Diego Tribune*. [Online] Available at: www.sandiegotribune.com/sdut-slovenias-prime-minister-accused-of-corruption-2013jan11-story.html.

Timmers, M. 1998. *The Power of the Poster*. London: V&A Publishing.

At the crossroads of cultural and ideological exchange 95

Tomšič, S. 2013. The People Returns: A Footnote to Protests in Slovenia. *Critical Legal Thinking – Law & the Political*, January 16. [Online] Available at: http://criticallegal thinking.com/2013/01/16/the-people-returns-a-footnote-to-protests-in-slovenia/.

Ugrešić, D. 2007. *The Ministry of Pain*. New York: Harper Perennial.

Znidarčič, A. 2013. Slovenska biografija: Vavpotič, Ivan (1877–1943). *Slovenska akademija znanosti in umetnosti, Znanstvenoraziskovalni center SAZ*. [Online] Available at: www.slovenska-biografija.si/oseba/sbi764889/.

Žužek, A. So med nami levi fašisti? [Are Left Fascists Among Us?] *SiolNet*. [Online] Available at: https://siol.net/novice/slovenija/so-med-nami-levi-fasisti-174255.

6 Social media and the 'Balkan spring'

Željka Lekić-Subašić

Society, information and 'information society'

The necessity of information for the functioning of democratic communities is not a recent discovery. From Gutenberg onward, this need has been to a great extent satisfied by so-called traditional or mainstream media – newspapers, radio and television – which are based on a one-way transmission model of communication. In this model, the sender was often the organisation itself, a professional communicator whom it employed, or another voice within society given or sold access to media channels; potential audiences were viewed as large aggregate or more or less anonymous consumers. The growth of the Internet, 24-hour television and mobile phones has significantly increased the volume of information we receive. Research undertaken by Martin Hilbert and his team at the University of Southern California, which used more than 1,100 sources from national statistical offices and international agencies, has shown that the average person is bombarded by the equivalent of 174 newspapers of data a day – five times as much as in 1986 (Alleyne 2011). Even more stunning is that, in 2007, the average person consumed six newspapers' worth of information every day, thanks to email, digital photography, and social network sites, compared with just two and a half pages 24 years before (Alleyne 2011).

New technologies have not only changed the quantity, but also the way in which information is consumed, and consequently, the effect of this information. The digital revolution cannot be considered just a technical change; it has potential for the creation of a huge democratic space open to everyone with Internet access, currently almost 40% of the world's population (International Telecommunication Union 2013). The benefits of the Internet for democratic politics include: an interactive, as opposed to one-way, flow of information; simultaneous vertical and horizontal communication, or the promotion of equality; disintermediation, meaning a reduced role for journalism to mediate the relationship between citizen and politicians; low costs for senders and receivers; a speed greater than that possible with traditional media, and an absence of boundaries (Bentivegna 2002). Internet access has gained the status of a human right, given that it 'has become an indispensable tool for realising a range of human rights, combating inequality, and accelerating development and human progress' (La Rue 2011: 22). Still, the digital revolution has also created the 'digital divide' and the question of whether the informational content made available by new technology and the rates of participation in consulting and exchanging information strongly favour the 'have' regions and nations, as opposed to the 'have nots' – reinforcing the economic divide and, at the individual level, those educated and politically interested (Norris 2001).

Web 2.0

A new significant change has been brought by the rise of so-called 'Web 2.0' sites. Thomas Pettitt (2010) established a theory, the 'Gutenberg Parenthesis', according to which the entire history of media has been merely 'interrupted by the age of print', characterised by the 'imprisonment' of words. So today's communication is in some ways similar to storytelling and other kinds of cultural production in previous times, 'when oral traditions meant dynamically changing texts and performances', Pettitt (2010) argues. For 500 years, knowledge was contained in a fixed format believed to be a reliable version of the truth; now, entering the post-print era, we are returning to an age in which information, whether factual or not, is more likely to be received from individuals than from official mediums. Pettitt points out that the way we think now is reminiscent of a medieval peasant, based on gossip, rumour and conversation. Dick Costolo, at the time the CEO of Twitter, expressed a similar view: 'If you went back to Ancient Greece, the way that news and information was passed around was that you went to the agora after lunch in the town square. This was unfiltered, multi-directional exchange of information' (Nisenholtz, 2013). More broadly, many believe that peer network architecture and collaboration is an ancient tradition, with a rich and illustrious history including the 18th-century coffeehouse or urban neighbourhood formation, with the Internet as the most visible recent achievement in that tradition (Johnson 2012).

'Web 2.0' is a label coined by Tim O'Reilly to refer to the transition of the World Wide Web to a new phase of use and service development (Harrison and Barthel 2009). According to O'Reilly, the major distinction between Web 1.0 – original Internet websites that allowed only one-way communication through static web pages – and Web 2.0 is the 'collective intelligence' and 'architecture of participation' created through applications that invite, facilitate, encourage or make it possible for users to interact, share knowledge and information with each other and construct content. According to Hardey (2007), 'it is the content provided by other users' that is responsible for the popularity of the Web 2.0 application Facebook and other social networking sites. According to Tim Berners-Lee, the creator of the World Wide Web, this phase represents web adolescence (Potts 2007). The access to user-generated content, enabled by Web 2.0 technologies, brings the web closer to an ideal personal, democratic and do-it-yourself communication medium (Rheingold 2003). There are thousands of Web 2.0 applications and specialised sites. Typical categories include the various types of social networks, business networks, collaborative encyclopaedias and many other specialised sites.

98   *Željka Lekić-Subašić*

In this chapter, I analyse the use of three social media sites – Facebook, Twitter and YouTube – by activists and the general public during the 2012–2013 social movements in Southeast Europe. All three sites, which have attracted the largest number of users of all social networking sites, allow for sharing content, with Facebook and Twitter being used more for communication and message exchange, and YouTube for uploading, viewing and reviewing video clips. These platforms have increasingly become the 'vox populi' of modern times (Guerrini 2013). The content published on these sites and their usage models are investigated to determine the role of social media and online activism in the social movements in Southeast Europe. The methodology includes case study analysis, content analysis, interviews and surveys.

Social media and online activism

The ability of the non-mainstream media to disseminate information, galvanise public opinion and bring about change effectively was quickly recognised. The use of alternative and instant communication to spread political messages predates Twitter and Facebook. Shirky (2011) points out that Filipinos used Short Message Services (SMS) on mobile phones in 2001 to express political dissent during the impeachment trial of then President Joseph Estrada. The protest was organised through text messages shortly after the country's congress voted to set aside key evidence against Estrada. In her words: 'The public's ability to coordinate such a massive and rapid response – close to seven million text messages were sent that week – so alarmed the country's legislators that they reversed course and allowed the evidence to be presented [. . .] [B]y January 20, he was gone. The event marked the first time that social media had helped force out a national leader' (Shirky 2011). Fahmi (2009) traces the evolution of the new media phenomenon as tool for public dissent even before this. Referring to the protests against the World Trade Organisation (WTO) in Seattle in 1999, he claims that using blogs and collaborative web pages created a 'virtual geography', which displaced the constraints of distance.

The term 'Twitter revolution' was coined by Western media when two mass protests happened in 2009 in a matter of months – in Moldova in April, when more than 10,000 young Moldavians protested against the country's communist leadership, ransacking government buildings and clashing with the police, and in Iran in June 2009, when hundreds of thousands of people took to the streets to oppose the official results of the presidential election. Both protests were backed by social messaging sites. In Moldova, the protesters created their own searchable tag on Twitter, rallying people to join and propelling events in this small former Soviet state onto a Twitter list of newly popular topics, so people around the world could keep track (Barry 2009). In Iran, although sceptics note that only a small number of people in the country actually use Twitter to organise protests and that other means – individual text messaging, old-fashioned word of mouth and Farsi-language websites – are more influential, social media has been crucial for protesters in directing the public and for journalists to find video, photographic and written material related to the protests because the Iranian government restricted journalists' access to events (Cohen 2009). The video of Neda Agha Soltan dying after being shot in the chest, captured by a mobile phone camera and uploaded to the Internet, became the most powerful and recognisable symbol of the protests.

The role of social media became even more significant during the so-called Arab Spring – unprecedented protests in North Africa and the Middle East that caused the fall of long-time regimes in Egypt, Tunisia and Libya. The self-immolation of Mohamed Bouazizi, a Tunisian street seller, was one of 'several stories told and retold on Facebook, Twitter, and YouTube in ways that inspired dissidents to organise protests, criticise their governments, and spread ideas about democracy' (Howard et al. 2011: 2). One study on the role of social media in these uprisings finds that, first, social media played a central role in shaping political debates in the Arab Spring; second, a spike in online revolutionary conversations often preceded major events on the ground; and third, social media helped spread democratic ideas across international borders (Howard 2013).

Yet the use of social media for political uprisings is not something exclusively linked to non-Western or less developed parts of the world; it has also happened in Western liberal democracies, particularly in the aftermath of the financial crisis (Gonzalez-Bailon et al. 2011). One can hardly overestimate the role of social media as the mobilisation tool in the Occupy Wall Street protest, which began in New York City on 17 September 2011 and turned into a movement that has spread to hundreds of locations around the globe. Neal Caren and Sarah Gaby (2011) tracked the role of social networking sites, such as Facebook and Twitter, in linking supporters and distributing information. By the end of October 2011, they found that more than 400 US Occupation-related Facebook pages had been established, with at least one page for each of the 50 states. Based on data acquired from Facebook, they found that Occupy groups have recruited over 170,000 active Facebook users and more than 1.4 million 'likes' in support of occupations. Protesters also uploaded photos and videos to YouTube and image-sharing sites like Bambuser and Yfrog, and broadcasted their gatherings live using the Livestream service, mainly through a channel called Global Revolution. Twitter was also used massively, especially during ongoing and significant events, and the highest tally of 55,663 tweets was reached on 15 November 2011, when the New York Police Department removed all activists and protesters from Zuccotti Park and the surrounding streets (Carleton 2011).

Social media was also used extensively during the riots in London, although protestors mostly used BlackBerry messenger, a free mobile phone messaging service open to anyone with a BlackBerry smartphone (Ball and Brown 2011). But the video of a Malaysian student being beaten and then robbed by fake Samaritans pretending to help him, which spread over social media sites, seemed to represent 'the evil without reason and the greed that many of the official explanations highlighted as the main reason for the rioting' (Guerrini 2013). The video was shot from above by a person living in a nearby building, who then, 'shocked by what he had seen', uploaded the footage to his Facebook page, where it was later picked up by his 'friends' and went viral, especially after being reposted on YouTube,

100   *Željka Lekić-Subašić*

where during the next few days it was viewed more than 3 million times. On Twitter, people were sending messages of support to the injured student and donating money to help him via a Tumblr blog called 'Something nice for Ashraf'. Twitter was also used and proved to be capable of mobilising large numbers of people to organise a clean-up of riot-damaged streets (Ball and Lewis 2011).

Evidence shows that social media and new media technologies have brought very concrete changes to people's lives. When street shootouts between warring Mexican drug cartels made cities like Monterrey inhospitable, citizens developed their own emergency notification networks with Twitter. Urban governments failed to provide public warning systems, so citizens created their own public communication system via digital media. After the Haiti earthquake, 35 million USD were collected in the United States for the relief efforts through 10 USD-each SMS donations. 'If you give to citizens an easy way for connection and engaging, they will do it', Alec Ross (2010), Senior Adviser on Innovation to former US Secretary of State Hillary Clinton and an architect of Barack Obama's digital campaigning in the 2008 presidential election, explained. Colombo (2012) shows that, in addition to greater interest, the Internet positively affects internal political efficacy – the degree with which people consider themselves more or less knowledgeable regarding politics. The change in the communication method occurs at both the individual and collective level; that is, technology not only empowers particular citizens, but also provides them with new tools with which they can build new forms of collective action (Noveck 2005). Baker (2011) introduces the term 'mediated crowd', a collective action that occurs in the virtual (and geographic) arena as opposed to a traditional crowd, which is typically limited to physical congregation in a shared geographical location. She underlines that these two public domains are not mutually exclusive, 'with the "mediated crowd" able to traverse from the virtual public sphere into geographical public space, or to occupy both spheres simultaneously via new social media'; the very notion of the 'mediated crowd' is distinguished from a standard crowd by 'its reliance on media communication technologies to mobilise and sustain collective action' (Baker 2011). Obviously, one of these new forms of collective action involves the use of the Internet for political purposes. The use of the Internet may involve the dissemination of information on activities and events to a broader public and facilitate coordination for activists (Ayres 1999), as well as provide electronic versions of traditional forms of participation, such as online voting or petition signing, and new forms of cyber involvement such as politically motivated hackings (Jordan and Taylor 2004). Social media has become a place for politicians to engage directly with the people; when former US President Barack Obama won against Republican rival Mitt Romney, the tweet of Obama hugging his wife broke records to become the most retweeted ever (Lee 2013).

Cyber-utopianism and slacktivism

However, not all scholars agree on the Internet's transformative political potential and radically positive effects on democracy (see Hindman 2009; Berkhout

Social media and the 'Balkan spring' 101

and Jansen 2012; Morozov 2013). Most people admit that social media can be very successful in providing information, but the issue remains that many political institutions regularly confront problems that are not the result of deficiencies in knowledge. According to Morozov (2013), the theory of 'cyber-utopianism' that believes that 'the Internet will destroy dictatorships, undermine religious fundamentalism, and make up for failures of institutions' is fundamentally wrong. Morozov raises the concerns of privacy and security and, taking the same example of the events in Iran, he reminds us that, once the protests diminished, the Iranian authorities embarked on a digital purge of their opponents and, in just a few months, formed a high-level cybercrime team and tasked it with finding any false information – or, as they put it, 'insults and lies' – on Iranian websites. Those spreading false information were to be identified and arrested. Similarly, leading US human rights lawyer John Cooper QC warned that political activists must watch what they say on the likes of Facebook and Twitter, sites that will become the 'next big thing in law enforcement', after a New York court ordered Twitter to hand over messages posted on the site by a demonstrator belonging to the Occupy Wall Street movement (Rawlinson 2012). Morozov also gives other examples of the Internet's non-democratic usage, like in Russia, where the 'Movement against Illegal Immigration' uses Google Maps to create mash-up maps of ethnic minorities' homes, urging people to find and harass them; or in Japan, where, after intense pressure from Japanese anti-discrimination non-governmental organisations (NGOs), Google requested that the owners of the maps remove the legend that identified the Burakamin ghettos as 'scum towns' (Morozov 2011).

Further criticism is related to the political and citizen activism that has been facilitated and transformed by social networking sites.

> All of a sudden, people were getting interested in everything and nothing at the same time; all subjects, no matter how ridiculous or sublime, were getting equalised in such a way that nothing mattered enough to want to die for.
>
> (Morozov 2011)

The derogatory epithet used for these activities is *slacktivism*, which refers to political activities that have no impact on real-life political outcomes, but only serve to increase the feel-good factor of the participants. The citizens satisfy their need to engage politically by getting involved in almost pointless and isolated actions, either by signing an online petition, forwarding a message or re-tweeting a tweet, or 'liking' or commenting on content shared on a social networking site, blog or mass media website. In this sense, the availability of electronic forms of 'activism', scholars warn, may even lead to deterioration in the quality of participation, as people who would otherwise become involved through traditional means may instead opt for digital opportunities, believing that these activities are a sufficient replacement. According to this critique, the Internet, at best, merely provides another tool for the already active; it does not help mobilise previously

102 Željka Lekić-Subašić

passive citizens. According to Gladwell (2010), the platforms of social media are built around 'weak ties [. . .] that seldom lead to high-risk activism'. In other words, Facebook activism succeeds 'not by motivating people to make a real sacrifice but by motivating them to do the things that people do when they are not motivated enough to make a real sacrifice' (Gladwell 2010). The second crucial distinction he finds between traditional activism and its online variant is a lack of hierarchical organisation, centralised leadership and discipline in the latter. Decisions are made through consensus, and the ties that bind people to the group are loose. 'How do you make difficult choices about tactics or strategy or philosophical direction when everyone has an equal say?' Gladwell (2010) asks. He concludes that high-risk strategies that leave little room for conflict and error, like boycotts, sit-ins and non-violent confrontations – all weapons of choice for the civil-rights movement – are not possible through online social media. Therefore, according to critics, although social media-based mobilisation occasionally leads to genuine social and political change, this is mostly accidental, a statistical certainty rather than a genuine achievement.

There is, however, yet another approach, made at the collective level, and emphasising the side of the receiver, to whom the citizens' clicks, re-tweets or 'likes' are addressed. At the collective level, these *slacktivists* are the same individuals who are involved in political actions outside of social networking sites (Peña-López 2013), providing cohesion to the group and a sense of collective identity. Their specific actions come to complement, not replace, other actions of political participation, and the passive visibility of these actions – as they appear in the activists' profiles on social networking sites – 'ends up providing these actions with a life of their own, making involvement in civic causes be spread and resulting in behavioural changes both at the individual level as in the social circle next to the citizen' (Peña-López 2013: 347). Slacktivism is not as important in relationship to the issuer – who simply clicks a link – but in relationship to the receiver, i.e. the institution that feels questioned or challenged by millions of micro-actions that are also, in essence, the echo of a compacted movement. A movement that, as it is not institutionalised, does not fall within our usual parameters to measure the impact of political participation: working hours 'lost' by a strike, how many protesters there are on the streets or the number of votes that changed sides in an election. Peña-López believes that *slacktivism* does not actually take place in the periphery of new social movements in the sense of something marginal, but in the sense of something that is actually part of the whole, 'as smoke is part of the fire' (Peña-López 2013). In this sense,

> slacktivism is not a weak engagement, but just a part of the new digital toolbox of political participation, which sometimes is more committed and sometimes is not [. . .] [It] does not define the activist, but, in general, the activist individually uses slacktivism as yet another tool to reinforce a much more comprehensive and collective strategy of political engagement.
>
> (Peña-López 2013)

Case study: social media and the 'baby revolution' in Bosnia-Herzegovina

The 'baby revolution', the name given to protests held from 5 June to 1 July 2013 in front of the parliament building in Sarajevo and many other towns in Bosnia-Herzegovina, was unprecedented in the post-war period in this country. In a country where no cause has been significant enough to unite ruling and opposition political forces and all three main ethnic groups (Bosniaks, Serbs and Croats), almost everyone agreed that 'the painfully incompetent, wilfully corrupt and supremely arrogant political elite' (Medic 2013), who could not find a solution regarding how to redraw the districts that determine the 13-digit identification number assigned to each citizen, had to be removed from power, and this resulted in tens of thousands of people going out onto the streets. The protests were sparked by the desperate bid of the mother of a 3-month-old baby, Belmina Ibrisevic, who had urgently needed a stem cell transplant in Germany. But because the national law on ID numbers had not yet been adopted after the old law's expiration in February, newborns were no longer being issued the ID numbers required to obtain a passport and health insurance.

Following the chronological order of the most important events in the period 5 June to 1 July 2013 and material published on social media related to the protests, together with interviews with the organisers of the protests and surveys with university students as representatives of the general public, this case study aims to determine the role of social media[1] in the organisation of the protests and how important online activism was for this particular cause.

On 4 June 2013, the story about Belmina's problem appeared on the website of a local radio station, on a page dedicated to stories posted by members of the audience, which spread on Facebook. Later in the evening, the story was picked up by popular web portal klix.com, which published the story with the title 'Politicians, do you have a conscience? Baby cannot receive surgery because she does not have an ID number'.[2] The article was shared 8,170 times on Facebook, 75 times on Twitter, and received 156 online comments, most of them posted the very same evening. Many commenters called for street protests as a solution to the problem. At 01:27 on June 5, one post declared that the Facebook group 'JMB'[3] had been formed as a sign of support for the baby. That was the first of more than 20 pages and communities established on Facebook in the following days,[4] a sign that online discussion on this subject was intense. The same day, several people, many of them parents with babies, assembled in front of the parliament and blocked the exits of the garage, protesting over the plight of baby Belmina, who was unable to leave Bosnia for a life-saving operation. That day, the Council of Ministers adopted a temporary measure that allowed personal numbers, the basis for all documents, to be issued for the next six months. The story had already been picked up by mainstream media, both local and international. As a show of support, on June 6, 3,000 people joined the first protesters in demanding that parliament, which was in session that day, adopt a permanent law so the problem would not arise again. They formed a human chain around the building and

104   *Željka Lekić-Subašić*

prohibited any politician from exiting the parliament until an agreement had been reached, effectively trapping 1,500 politicians inside the building. The satirical article 'Fifty babies arrested on protests in Sarajevo',[5] published that evening, was shared on Facebook 7,490 times, and the tweet accusing 'Bosniak parties' for a planned 'lynching' of representatives from Republika Srpska, posted on the personal Twitter account of MP Aleksandra Pandurevic, provoked 245 bitter online comments.[6] In fact, all the Facebook groups created at that time stated precisely the contrary, that 'no flags, religions, parties, politicians, advertisements' were allowed,[7] that they were 'citizens [. . .] regardless of ethnic and religious belonging',[8] and that 'they do not represent any party or organisation'.[9] Pandurevic's tweet provoked another online petition requesting her resignation, signed by 20,995 persons.[10] The blockade of the parliament building lasted until the early morning hours of June 7 and protestors gave parliament until June 30 to adopt the law on ID numbers and establish a solidarity fund for citizens in need of medical treatment.

In the meantime, the movement created a website (www.jmbg.org) and several recognisable hashtags on Twitter, such as #svismomibelmina [We are all Belmina] and #JMBG (the local acronym for the ID numbers). The most numerous protests were held on June 11, the day when the Peace Implementation Council for BiH held a session about the issue of identification numbers, with almost 10,000 people gathering in front of the parliament building in Sarajevo. On June 16, people gathered to pay tribute to one-and-a-half-month-old baby girl Bermina Hamidovic, who died of sepsis on June 13 after a delayed medical evacuation abroad. The posts announcing the gathering on June 16 on the Facebook page 'Ja.BIH.JMBG' received more than 1,000 'likes' and more than 128 'shares', meaning that it appeared on the personal profiles of numerous Facebook users. The page itself now has more than 21,000 'likes' and nearly the same number of "follows", meaning that this many Facebook users receive posts from this page in their news feeds. Twitter analysis shows that in the period June 4 to June 30, there were 19,933 tweets originating from Bosnia-Herzegovina with protest-related hashtags,[11] with a peak point on June 6–7 of 5,110 tweets, and another on June 11–12 of 2,514 tweets. The number of tweets significantly decreased towards the end of the month. Results of a video search on YouTube show more than 2,000 video materials related to the JMBG protests,[12] with a six-minute video from the protests in Sarajevo on June 6 having more than 14,000 views.[13] The next most viewed video was uploaded on June 17, and shows children from different parts of the world expressing their support for children and babies in Bosnia-Herzegovina: it had more than 9,000 views.[14] The majority of videos were uploaded during the first two days of the protests, June 5–6, from the largest protest in Sarajevo on June 11, and from the concert of Bosnian groups held within the protest in Sarajevo on June 18.

For the purpose of this paper, a survey was conducted with a group of 30 students, ages 18–20, from the Faculty of Philosophy at the University of Sarajevo.[15] Although the sample is small and the applicability of the results to the whole population of BiH rather limited due to the narrow age range, the results are still

Social media and the 'Balkan spring' 105

interesting and worth mentioning. To the question 'what were the sources of information used about the protests in Bosnia-Herzegovina, June 5–30, 2013?', 40% of students responded that they found information online, on social media (mostly Facebook), and on web portals; 27% received information from social media combined with traditional media, mostly television; and 30% received information through traditional media only. Only one student received information from friends or family members in person. One third of the questioned students were actually present at the protests, with 80% of those indicating they participated on their own personal initiative rather than from content or invitations posted on social media. A small number were invited by friends or family members in person.

According to the organisers of the protests, social media – especially Facebook – was of crucial importance for spreading information and popularising the protests, especially at the very beginning, on June 5, when the information on mainstream media was 'censored'.[16] Afterwards, the organisation and coordination of the protests were conducted in person at meetings in front of the parliament building and other locations, and Facebook served more as a communication tool and a 'mailing list'.[17] Both interviewed organisers underline that online activism *per se* has no purpose at all if it is not accompanied by concrete action in real life, and that one click or 'like' is simply not good enough, but at the same time, Zoran Ivancic, one of the organisers of the protests, believes that the correspondence rate between online and real-life activism in Bosnia at that time was quite high. Still, he warns, the same tools are also available to 'fascists and attackers of minority groups [. . .] who seem to use it more efficiently'.[18] Social media sites were also used by state authorities during the protests: the Republika Srpska Minister for the Interior confirmed that police were following the activities on social media to find those who took the initiative in 'spreading misinformation about Republika Srpska'.[19]

Although a direct cause-and-effect relationship cannot be confirmed, it may be noted that the intensity of discussion on social media sites about the 'baby revolution' in Bosnia-Herzegovina corresponded to the activities of protestors in real life, and that social media – particularly Facebook – served as a communication tool for the protest organisers, especially during the first days of the protests, and as a source of information for the general public during the whole period.

'Slovenia's uprising' and other protests in Southeast Europe

The protests in Slovenia began on 2 November 2012 in Maribor as a response to the actions of Mayor Franc Kangler, initially in a dispute over the placement of new traffic enforcement cameras. During the following three months, there were 98 protests in all major Slovenian cities, with more than 100,000 participants altogether. On 21 December 2012, the first All-Slovenian Uprising against the political elite took place, with 10,000 peaceful protesters. Many of the protesters were singing revolutionary songs such as the *Internationale*, which prompted the ruling Slovenian Democratic Party (SDS) to tweet that the protests were 'an

106 Željka Lekić-Subašić

uprising of communist zombies'. This evoked a reaction at the second uprising in Slovenia on 11 January 2013, in which many of the protesters came wearing zombie masks. In a way, the situation was reminiscent of that in 2011, when the so-called 15 October movement (15O) organised similar protests as a response to austerity measures, and occupied the platform in front of the Slovenian stock exchange for a few months. Similarly to those in 2011, but to a greater extent, the organisation of the protests in 2012 and the spread of information about them were largely conducted via social media.[20]

The Facebook page '*Franc Kangler naj odstopi kot župan Maribora*' [Franc Kangler to resign as Maribor mayor], created in October 2012, had more than 40,000 'likes' at its peak, with many of those Facebook users also 'following' the page.[21] On the question of whether Kangler should resign from his position, posted by the page's administrators on October 28, 1,810 people answered positively. On the Facebook event announcement of the protests on November 21, 'the first Maribor uprising', 1,970 people confirmed their presence,[22] although according to media reports, around 1,000 actually attended the protests. The next protest, on November 26, was also announced on Facebook,[23] and this time, almost 10,000 attended. Twitter analysis shows there were 10,845 tweets originating from Slovenia with protest-related hashtags[24] in the period November 1 to 21 December 2012, with the peak period being November 30 to December 1 eliciting 2,255 tweets, when protests spread to five other cities in Slovenia, including the capital, Ljubljana. Protestors requested the resignation of Slovenian Prime Minister Janez Janša and his Cabinet, accusing them of corruption and fraud.

Presiln's (2013) research shows that Facebook played a significant role in the organisation of protests in Slovenia, especially in spreading protest messages and inviting people to active participation. Of the survey participants, 66% received information about the protests via the Internet, 34% by television, and newspapers and radio had rather insignificant roles. More importantly, 88% of those receiving information via the Internet have done so via Facebook, which, taking into account the huge number of Facebook users in Slovenia, leads this author to conclude that the importance of this social media site for informing and recruiting protest supporters is undoubtable. Of the survey participants, 70% were exposed to information about protests on Facebook between one to five times per day, and 21% were exposed more than five times per day. Among those who actively participated in the protests, the percentage of those who have been exposed to information about the protests on Facebook more than five times per day rises to 33%. Furthermore, according to Presiln's findings, although Facebook contributed to the organisation and coordination of active supporters, the general population used it as an information resource for past as well as current happenings. Of the survey participants, 66% received information about future protest-related events on Facebook, 64% received information about what has already happened, 24% used it to alert friends about current events, and 23% communicated and shared experiences with other protest participants. Most of the survey participants found the information they received from Facebook to be useful and trustworthy.

The results of this survey confirm the same results as in Bosnia-Herzegovina: that social media has been largely used as a source of information and as an organisational tool for protestors. However, as in Bosnia-Herzegovina, Facebook has been used by authorities as well: the media reported that police in Slovenia have searched Facebook profiles to identify protest organisers.[25]

The use of social media during protests certainly did not end in Slovenia and Bosnia-Herzegovina. Many Bulgarians credit the Internet and social media for inspiring and spreading the #ДАНСwithme protests, as they were known on social media, during June and July 2013. #ДАНСwithme has become the main hashtag – along with #Bulgaria – around which tweets, videos, Facebook and blog posts and messages about the demonstrations have been focused. The hashtag is a pun: ДАНС in Bulgarian is the acronym of the State Agency for National Security – the country's secret service – and the protests were sparked by the controversial appointment, later cancelled, of businessman and MP Delyan Peevski as its new head. #ДАНСwithme sounds like 'dance with me' in English. Maxim Behar, the author of the recent book *Generation F* about Bulgarian youths, believes that it is 'Generation F's connectedness, the result of extensive high-speed broadband networks in Bulgaria, which led to the protests' (Troev and Buckley 2013). Social media was also used previously in Bulgaria, during the series of mass protests in January–February 2013,[26] which were initially triggered by the shockingly high electricity bills in the EU's poorest member state. However, many protesters also demanded the resignation of the centre-right GERB government of Boyko Borisov, and the government resigned on February 20. The same day, a new Facebook page was created, '*Протест В Подкрепа На Бойко Борисов*' [Protest in support of Boyko Borisov], with a call to Bulgarian citizens to express their support for Borisov and to go out on protests; the page gathered more than 1,700 users in less than an hour and more than 36,000 'likes'.[27] Another prominent example of the use of social media was during the protests in Turkey, where it became so significant that Turkish Prime Minister Recep Erdoğan called social media 'the curse of society today' and accused protesters of spreading lies and rumours (Russel 2013). The irony of his claims is that he himself is one of the highest-profile figures online in the country. In Hungary, a Facebook group turned into the largest grassroots opposition movement: the demonstrative 'One Million for the Freedom of Press in Hungary', created in December 2010 as a response to the introduction of the very controversial media law by the Fidesz party under Viktor Orban and his increasingly authoritarian government, has organised numerous significant offline demonstrations in Budapest and in other cities in Hungary, and eventually spawned into a political movement (Bognar et al. 2013).

Conclusion

Social media platforms have various functionalities that can be effectively used by social movements: they encourage innovative use; permit the integration of various sources and materials (e.g. text, images, video and sound); allow for the creation of flexible information-environments, in which individuals can tailor their

108   *Željka Lekić-Subašić*

encounter with the content in a way that best suits their learning styles; and offer on-demand access to current information, providing individuals access to relevant information quickly and easily (Garrett 2006). Furthermore, the instant communication with low costs offered by social media in turn tremendously reduces the cost of collective action and increases social movements' ability to reach a greater audience. Additionally, simultaneous interaction with people from different social networks, such as family, friends, co-workers or old classmates, results in individuals being exposed to a variety of sources and views shared and discussed amongst their Facebook friends. By facilitating many-to-many communication, social media platforms can also encourage communication between groups and possibly decrease group polarisation. As could be seen in the description of the Facebook groups created during the 'baby revolution' in Bosnia-Herzegovina, the joint motive – a baby's life – circulated through social media platforms contributed to the creation of groups on grounds other than those usually used in the country, such as ethnicity, religion and political affiliation.

The cases presented in this paper confirm previous research evidence that online activities do not substitute but rather present yet another component of political actions that engaged citizens may perform in real life (Christensen 2011). Although most Internet users or *slacktivists* never develop deeper forms of involvement, and despite the fact that (too) much time and effort was spent on pointless discussions (such as that about what the state officials in Bosnia-Herzegovina were doing during the protestors' siege of the parliament building), there was no evidence that Internet activities were damaging civic engagement by replacing more effective forms of participation.

Although online political information's direct impact on motivation or activism is small compared to other socio-economic factors, Internet use and information access have been linked to greater citizen involvement in political discussions. In both Bosnia-Herzegovina and Slovenia, social networking sites presented a very important source of information for the wider public and a communication tool for the protests' organisers, especially in the early stages of organisation. Online activities during the recent protests in Southeast Europe rendered communication more frequent and intense and created feelings of empathy and belonging to larger groups, confirming the capacity for mediated communication to evoke collective emotional responses. As Stone (2010) puts it, 'rudimentary communication among individuals in real time allows many to move together as one – suddenly uniting everyone in a common goal'. Of course, to avoid the traps of cyber-utopianism and slacktivism, it has to be noted that, first, not only collective action and activism changes in the course of technological development, utilising new capabilities for their advantage, but opponents can utilise the same tools for their own advantage as well; and second, collective action is a much more complex and multi-faceted process than creating a Facebook group. Social media does not facilitate collective action or social change by itself. These should be considered tools used by people who may have different goals and actions.

Notes

1 Of all social media sites, Facebook and YouTube are the most popular in Bosnia-Herzegovina. There are 1.16 million Facebook users in the country and Facebook receives more than 500,000 unique visits a day from Bosnian users (MVF 2013a).
2 See www.klix.ba/vijesti/bih/politicari-imate-li-savjesti-tromjesecna-beba-ne-moze-na-operaciju-jer-nema-jmb/130604130.
3 See www.facebook.com/groups/134792740053466/.
4 See www.facebook.com/search/str/jmbg/pages-named.
5 See www.klix.ba/vijesti/bih/pedeset-beba-uhapseno-na-protestima-u-sarajevu/13060 6139.
6 See www.klix.ba/vijesti/bih/sramotno-ponasanje-aleksandre-pandurevic-u-jeku-protesta-pred-parlamentom/130606084, accessed on 8 November 2013.
7 See www.facebook.com/groups/133926063478214/.
8 See www.facebook.com/groups/495617230509250/.
9 See www.facebook.com/Ja.BiH.JMBG.
10 See www.onlinepeticija.com/trenutni_otkaz_aleksandri_pandurevic.
11 #JMBG, #JMBGzasve, #svismomibelmina, #Sarajevo, #protesti, #BIH
12 See www.youtube.com/results?search_sort=video_date_uploaded&search_query=jm bg+sarajevo&filters=video&page=2.
13 See www.youtube.com/watch?v=YzriK2UUzY8.
14 See www.youtube.com/watch?v=iCGe22jnwGs.
15 The anonymous paper survey was administered before class to 30 students in their first year of the Faculty of Philosophy, University of Sarajevo, on 15 November 2013.
16 Author's interview with Darjan Bilic, an organiser of the protest, 8 November 2013.
17 Author's interview with Zoran Ivancic, an organiser of the protest, 10 November 2013.
18 Author's interview with Zoran Ivancic, an organiser of the protest, 10 November 2013.
19 See http://abrasmedia.info/content/borenovi%C4%87-tra%C5%BEi-od-ministra-policije-adrese-korisnika-dru%C5%A1tvenih-mre%C5%BEa-koji-su-podr%C5%BEavali.
20 At the time of the protest, 1.4 million Slovenians were online, which represents a 70% Internet penetration; 98% of Internet users in Slovenia use it most often to access social media sites (Mesko 2011). Facebook is the most popular social media site in Slovenia: there are 745,000 Facebook members in Slovenia, which represents 31% of the whole population and 52% of the Slovenian Internet population. Facebook has more than 500,000 unique visitors to the site per day, compared to Twitter, which only receives around 10,000 unique visitors daily (MVF 2013b).
21 See www.facebook.com/kangler.naj.odstopi.
22 See www.facebook.com/events/364296646990871/.
23 See www.facebook.com/events/112860042210284/.
24 #gotofje, #ljprotest, #mprotest, #fertikje, #slovenia, #ljubljana, #maribor
25 See www.delo.si/novice/slovenija/policija-na-fb-isce-udelezence-in-organizatorje-pro testov.html, accessed on 12 November 2013.
26 See http://spotlight-universityofbedfordshire.blogspot.com/2013/03/bulgarian-protests-and-social-media.html, accessed on 12 November 2013.
27 See http://ernoblogger.blogspot.com/2013_02_01_archive.html, accessed on 12 November 2013.

References

Alleyne, R. 2011. Welcome to the Information Age – 174 Newspapers a Day. *Telegraph*, February 11. [Online] Available at: www.telegraph.co.uk/science/science-news/8316534/Welcome-to-the-information-age-174-newspapers-a-day.html.

110 Željka Lekić-Subašić

Ayres, J.M. 1999. From the Streets to the Internet: The Cyber-Diffusion of Contention. *The Annals of the American Academy of Political and Social Science* 566(1): 132–143.

Baker, S.A. 2011. The Mediated Crowd: New Social Media and New Forms of Rioting. *Sociological Research Online*, November 30. [Online] Available at: http://www.socresonline.org.uk/16/4/21.html.

Ball, J. and S. Brown. 2011. Why Blackberry Messenger was Rioters' Communication Method of Choice. *The Guardian*, December 7. [Online] Available at: www.theguardian.com/uk/2011/dec/07/bbm-rioters-communication-method-choice.

Barry, E. 2009. Protests in Moldova Explode, With Help of Twitter. *The New York Times*, April 7. [Online] Available at: www.nytimes.com/2009/04/08/world/europe/08moldova.html?pagewanted=all&_r.

Bentivegna, S. 2002. Politics and New Media. In: *The Handbook of New Media: Social Shaping and Consequences of ICTs*, eds. L. Lievrouw and S. Livingstone. London: Sage, pp. 50–61.

Berkhout, R. and F. Jansen. 2012. Introduction: The Changing Face of Citizen Action. *Development* 55(2): 154–157.

Bognar, E., L. Denick, and P. Wilkin. 2013. *Social Media, Virtual Politics and Inclusion – the Case of Hungary's 'Milla' Group*. Conference Paper, IAMCR 2013 Conference Dublin, 25–29 June 2013.

Caren, N. and G. Sarah. 2011. Occupy Online: Facebook and the Spread of Occupy Wall Street. [Online] Available at: http://ssrn.com/abstract=1943168.

Carleton, W. 2011. On the Scene: A Geek's Guide to the Wall Street Occupation. *Geekwire*, October 16. [Online] Available at: www.geekwire.com/2011/occupy-wall-street-geeks-guide/.

Christensen, H.S. 2011. Political Activities on the Internet: Slacktivism or Political Participation By Other Means? *First Monday*, February 16. [Online] Available at: http://firstmonday.org/htbin/cgiwrap/bin/ojs/index.php/fm/article/view/3336/2767.

Cohen, N. 2009. Twitter on the Barricades: Six Lessons Learned. *The New York Times*, June 20. [Online] Available at: www.nytimes.com/2009/06/21/weekinreview/21cohenweb.html?_r=0.

Colombo, C., C. Galais, and A. Gallego. 2012. El uso de Internet y las actitudes políticas. Datos cuantitativos y cualitativos de España. *Arbor: Ciencia, Pensamiento y Cultura* 188(756): 751–766.

Fahmi, W. 2009. Bloggers' Street Movement and the Right to the City. (Re)claiming Cairo's Real and Virtual 'spaces of freedom'. *Environment and Urbanisation* 21(1): 89–107.

Garrett, R.K. 2006. Protest in an Information Society: A Review of Literature on Social Movements and New ICTs. *Information, Communication & Society* 9(2): 202–224.

Gladwell, M. 2010. Why the Revolution Will Not Be Tweeted. *The New Yorker*, October 4. [Online] Available at: www.newyorker.com/reporting/2010/10/04/101004fa_fact_gladwell?currentPage=all.Gonzalez-Bailon, S., J. Borge-Holthoefer, A. Rivero, and M. Yamir. 2011. The Dynamics of Protest Recruitment Through an Online Network. *Scientific Reports* 1(197). [Online] Available at: www.nature.com/articles/srep00197.

Guerrini, F. 2013. Newsroom Curators & Independent Storytellers: Content Curation as a New Form of Journalism. *Reuters Institute Fellowship Paper*. [Online] Available at: https://reutersinstitute.politics.ox.ac.uk/our-research/newsroom-curators-and-independent-storytellers.

Hardey, M. 2007. The City in the Age of Web 2.0: A New Synergistic Relationship Between Place and People. *Information, Communication and Society* 10(6): 867–884.

Harrison, T.M. and B. Barthel. 2009. Wielding New Media in Web 2.0: Exploring the History of Engagement With the Collaborative Construction of Media Products. *New Media Society* 11(155).

Hindman, M. 2009. *The Myth of Digital Democracy*. Princeton: Princeton University Press.

Howard, P.N. 2013. If Your Government Fails, Can You Create a New One With Your Phone? *The Atlantic*, July 31. [Online] Available at: www.theatlantic.com/international/archive/2013/07/if-your-government-fails-can-you-create-a-new-one-with-your-phone/278216.

Howard, P.N., M.M. Hussain, J. Earl, and K. Kimpor. 2011. *Opening Closed Regimes: What Was the Role of Social Media During the Arab Spring?* [Online] Available at SSRN: https://ssrn.com/abstract=2595096.

International Telecommunication Union. 2013. *Measuring the Information Society Report.* [Online] Available at: www.itu.int/en/ITU-D/Statistics/Documents/facts/ICTFactsFigures 2013.pdf.

Johnson, S. 2012. *Future Perfect: The Case for Progress in a Networked Age*. New York: Riverhead Hardcover.

Jordan, T. and P. Taylor. 2004. *Hacktivism and Cyberwars: Rebels With a Cause?* New York: Routledge.

La Rue, F. 2011. Report of the UN Special Rapporteur on the Promotion and Protection of the Right to Freedom of Opinion and Expression. [Online] Available at: http://www2.ohchr.org/english/bodies/hrcouncil/docs/17session/A.HRC.17.27_en.pdf.

Lee, D. 2013. How Twitter Changed the World, hashtag-by-hashtag. *BBC*, November 7. [Online] Available at: www.bbc.co.uk/news/technology-24802766.

Medic, R. 2013. Babylution: Facebook's First 'Hashmob' Is Happening in Bosnia. *Netocratic*, June 18. [Online] Available at: http://netocratic.com/babylution-facebook-hashmob-1408.

Meško, G. 2011. Internetna študija poznavanja kibernetskih groženj in strahu pred kibernetsko kriminaliteto. *Revija za kriminalistiko in kriminologijo* 62(3): 242–252.

Morozov, E. 2011. *The Net Delusion: The Dark Side of Internet Freedom*. New York: Public Affairs Books.

Morozov, E. 2013. Why Social Movements Should Ignore Social Media. *New Republic*, February 25. [Online] Available at: www.newrepublic.com/article/112189/social-media-doesnt-always-help-social-movements#footnote-1.

MVF. 2013a. *Internet Marketing and Lead Generation in Bosnia-Herzegovina*. [Online] Available at: www.mvfglobal.com/.

MVF. 2013b. *Lead Generation and Internet Marketing in Slovenia*. [Online] Available at: www.mvfglobal.com/.

Nisenholtz, M. 2013. Interview with Dick Costolo, CEO of Twitter. *Nieman Lab*. [Online] Available at: www.niemanlab.org/riptide/person/dick-costolo/.

Norris, P. 2001. *Digital Divide: Civic Engagement, Information Poverty, and the Internet Worldwide*. Cambridge: Cambridge University Press.

Noveck, B.S. 2005. A democracy of groups. *First Monday* 10(11). [Online] Available at: http://firstmonday.org/htbin/cgiwrap/bin/ojs/index.php/fm/article/view/1289/1209.

Peña-López, I. 2013. *Casual Politics: From Slacktivism to Emergent Movements and Pattern Recognition*. Proceeding of the 9th International Conference on Internet, Law & Politics, Universitat Oberta de Catalunya, Barcelona, 25–26 June 2013.

Pettitt, T. 2010. *MIT Communications Forum: The Gutenberg Parenthesis – Oral Tradition and Digital Technologies*. [Online] Available at: http://video.mit.edu/watch/the-gutenberg-parenthesis-oral-tradition-and-digital-technologies-9566/.

112   Željka Lekić-Subašić

Potts, A. 2007. Watching the Web Grow Up. *The Economist*, March 8. [Online] Available at: www.economist.com/node/8766093.

Presiln, K. 2013. Vpliv spletnih socialnih omrežij na dinamiko protestov. *Varstvoslovje* 15(1): 9–28.

Rawlinson, K. 2012. Activists Warned to Watch What They Say as Social Media Monitoring Becomes 'Next Big Thing in Law Enforcement'. *The Independent*, October 1. [Online] Available at: www.independent.co.uk/news/uk/crime/activists-warnedto-watch-what-they-say-as-social-media-monitoring-becomes-next-big-thingin-law-enforcement-8191977.html.

Rheingold, H. 2003. *Smart Mobs: The Next Social Revolution*. New York: Basic Books.

Ross, A. 2010. 21st Century Statecraft. *Grid Talks*. [Online] Available at: www.bonnier grid.com/speakerevent.php?event=52.

Russel, J. 2013. Turkish PM Blasts Twitter and Social Media for Spreading 'lies' During Weekend Protests. *The Next Web*, June 2. [Online] Available at: http://thenextweb.com/eu/2013/06/02/turkish-pm-blasts-twitter-and-social-media-for-spreading-lies-during-weekend-protests/.

Shirky, C. 2011. The Political Power of Social Media: Technology, the Public Sphere and Political Change. *Foreign Affairs*. [Online] Available at: www.foreignaffairs.com/articles/2010-12-20/political-power-social-media.

Stone, B. 2010. Exclusive: Biz Stone on Twitter and Activism. *The Atlantic*, October 19. [Online] Available at: www.theatlantic.com/technology/archive/2010/10/exclusive-biz-stone-on-twitter-and-activism/64772/.

Troev, T. and N. Buckley. 2013. Bulgaria's 'Generation F' Leads Protests Against Corruption. *Financial Times*, July 15. [Online] Available at: www.ft.com/intl/cms/s/0/75920 b00-ec0d-11e2-bfdb-00144feabdc0.html.

7 'Missing the forest for the trees'

From single-issue protests to resonant mass-movements in Greece, Turkey and Bosnia-Herzegovina

Chiara Milan and Leonidas Oikonomakis

Introduction

A global cycle of protest has shaken the world since 2011. Mobilisations have taken off in hundreds of cities, from North Africa to Southern Europe and the US. On the streets and in the squares, demonstrators have denounced the unresponsive attitudes of politicians, banks and corporations, and demanded changes to current social and economic policies. These protest movements have been typified by the occupation of public spaces, the establishment of encampments, and self-organised popular assemblies. Some scholars have referred to this transnational movement family (as Della Porta and Rucht [1995] define a set of coexisting movements with similar basic demands and a common constituency) as the Real Democracy Movement (Hardt and Negri 2011; Oikonomakis and Roos 2013; Sitrin 2016). This name originates in the slogan of the Spanish grassroots platform *¡Democracia Real YA!* (Real Democracy Now), which sparked the 15-M Movement, known also as the *Indignados*, in Spain in March 2011. According to these scholars, the unifying element that connects the different movements springing up around the world is a critique of the representational political system, which is deemed inadequate to respond to salient popular concerns. The movement's participants protest against the lack – or failure – of political representation (Hardt and Negri 2011), and prefigure the creation of a different democratic model based on decentralised autonomous workshops, thematic groups, collective assemblies, and independent citizens' platforms (Oikonomakis and Roos 2013).

The protest wave also reached several countries in Southeast Europe. Following in the footsteps of similar movements elsewhere, Greece, Turkey and Bosnia-Herzegovina (BiH) experienced significant protests between 2011 and 2013. Upon closer examination, it becomes apparent that the mobilisations in these three countries share several similarities. The movements' participants expressed dissatisfaction with a political system deemed incapable of addressing issues of concern to them. Moreover, the repertoires and organisational model adopted were similar to those of other movements in the Real Democracy family. Furthermore, there was a single issue that triggered all the protests. The Movement of

114   Chiara Milan and Leonidas Oikonomakis

the Squares in Greece in summer 2011 was spawned by opposition to externally imposed austerity measures; Turkey's Occupy Gezi movement in May 2013 was triggered by the demolition of a park in Istanbul's Gezi neighbourhood; and the #JMBG movement in Bosnia-Herzegovina (June 2013) was provoked by the government's inability to issue ID numbers.

Nevertheless, the three movements evolved in different fashions. The Movement of the Squares in Greece and the Occupy Gezi movement in Turkey brought together a wide array of social and economic grievances. The protests in these two countries culminated in broad-based mass mobilisations that involved various social groups, and subsequently challenged the legitimacy of the representational political system. By contrast, despite inspiring massive mobilisation, the #JMBG movement did not succeed in moving beyond the single issue of ID numbers to formulate a critique of the existing structures of political representation. The demonstrators in the squares of the former Yugoslav country did not consist of diverse social groups, nor did they reproduce the alternative practices of direct democracy and forms of autonomous self-organisation that characterised the protests in Greece and Turkey.

Our argument

With reference to the metaphor that gives this chapter its title, we argue that the austerity measures in Greece, the destruction of Gezi Park and the failure to disburse national ID numbers in Bosnia-Herzegovina are to be considered 'trees', that is, specific symptoms of the inadequacy of liberal parliamentary democracy to accommodate the citizens' demands for greater participation in the decisions that affect their lives. The legitimation crisis of the representational political system is the 'forest', the overarching theme behind the rise of movements in Greece, Turkey and BiH, but also in Spain and Brazil since 2011. Hence, we argue that the movements analysed in this chapter were a reaction to governments who were facing a crisis of representation, of which the austerity measures, the dismantling of the park and ID numbers were but specific traits. Whereas the demonstrators in Greece and Turkey managed to successfully connect a single-issue protest over austerity and the destruction of a park, respectively, to the inadequacy of the model of representational political system, the Bosnian movement remained limited to the narrow issue of ID numbers without developing a wider critique of the representational political system. Recalling the title of the chapter, the #JMBG movement 'missed the forest for the trees', failing to light the fire of social discontent.

In this chapter, we attempt to explain the patchy evolution of the three movements through a comparative analysis. To that end, we explore the wave of protest through the lenses of social movement studies. We draw on the concepts of frame resonance (Snow and Benford 1988; Tarrow 2011), networks (Diani 2004) and resources (McCarthy and Zald 1977). Throughout the chapter, we analyse the way in which the movements' organisers constructed collective action frames, namely 'defin[ing], creat[ing], and manipulat[ing] grievances and discontent'

(McCarthy and Zald 1973, 1977) to make sense of reality in a way that persuades the participants that their cause is just and important (Benford and Snow 2000). We thus investigate the extent to which these frames resonated with the cultural environment in which they emerged, and with the shared cultural understandings of the population they were addressed to (Snow and Benford 1988; Tarrow 2011). Drawing on Diani's (2004: 339) argument that 'social movement activities are usually embedded in dense relational settings', and are made up of a web of multiple ties that facilitate participation, we investigate the extent to which connective structures such as pre-existing movement organisations and the aforementioned strong interpersonal linkages facilitated (or hindered) mobilisation in the three cases. Social network scholars claim that social networks affect participation in collective action, insofar as the ability to create networks of groups and individuals facilitates the recruitment and aggregation of resources necessary for mobilisation (Diani 2004; Della Porta and Diani 2009). In particular, social bonds and the existence of previous networks are said to encourage further participation in social movement activities, and to foster the sustenance of collective action over time (Della Porta and Diani 2009). As Zibechi (2013a, 2013b) writes in two articles about the 2013 uprising in Brazil, mobilisations that do appear to start spontaneously, frequently triggered by a single issue that becomes the spark lighting the fire, very often have their roots in 'hidden spaces/transcripts' (Scott 1990), 'the acts of daring and haughtiness that [. . .] had been long and amply prepared in the hidden transcript of folk culture and practice' (Scott 1990: 264). In studying networks and linkages, we also explore the ability of movement organisers to aggregate and mobilise the human, material and organisational resources necessary for collective action.

We argue that the reduced potential for sustained nationwide mobilisation surrounding the question of democracy in Bosnia-Herzegovina can be attributed to the absence of two critical conditions: (1) the resonance of the overarching frame with the target group and broader culture, and (2) strong local and transnational movement networks, as well as previous experience of collective action, which translates to a lower capacity to aggregate and mobilise necessary resources.

Methodological approach

To provide evidence for our argument, we drew upon multiple data sources and used a triangulation of methodological tools for data collection. Our empirical research relies on extensive participant observation of 56 out of 72 popular assemblies at Syntagma Square in the period between May and August 2011, in-depth interviews with key informants (activists, academics and journalists) participating in the waves of protests in Athens and Sarajevo, and an analysis of the minutes of the Popular Assemblies of Syntagma Square. Regarding the Turkish case study, we relied mostly on desk research. We also consulted existing literature on the three mobilisations, archival material, press releases and articles, flyers, and movements' bulletins collected both from the websites of the initiatives and in person during field trips in Greece and BiH. Given the sensitivity of the topics and

116 *Chiara Milan and Leonidas Oikonomakis*

owing to the potentially easy identification of our informants, we have chosen not to report interviewees' private data, with the exception of public figures.

Turkey: meet the *çapulcular*[1]

> International Human Rights Organisations and Dear Friends, Comrades, Press Members from all over the world. [. . .] This is an urgent call from human rights defenders, activists, NGOs, professional chambers, grassroots, neighbourhood associations and Istanbulites.

So began the message the authors received on 31 May 2013, signed by 'Urban Movements Istanbul/Habitat International Coalition'. The message was written in the aftermath of a police crackdown against demonstrators occupying the city's largest public park, located in the Gezi neighbourhood. The Turkish government had sent the police to violently break the citizens' resistance, ongoing since the 27th of that month, to the demolition of Gezi Park. In its place, the government planned to erect a large mall in the form of a replica of the former Ottoman Artillery Barracks (*TopçuKışlası*). A number of videos and pictures – including the famous 'sprayed red-skirt girl' – accompanied the message, which went viral during the following days on activists' mailing lists as well as on social media. The message was also translated into a number of languages other than English. The increasing attention paid to the fate of Gezi Park, as well as the coverage the news received, suggested that the 'Urban Movements Istanbul' were very well networked within the local and international activist world. Further research on the 'Habitat International Coalition' proved this hypothesis correct. Habitat International is a global network of social movements, activists, academics and community-based organisations, working for more than 30 years on issues related to the right to habitat and social justice.

Gezi Park, and the nearby Taksim Square, represent a symbolic place for the Istanbulites, as Cassano (2013) noted in an article written for the free E-zine *Jadaliyya* a few days after the beginning of the protests:

> Taksim Square is the heart and soul of Istanbul. It is common sense to Istanbulites that if a revolution is to come to Turkey, it would begin in Taksim. Protests are regularly held in the square, and issues run the full gamut of concerns of Turkish citizens: LGBT equality, recognition of the Armenian Genocide, an end to the Kurdish conflict, an end to military conscription, economic justice, and more. In 2011, there was a massive one-day protest in support of a free and open Internet that drew upwards of thirty thousand people.

The main issue driving *ResIstanbul*, as the struggle opposing the dismantling of Gezi Park was also named (Gambetti 2013), was not simply the trees in the park, and the revolt did not concern only the 'right to the city'. The movement's participants targeted the failure of representative parliamentary democracy, even in

'*Missing the forest for the trees*' 117

its most powerful form, the type of government led by the social conservative 'Justice and Development' party (AKP). Elected with more than 50% of the vote in the 2011 legislative elections, the AKP government failed in accommodating the demand of the citizens, living both in the city and rural areas, to have a say in all the decisions that influence their lives. Instead, the party embarked on a neoliberal transformation of the country's social and economic life. As Christofis (2013) notes, the strong authoritarian government of Tayyip Erdoğan reduced the Turkish citizen to 'nothing more than a voter' every five years (four, after the 2007 Constitutional Amendment referendum).

Who were the participants in the massive movement in 2013? All international and national commentators and journalists agree that the protestors came from diverse backgrounds, hailing from all layers of social stratification. The rebellion in Turkey included movements, with the participation mainly of youth and students, protesting against the increasingly authoritarian character of Erdoğan's government. Student groups had long been involved in this struggle, at times openly challenging the premier himself during his visits to their universities, which resulted in more than 700 students being in prison at the time of the uprising, according to the Solidarity for Arrested Students Platform (Hurriyet Daily News 2012). At that time, the issue of freedom of expression was already a hot topic, with Turkey holding more imprisoned journalists than any other country (Roos 2013a). However, those who played the most prominent and active role were women, including feminist groups, who saw in the Occupy Gezi movement an opportunity to protest against the neoliberal, conservative transformation that Turkish society was undergoing under the patriarchal leadership of Erdoğan (Navaro-Yashin and Yildirim 2013). Together with women, the LGBTQ groups of Turkey (Açıksöz and Korkman 2013; Zengin 2013), and the mainly well-educated youth (Gokay and Xypolia 2013), also took to the street. The Kemalist and nationalist opposition was also present, as were the fan clubs of the country's biggest sports teams (namely *Fenerbahce, Galatasaray and Besiktas*), and the Kurds – although divided and careful not to endanger their ongoing peace talks with the government. As Wallerstein (2013: 32) wrote about the presence of the Kurds on Taksim Square:

> What then should the Kurdish movement do politically? There are some Kurdish militants, particularly in Istanbul and other large cities, who have joined the rebellion, as individuals. But the PKK has carefully avoided any statement on the uprising. And in Diyabarkir, the largest Kurdish city, the number of protesters has been very few. It could well be that a major victim of the anti-authoritarian uprising in Turkey will be the Kurds.

How did it come to pass that such diverse groups should gather together to protest, starting from the destruction of a park in Istanbul? These movements did not emerge out of nowhere, but were the result of tireless activist groundwork in Turkey that had been ongoing unnoticed for an extended period of time. They only needed a spark to mobilise and challenge the democratic legitimacy of the Turkish

118 *Chiara Milan and Leonidas Oikonomakis*

parliamentary political system. Before Gezi Park, other social movements that had mobilised over local issues had emerged in the rest of the country, with a prominent example being that against the construction of a large dam that would bury the ancient city of Hasankeyf under water. Just two days before Gezi Park, youth groups in Ankara had staged a 'subway kissing protest', organised through social media, which was triggered by an announcement made some time earlier in the capital's subway urging couples to 'behave in accordance to public moral codes' (Sehlikoğlu 2013). Occupy Gezi was also followed by several citizen initiatives and protest waves. In Istanbul alone, more than 35 self-organised horizontal neighbourhood assemblies were formed and already operating a few days after the uprising began (Roos 2013b), challenging the political system of the country that diminishes the citizen's participation to that of mere voters.

The scale and frequency of demonstrations decreased over the summer, and the protest ended on 30 August 2013 after the eviction of Taksim Square, the epicentre of the protests. A few months after Gezi Park, another movement emerged, opposing the attempt to chop down the 3,000 trees of the campus of Middle East Technical University (METU) in Ankara to make room for a highway. The movement, which witnessed the active participation of METU students, as well as the locals of the nearby 100.Yıl and Çiğdem neighbourhoods, was again faced with government repression.[2] Furthermore, Occupy Gezi was embedded in transnational movement networks. The initial call for solidarity with the demonstrators in Turkey passed through the vast Habitat International Coalition network, which facilitated its diffusion and enhanced the organisation of rallies and protests in more than 70 cities both within Turkey and abroad.

Greece: the Movement of the Squares

Unlike Occupy Gezi, the 'Movement of the Squares' in Greece did not begin because of a park, but it did have its own 'trees'. Even at the beginning of May 2010, strikes and rallies had been staged in Athens to oppose the crisis-related austerity measures imposed on the country's citizens by its government(s) and the 'troika' of foreign lenders. In May 2011, activists organised another wave of demonstrations in Athens' central Syntagma Square, and in the other main urban centres of Greece, which lasted until August 2011.

Before moving on to analyse the movement's characteristics, we explain why we prefer to adopt the term 'Movement of the Squares' instead of 'Greek Indignados' or 'Αγανακτισμένοι/*Aganaktismenoi*', which are in use in the relevant literature and media coverage. In our opinion, the latter terms risk misleading the reader by implying the movement is an imitation of that which unfolded in Spain in 2011. As a matter of fact, although the Facebook calls to Occupy Syntagma Square (or Lefkos Pyrgos in Thessaloniki) were titled '*Aganaktismenoisto Syntagma/Lefko Pyrgo*', meaning 'The Indignados in Syntagma/Lefko Pyrgo', the people who made those calls never revealed their faces, nor were they the same activists who occupied the square and organised assemblies. The occupiers of Syntagma actually rejected the name 'Indignants' in any language, and never signed any of their communications as *aganaktismenoi*. This label was perceived as an externally imposed term; instead, they preferred the signature 'Syntagma Popular Assembly' (Syntagma Popular Assembly 2011). In addition, the Syntagma Popular Assembly of 31 May 2011 voted in favour of placing a huge banner at the upper part of Syntagma Square, and one participant suggested that the movement 'not to be called *aganaktismenoi* (indignants), but rather *apofasismenoi* (determined)' (Syntagma Popular Assembly 2011). A few days later, a banner reading in huge capital letters 'WE ARE NOT INDIGNANT, WE ARE DETERMINED' was placed such that it would be visible during the large general strike and mobilisation of 15 June 2011. However, most of the mainstream media did indeed use the label *aganaktismenoi* and some people who either participated or passed by the Movement of the Squares also adopted it.

The occupation of Syntagma Square lasted for 72 days, making it the longest occupation of public space. The 'lesson in direct democracy' of the Movement of the Squares, as Manolis Glezos[3] put it, translated into a critique of the representative parliamentary system of the country, both in theory and practice, for as long as the movement lasted. As a participant in the Syntagma Popular Assembly of 5 June 2011 said, 'What we are going through is an oligarchy; it is not democracy to [just] vote every four years for the one that will represent us; democracy cannot be locked into Parliaments' (Syntagma Popular Assembly 2011).[4]

In the same line of reasoning, several speakers of the Syntagma Popular Assembly brought forward a demand for direct democracy, even beyond the reversal of austerity measures. As another participant said the day after the parliamentary approval of the latest austerity package, and therefore once one of the main objectives of the movement had been lost, 'Those who were obsessed with the mid-term agreement [which had been passed on 29 June 2011] that's over now. What is now at stake is something deeper, a bigger crack. [And it is] that of autonomy and direct democracy' (Syntagma Popular Assembly 2011 on 30 June 2011).[5]

Or, as the Syntagma Popular Assembly itself officially declared with its decision of 30 May 2011:

> It was unanimously agreed [that] our strength is [our] self-organisation, that all the actions are ours, that there need to be organised thematic assemblies, that we need to strengthen the working groups, make this initiative massive, [and turn it into] a movement that will mobilise all the people until social liberation becomes reality.[6]

How did the Movement of the Squares, out of a single-issue protest over austerity measures, develop a general critique and rejection of the political class and representative parliamentary political system? In other words, how did the Movement of the Squares manage not to miss the forest for the trees, and how did it create what Johnston (2011) calls pre-figurative 'free spaces', 'Temporary Autonomous Zones' (Bey 1997), or 'cracks' (Holloway 2010) in which a horizontal, leaderless, direct-democratic and participatory form of decision-making could be experimented with and diffused?

120 Chiara Milan and Leonidas Oikonomakis

The assembly form and overall dismissal of the representative parliamentary system that the Movement of the Squares adopted from their very first day were anything but coincidental. On the contrary, they were part of the 'hidden transcripts' that had been practiced in Greece long before the beginning of the movement on 25 May 2011, and were maintained after the eviction from the square on 30 July 2011. The most visible example is the anarchist space, one of the strongest in Europe, with a number of squats across the country. The Greek anarchists, although reluctant in the beginning, joined the Movement of the Squares, providing it with their horizontal organisational experience and resources.[7] Furthermore, many other movement participants had taken part in the Global Justice Movement a decade before. Others, especially newly unemployed former students, had also experienced the leaderless and consensus-based decision-making form of assembly during the 2008 December rebellion, which some define as a social movement in itself (Sotiris 2013). In December 2008, the assassination of 16-year-old Alexandros Grigoropoulos in the anarchist Exarhia neighbourhood of Athens triggered a general uprising, led mainly by the country's youth and coordinated through horizontal assemblies, in which immigrant groups also participated, perhaps for the first time. During that uprising, some pre-existing activist networks were strengthened even further, as the 2011 Movement of the Squares experience also suggests.

All those political realities joined the Movement of the Squares, offering their horizontal movement experience, which in turn was transferred to the younger activists who took their 'baptism of fire' at Syntagma and other squares of the country. This direct-democratic form of decision-making later resonated with other horizontal movement experiences born after the evacuation of the squares; for instance, the movements against water privatisation in Athens and Thessaloniki, or the antifascist movement-coordinating platform, which adopted the same practices developed during the square assemblies.

Apart from their leaderless and consensus-based political experiences, these activists also brought into the squares another asset: access to their activist networks within and outside the country. From the beginning, the Movement of the Squares created their own communication groups, responsible for building a network for the exchange of information with the other squares of the country and the world. Through those networks, and at times thanks to the help of the 'Take the Square Collective',[8] Syntagma Square was put in direct Internet communication with the squares of Madrid, Barcelona and Sevilla. These networks facilitated contact with theorists and activists from around the world, providing them with the opportunity to communicate directly with the movement's participants. Through the same means, the massive demonstration #15O *United for Global Change* was organised in October 2011. Called for by the Spanish platform 'Real Democracy Now!' to mark the five-month anniversary of the first protest in Spain, the demonstration of 15 October 2011 included occupations and protests that were held in more than 1,000 cities and 80 countries worldwide, in which the Greek movement also participated. That day, the demonstrators targeted growing economic inequality and the lack of truly democratic institutions that would allow direct public participation at the local and global level.

In summary, from our analysis of the Greek case, it emerges that the Movement of the Squares did not appear out of the blue. On the contrary, its assembly form and its critique and rejection of the country's representative parliamentary political system are deeply rooted in Greece's 'hidden spaces', where they had long been practiced outside the focus of the general public and mainstream media. The country's anarchist political space, the veterans of the Global Justice Movement, and the newly unemployed former student activists of the 2008 rebellion played a preeminent role in what later became Greece's long summer of 2011 by enriching the movement with their political experiences and networks. The Movement of the Squares themselves further reinforced their ties, as the movement had, since the beginning, set up communication committees and a website to allow for better coordination amongst themselves, as well as with the squares of Spain and the world. Those networks allowed the Greek movement to co-organise and participate in massive transnational mobilisations, the spearhead of which was the *#15O United for Global Change*. In the words of one Syntagma Popular Assembly speaker on 30 June 2011, after the lost battle of 28–29 June: 'What I mean to say is that we did not find the square ourselves – *it* found *us*. The characteristics were already there'.[9]

Bosnia-Herzegovina: the #JMBG protests

Popular protests erupted in Sarajevo on 5 June 2013, when several people parked their cars in front of the garages of the BiH National Parliament. The spark that ignited the protests was the case of a seriously ill 3-month-old baby girl, Belmina Ibrišević. In need of urgent medical treatment outside BiH, she was prevented from leaving the country due to the inability of the Ministry of the Interior to allocate her a 13-digit Unique Master Citizens Number (*Jedinstveni matični broj građana*; JMBG), assigned to every Bosnian citizen. Like Belmina, all Bosnian children born after February 2013 were denied new IDs. In turn, no passports or other documents necessary to travel abroad could be issued to them. The deadlock originated when a pronouncement from the Constitutional Court erased the Law on Personal Identification Numbers on 13 February 2013, thus freezing the newborns' registration. Such a decision resulted from six months of disagreement among Bosnian Members of Parliament (MPs) regarding the definition of registration areas, necessary for the allocation of identification numbers.

The car blockade prevented nearly 1,500 persons from leaving the premises, including civil servants, MPs, and foreign investors who were attending a finance conference inside the building. On the night of 6 June 2013, a human chain surrounded the building. Only the overnight intervention of the High Representative Valentin Inzko, the international civilian supervisor for the peace process in BiH, allowed for the evacuation of the 'hostages' trapped inside (Milan 2013). Notwithstanding Inzko's promise to find a solution to the stalemate, the demonstrators refused to step back. For 25 consecutive days following this, several

122 *Chiara Milan and Leonidas Oikonomakis*

thousand demonstrators of different age groups, including children with their parents, peacefully occupied the square in front of the parliament at the outskirts of the city centre, and continued doing so day and night until 1 July 2013.

The #JMBG protests, as they rapidly became known owing to the blogging service Twitter, sprung up in Sarajevo and expanded to the main cities of BiH. Citizens from neighbouring cities joined the protests in the capital, and rallies were organised in the main urban centres of the country. Reports of similar manifestations came from smaller towns as well, 'in smaller cities where nothing similar has ever happened'.[10] On the squares, the demonstrators urged the adoption of a legal framework allowing the allocation of JMBG at the state level for newborns to obtain their IDs and therefore access civil rights. The agenda of the protesters rapidly expanded to include other issues, such as the creation of a solidarity fund to finance the treatment of critically ill children abroad in case of unavailable proper treatment in BiH, the reduction of MPs' and members of the Council of Ministers' salaries by 30% for the whole duration of their term in office, and the granting of the difference to the aforementioned solidarity fund. Finally, they demanded that protestors not be persecuted by the authorities, as well as the guarantee that repressive measures would not be used against them.

Although in Greece and Turkey the demonstrators adopted direct-democratic practices, in Bosnia-Herzegovina autonomous self-organisation proved sparse. In Sarajevo, bystanders gathered daily at noon in the square in front of the BiH National Parliament for coffee sessions known as 'Coffee for the ID number' (*Kafa za JMBG*). However, movement organisers did not succeed in organising the debate through assemblies in the squares or neighbourhoods. Relying on the words of an active participant,

> It was a great chaos, nothing similar to Zuccotti Park. There was no procedure to decide who could speak and for how long, how to divide among groups, or how to organise large assemblies. It was chaotic and completely unorganised: whoever was close to somebody with a paper and a pen was shouting what should be written.[11]

Although rallies proceeded in an unstructured way, the #JMBG demonstrators in Sarajevo appointed four working groups to deal with planning, logistics, media communication, and contact with other cities in BiH. Nevertheless their large dimension prevented them from working efficiently. No contact was established with similar movement elsewhere, although international support came from neighbouring Croatia and from the Bosnian *dijaspora* spread outside the country's borders. The protest also received scarce coverage by mainstream and international media, with the exception of the broadcaster *Al Jazeera Balkans* (Al Jazeera Balkans 2013).

The protest ended on 1 July 2013 with what was termed the 'Dismissal Day' (*Otkaz*). On that day, the demonstrators, although in a smaller number compared to the previous days, took to the square in front of the BiH National Parliament and declared the incumbents' wholesale dismissal, on account of their being 'no longer credible representatives of the citizens of Bosnia Herzegovina' (JMBG.org 2013). Eventually, the protestors released a communiqué on behalf of the citizens of BiH, urging the international community to 'withdraw all previous invitations to the representatives of BiH to meetings, conferences and other formal events [. . .] to clearly show the BiH politicians that they finally have to take responsibility and do the job they were elected to do'. In their open letter, they also invited the international community 'to cancel all planned official visits to our country, because, from today, [the international community] do[es] not have legitimate interlocutors in Bosnia and Herzegovina' (#JMBG Manifesto 2013).

Analysis

In summary, the Movement of the Squares in Greece proved capable of developing an overall critique and rejection of the country's representative parliamentary democratic system, and proposed direct – or *real*, as the Greek protestors called it – democracy as an alternative model, while also practicing it in the squares and neighbourhood assemblies in a pre-figurative manner. In addition, it managed to reach most of the squares of the country's main cities and become the focus of national and international public and media attention for weeks. In a similar fashion, the Turkish Occupy Gezi movement diffused to more than 70 cities across the country, with a significant number of European and global solidarity actions emerging in several cities abroad. In Bosnia-Herzegovina, by contrast, although the #JMBG movement lasted for approximately a month – which is not a minor achievement, becoming the largest popular movement in the country since the 1992–1995 war[12] – it did not manage to connect the ID number issue with the failure of the post-Dayton political system, and it only partially formulated alternative practices of direct democracy and autonomous self-organisation.

In this chapter, we argue that the negligible success of the Bosnian-Herzegovinian #JMBG movement can be attributed to the low resonance of the frame used by the movement's organisers, and the absence of strong local and transnational movement networks as well as previous experience of collective action, which resulted in a lower ability to aggregate or mobilise the resources necessary for collective action. In what follows, we explore each of these factors in depth.

Low resonance of frame

For single-issue protests to evolve into resonant mass-movements, they ultimately have to confront the structural context in which they arise. Accordingly, we investigated the cultural milieu in which the three protest waves took place. In the squares of Greece and Turkey, as well as in other squares around the world, the 'real democracy' call was adopted and resonated with the wider population. The call for greater citizen participation urged to change 'a dominant and oppressive system, led by a political class working for banks and big corporations' (About Us | Take the Square 2011). Although this call to end an oppressive

124 *Chiara Milan and Leonidas Oikonomakis*

system resonated in Greece and Turkey, in BiH the cultural and political context limited its resonance.

Bosnia-Herzegovina is a post-war country that hangs in the balance of a delicate system of equilibrium among ethno-national quotas. The 1992–1995 war ended more than 20 years ago, yet the level of social trust among people is still low. In such a context, the movement's organisers perceived that an encompassing frame questioning the model of representative democracy, although in the distorted and dysfunctional version foreseen by the Dayton Peace agreement,[13] would not appeal to the broader population. By contrast, they perceived it would be understood as an attempt to undermine the precarious equilibrium upon which the country is based. Furthermore, they deemed that the use of such a discourse would easily lend itself to discrediting the demonstrators as undermining the stability of the country.[14] The widespread fear of instability originates from having lived through a war, an experience that created 'a huge longing for stability which has transformed into a fear of instability. Since people are so afraid of instability, they feel any stability is better, even if it consists of misery and insecurity' (BiH protest files 2014). For these reasons, activists explain, the movement's organisers preferred to narrow the nature of the demands to basic human rights, as they perceived that the time was not ripe for the development of a more radical, anti-system critique of the representative system, nor for the use of an anti-austerity narrative. The target of the grievances was thus identified in an unresponsive political class that violates the rights to existence of all babies in BiH, without demanding any revolutionary change. As a protest leader stated, 'What is most unbelievable is that [we demanded] from elected politicians that they do what they were elected to do' (Arnautović 2013). Nevertheless, the particularistic nature of the demands, framed in terms of human rights, narrowed the appeal to a potentially larger audience.

Lack of previous collective action experience and loose ties to other movements

The second element we analysed was the organisers' previous experience of collective action and the strength of ties to other movements at the local and transnational level. We observed that both Greece and Turkey could count on extensive local horizontal movement experience and pre-existing local and transnational activist networks. By contrast, in the Bosnian case, such networks and experience appear to have been largely absent.

The #JMBG movement revealed the lack of horizontal movement experience amongst both organisers and protestors, as well as their loose ties nationwide and with movements elsewhere. By and large, Bosnia-Herzegovina does not count on a tradition of street activism or political engagement for social change, and the country has not experienced high levels of contention over the preceding years. Several protests were organised against the government and private companies in recent years; however, these remained mostly one-off events, and often did not succeed in reaching their goals. Previous attempts to join forces by means

'Missing the forest for the trees' 125

of contention were few, and most did not survive over time. Furthermore, the counter-cultural scene of BiH is very limited, and solidarity networks are active mostly at the local level. The underground scene consists of loosely connected groups. The *Dosta!* (Enough!) protest movement, which emerged in 2005 to tackle socio-political problems affecting Bosnian citizens, ran out of steam a few years later. Some local branches kept performing street actions, together with other oppositional groups, often connected through the network 'Antifascist Action Bosnia-Herzegovina' (*Antifašistička Akcija BiH*). These groups, however, were only loosely connected prior to the 2013 demonstrations. In the last decade, mass rallies took place in Sarajevo in 2008 when the citizens took to the streets again following the murder of a young student by a teenage gang (Touquet 2015), but in none of the cases did the rallies result in the articulation of a lasting horizontal network. This is at odds with the February 2014 uprising, during which protestors organised themselves into participatory assemblies called 'plenums' and, in the wake of the protests, gave birth to an informal network gathering together citizens, independent unions, and grassroots organisations (Milan 2014b).

Furthermore, the mushrooming of professional non-governmental organisations (NGOs) in the aftermath of the 1992–1995 war undermined the emergence of grassroots movements and contributed to dissuading citizens from civic engagement (Adamson 2002). As some informants claim, it transformed activism into a 9-to-5 job.[15] In the following excerpt, an activist highlights the negative outcome deriving from the dichotomy professional vs. grassroots, claiming that the third sector

> turned into a project base sector of the economy, where you fight for funds and spend them according to some regulations and then you type very nice reports. The credibility of civil society is one of the reasons why those protests did not take off and became stronger.[16]

As a result, and unlike in Turkey and Greece, in BiH, the protestors' front was polarised, rather than united. At first, the groups in the square ranged from students and families with babies to members of the patriotic 'Anti-Dayton' nationalist group. Although physically in the square, owing also to the proximity of the university to the parliament building, the youth – who made up the active core of the Greek and Turkish movements – were not involved in the decision-making processes, neither did they manage to organise themselves into an assembly, mainly due to a lack of relevant organisational experience. In an attempt by the movement organisers to keep control of the square, and undermine the attempts of nationalistic groups and political parties to interfere with the protests, a communiqué issued on behalf of the #JMBG movement invited all official organisations like labour unions, youth associations, and the like, to keep away from the square and join the protests exclusively at an individual level. An informant recalls:

> After one or two days of protests, instead of inviting civil society, labour unions, youth associations to join us [. . .] to get more people in the streets

and better logistics, as well as coverage in the entire country, as would be normal in civic protests in most of the country, here it was the opposite: we had to make a press release asking civil society organisations not to participate as organisations because it would be bad publicity for us, but to join us as individuals, if they want to help. That is the tragic part of the story. Some of them participated. This country is fragmented, and so is the government and civil society. Not so much [fragmented] by ethnic division, but by organisations that are active in order to achieve some goals and change in society, and those that are comfortable in spending huge amounts of money without actual results, and having insignificant projects.[17]

The deliberate choice to isolate formal actors weakened the protest front, alienating the human, logistical and organisational resources that were needed to build a more composite front, and discouraging the involvement of actors and social groups other than middle-class urbanities. Therefore, the movement's organisers did not manage to autonomously generate the human or organisational resources necessary for a successful mobilisation, nor build strong coalitions that might have helped the movement mobilise resources necessary to develop further. The movement's organisers had, in fact, few or no ties with transnational movements elsewhere, and were not connected with other squares of the Real Democracy Movement.

Conclusions

In this chapter, we strive to elucidate the reasons why the Bosnian #JMBG did not manage to elaborate, out of a local grievance, a broader, systemic critique of representation connecting the political deadlock over national ID numbers to the failure of the representational political system, in particular in the dysfunctional version foresaw by the post-war constitutional set-up.

The three cases we have examined offer several interesting insights into the emergence and development of resonant mass-movements. First, social movements, even those that at first glance seem to emerge spontaneously, do not appear out of a vacuum. They are products of tireless grassroots work that often takes place outside the mainstream and remains out of the spotlight until a spark, turning into a fire, brings it to the forefront. Siding with the work of Scott (1990), Zibechi (2013a, 2013b), and Oikonomakis and Roos (2013), we found that in two of our three cases (Turkey and Greece), the groups that participated in the uprisings and formed massive nationwide movements that challenged the whole political system of their respective countries had long been mobilising 'underground' and silently. They had only come to the forefront temporarily until then, when activated for their respective goals of focus. However, although those groups may have been working on different issues and in the 'hidden spaces' of their societies, they had managed to form powerful networks both nationally and internationally. When the moment came, those networks were activated, transforming a single-issue protest into mass popular movements. We thus maintain

'Missing the forest for the trees' 127

that the movements in Greece and Turkey took off due to the existence of these powerful movement networks that in the case of BiH were weak if not absent, as previously explained.

Another factor that explains the ability of the Greek and Turkish movements to formulate an overall critique of the representative democratic institutions of their respective countries, as well as perform alternative practices of direct democracy and autonomous self-organisation, was the existence of movements with experience in horizontal decision-making and direct democracy. The latter, with their practices, challenged the model of representative democracy, instead promoting a different direct-democratic model. This kind of movement was present in Greece and Turkey, and came to the surface in the horizontal and self-organised popular assemblies in the squares and neighbourhoods of both countries. By contrast, these elements were missing in the Bosnian case, accounting for the 'chaotic' character and more hierarchical organisational model of the #JMBG movement. As the Greek and Turkish examples demonstrate, these organisational capacities are not acquired from one day to the other, and the #JMBG movement, despite its temporary breakdown, was indeed a very important step in that direction, as it created new connections that paved the way for the following wave of protests that took place in 2014.

Notes

1 The term used by Turkish Prime Minister Recep Tayyip Erdoğan to describe the protestors, which translates to 'looters'.
2 The students' main slogan was 'There's only road passing through METU, and that is the road to revolution'.
3 Interview with Manolis Glezos, WWII Resistance hero and currently MP with SYRIZA political party, Athens, April 2013.
4 Authors' translation.
5 Authors' translation.
6 Authors' translation.
7 A year later, the country's Minister of Public Order Nikos Dendias targeted Greece's squats as 'centers of lawlessness' and forcefully evacuated a number of them (Oikonomakis 2013).
8 The international committee initiated by the Madrid's Puerta del Sol assembly following the anti-austerity protests of 15 May 2011. That day, some participants decided to camp in the main square of Madrid, Puerta del Sol. The encampment became known as Acampada Sol, and was exported to the rest of the cities of Spain and the world.
9 Authors' translation from the Syntagma Popular Assembly minutes. Emphasis added.
10 Interview with an activist participating in the car blockade. Sarajevo, October 2013.
11 Interview with an activist participating in the square occupation and protests. Sarajevo, October 2013.
12 Until the emergence of massive socio-economic protests in February 2014, which were sparked by a workers' demonstration in the city of Tuzla and gave birth to a grassroots mobilisation that spread across the country (Milan 2014a).
13 Three national communities populate BiH – Serbs, Croats and Bosniaks (Bosnian Muslims). The Dayton Peace Agreement, stipulated in 1995, divides BiH into two distinct and almost ethnically homogeneous areas – the 'entities' – and the autonomous district of Brčko. The Federation of BiH (FBiH) consists of 10 cantons, each of which has its own constitution and government. In turn, every canton is divided into smaller

128　*Chiara Milan and Leonidas Oikonomakis*

administrative units – the municipalities. By contrast, Republika Srpska (RS) has no cantons, only municipalities. Currently, Bosnia-Herzegovina appears as a consociational state and a triple power-sharing system (Bieber 2005). After the war, the majority of Bosniaks and Bosnian Croats settled in FBiH, whereas Serbs moved to RS.
14 Interview with local activists, Sarajevo, July and October 2013.
15 Interview with an activist, November 2013.
16 Interview with an activist working in a think tank, April 2014.
17 Interview with an activist, November 2013.

References

Açıksöz, S.C. and Z. Korkman. 2013. Masculinized Power, Queered Resistance. *Cultural Anthropology*. [Online] Available at: https://culanth.org/fieldsights/395-masculinized-power-queered-resistance.
Adamson, F.B. 2002. International Democracy Assistance in Uzbekistan and Kyrgyzstan: Building Civil Society from the Outside? In: *The Power and Limits of NGOs: A Critical Look at Building Democracy in Eastern Europe and Eurasia*, eds. S. Mendelson and J.K. Glenn. New York: Columbia University Press, pp. 177–206.
Al Jazeera Balkans. 2013. *Thousands Protest Over Bosnia Baby ID Row*. [Online] Available at: www.aljazeera.com/news/europe/2013/06/2013611152720320390.html.
Arnautović, A. 2013. *Dnevnik Aktiviste: Započeli Smo Nešto Veliko*. [Online] Available at: www.jmbg.org/dnevnik-aktiviste-zapoceli-smo-nesto-veliko/.
Benford, R.D. and D.A. Snow. 2000. Framing Processes and Social Movements: An Overview and Assessment. *Annual Review of Sociology* 26: 611–639.
Bey, H. 1997. T. A. Z.: The Temporary Autonomous Zone, Ontological Anarchy, Poetic Terrorism – Hakim Bey. *Hermetic Library*. [Online] Available at: http://hermetic.com/bey/taz_cont.html.
Bieber, F. 2005. *Post-War Bosnia: Ethnicity, Inequality and Public Sector Governance*. New York: Palgrave Macmillan.
BiH protest files. 2014. Stef Jansen: 'The Plenum Is a Roar of Enraged People'. [Online] Available at: https://bhprotestfiles.wordpress.com/2014/02/27/stef-jansen-the-plenum-is-a-roar-of-enraged-people/.
Cassano, J. 2013. The Right to the City Movement and the Turkish Summer. *Jadaliyya*. [Online] Available at: www.jadaliyya.com/pages/index/11978/the-right-to-the-city-movement-and-the-turkish-sum.
Christofis, N. 2013. Gezi Park: The Powerfully Symbolic Chance to Act Together! In: *Reflections on Taksim-Gezi Park Protests in Turkey*, eds. B. Gokay and I. Xypolia. Keele: Keele European Research Centre, pp. 47–50.
Della Porta, D. and M. Diani. 2009. *Social Movements: An Introduction*. Hoboken: Wiley.
Della Porta, D. and D. Rucht. 1995. Left-Libertarian Movements in Context: A Comparison of Italy and West Germany. In: *The Politics of Social Protest: Comparative Perspectives on States and Social Movements*, eds. J.C. Jerkins and B. Klandermans. Minneapolis: University of Minnesota Press, pp. 229–272.
Diani, M. 2004. Networks and Participation. In: *The Blackwell Companion to Social Movements*, eds. D.A. Snow, S.A. Soule, and H. Kriesi. Malden: Blackwell Publishing, pp. 339–359.
Gambetti, Z. 2013. Resistanbul: The Beginning of the End of an Era? *ROAR Magazine*. [Online] Available at: https://roarmag.org/essays/resistanbul-the-beginning-of-the-end-of-an-era.

'*Missing the forest for the trees*' 129

Gokay, B. and I. Xypolia (eds.). 2013. *Reflections on Taksim-Gezi Park Protests in Turkey.* Keele: Keele European Research Centre.

Hardt, M. and A. Negri. 2011. The Fight for 'real Democracy' at the Heart of Occupy Wall Street. *Foreign Affairs* 11. [Online] Available at: www.foreignaffairs.com/articles/north-america/2011-10-11/fight-real-democracy-heart-occupy-wall-street.

Holloway, J. 2010. *Crack Capitalism.* London: Pluto.

Hurriyet Daily News. 2012. RIGHTS – Number of Arrested Students 'on the Rise' in Turkey. *Hurriyet Daily News.* [Online] Available at: www.hurriyetdailynews.com/number-of-arrested-students-on-the-rise-in-turkey.aspx?pageID=238&nid=24337.

JMBG. 2013. #JMBG Manifesto. [Online] Available at: www.jmbg.org/jmbg-manifesto/.

JMBG.org. 2013. Open Letter of the Citizens of BiH to the International Community. [Online] Available at: www.jmbg.org/open-letter-of-the-citizens-of-bih-to-the-international-community/.

Johnston, H. 2011. *States and Social Movements.* London: Polity.

McCarthy, J.D. and N.Z. Mayer. 1973. *The Trend of Social Movements in America: Professionalization and Resource Mobilization.* Morristown: General Learning Press.

McCarthy, J.D. and N.Z. Mayer. 1977. Resource Mobilization and Social Movements: A Partial Theory. *American Journal of Sociology* 82(6): 1212–1241.

Milan, C. 2013. Occupy Sarajevo: Taking Parliament Hostage in Bosnia. *ROARMAG.* [Online] Available at: https://roarmag.org/essays/occupy-sarajevo-bosnia-herzegovina-protests/.

Milan, C. 2014a. Sow Hunger, Reap Anger: Why Bosnia Is Burning. *ROARMAG.* [Online] Available at: http://roarmag.org/2014/02/bosnia-protests-tuzla-workers/.

Milan, C. 2014b. New Social Movements Arise in Bosnia Herzegovina. *ROARMAG.* [Online] Available at: http://roarmag.org/2014/12/bosnia-february-protests-movements/.

Navaro-Yashin, Y. and U. Yildirim. 2013. An Impromptu Uprising: Ethnographic Reflections on the Gezi Park Protests in Turkey. *Cultural Anthropology.* [Online] Available at: www.culanth.org/fieldsights/391-an-impromptu-uprising-ethnographic-reflections-on-the-gezi-park-protests-in-turkey.

Oikonomakis, L. 2013. In Greece, the Criminals Live in Other Villas. *ROARMAG.* [Online] Available at: https://roarmag.org/essays/in-greece-the-criminals-live-in-other-villas/.

Oikonomakis, L. and J.E. Roos. 2013. *'Que No Nos Representan' The Crisis of Representation and the Resonance of the Real Democracy Movement From the Indignados to Occupy.* Canada: University of Montreal.

Roos, J.E. 2013a. The Turkish Protests and the Genie of Revolution. *ROARMAG.* [Online] Available at: https://roarmag.org/essays/tahrir-taksim-egypt-turkey-protests-revolution/.

Roos, J.E. 2013b. Assemblies Emerging in Turkey: A Lesson in Democracy. *ROARMAG.* [Online] Available at: https://roarmag.org/essays/assemblies-emerging-in-turkey-a-lesson-in-democracy/.

Scott, J.C. 1990. *Domination and the Arts of Resistance: Hidden Transcripts.* New Haven: Yale University Press.

Sehlikoğlu, S. 2013. Kissing the Mahrem in Ankara. *Cultural Anthropology.* [Online] Available at: www.culanth.org/fieldsights/405-kissing-the-mahrem-in-ankara.

Sitrin, M. 2016. 'Soon We Will Be Millions': From Paris With Love and Lessons. *ROARMAG.* [Online] Available at: https://roarmag.org/essays/from-paris-with-love-and-lessons/.

Snow, D.A. and R.D. Benford. 1988. Ideology, Frame Resonance, and Participant Mobilization. *International Social Movement Research* 1(1): 197–217.

Sotiris, P. 2013. Reading Revolt as Deviance: Greek Intellectuals and the December 2008 Revolt of Greek Youth. *Interface* 5(2): 47–77.

130 *Chiara Milan and Leonidas Oikonomakis*

Syntagma Popular Assembly. 2011. *Syntagma Popular Assembly's Minutes*. Athens: Syntagma Square.

Tarrow, S. 2011. *Power in Movement: Social Movements and Contentious Politics*. Cambridge: Cambridge University Press.

Touquet, H. 2015. Non-Ethnic Mobilisation in Deeply Divided Societies, the Case of the Sarajevo Protests. *Europe-Asia Studies* 67(3): 388–408.

Wallerstein, I. 2013. *Turkey: Dilemma of the Kurds*. In: *Reflections on Taksim-Gezi Park Protests in Turkey*, eds. B. Gokay and I. Xypolia. Keele: Keele European Research Centre, pp. 31–33.

Zengin, A. 2013. What Is Queer About Gezi? *Cultural Anthropology*. [Online] Available at: https://culanth.org/fieldsights/407-what-is-queer-about-gezi.

Zibechi, R. 2013a. Autonomy in Brazil: Below and Behind the June Uprising (Part 1). *Upside Down World*. [Online] Available at: http://upsidedownworld.org/archives/brazil/the-june-uprisings-in-brazil-below-and-behind-the-huge-mobilizations-part-1/.

Zibechi, R. 2013b. The June Uprisings in Brazil: Below and Behind the Huge Mobilizations (Part 2). *Upside Down World*. [Online] Available at: http://upsidedownworld.org/archives/brazil/the-june-uprisings-in-brazil-below-and-behind-the-huge-mobilizations-part-2/.

8 Are the Balkans different? Mapping protest politics in post-communist Southeastern Europe

Marius I. Tatar

Introduction

Transitions to democracy and EU integration processes in post-communist Europe have been accompanied by relatively low levels of protest mobilisation. However, in recent years, new waves of protests have emerged in the region, ranging from mass demonstrations to organised strikes and riots. The rise in elite-challenging activity suggests a revival of protest politics in former communist countries in the current economic crisis. This chapter comparatively examines the dynamics and determinants of different forms of protest activity in Southeast Europe.[1] Drawing on theoretical insights derived from the literature on political behaviour and social movements, this chapter analyses the profile of different types of protesters and the factors that may account for their preference for certain forms of protest actions over others. Research on Southeast Europe often investigates citizen participation from a cross-national perspective at a single point in time, with special emphasis on aspects of electoral participation. This study follows a longitudinal approach that captures the dynamic phenomena of protest participation using statistical analysis of survey datasets (such as the regularly published European Values Surveys and World Values Surveys) that allow for comparisons over time both cross-nationally and within a single country. Besides assessing the effects of individual-level variables, the chapter also considers country-level contextual factors such as the levels of democratic and economic development.

The countries I focus on in this chapter are new democracies. During their transition from communism, some of these societies experienced relatively long periods of political instability, economic distress,[2] inter-ethnic and inter-confessional tensions, and even armed conflicts. Thus, the question that arises is whether protest politics strengthens or weakens the prospects of democratic consolidation in this region. In other words, who is more prone to protest: those with authoritarian orientations, or those who share a democratic political culture? If, for instance, citizens oriented towards authoritarianism are more likely to be politically engaged in this region, the processes of democratic consolidation might be threatened. The massive involvement of authoritarian-minded citizens in the political process might provide good ground for the emergence of populist authoritarianism in these countries (Krajnc et al. 2012). If, on the other hand, citizens who participate

132 *Marius I. Tatar*

in protests are on average more democratically oriented – so-called *critical democrats* (Dalton and Welzel 2014) – they may challenge political elites, demanding more open, accountable and responsive democratic governance. In this case, protesters have the potential to play a pivotal role in the democratic consolidation process in post-communist countries (Guérin et al. 2004).

The rest of this chapter is structured in five main parts. First, I conceptualise protest politics within the framework of democratic theories, and then briefly review arguments derived from some of the most influential theoretical perspectives regarding protest participation. In the next section, I draw a general picture of the dynamics of protest politics in post-communist Southeast Europe before the economic crisis. I then focus on the characteristics of participants in two of the most common protest forms: signing petitions and demonstrating. The chapter then explores patterns of protest politics during the economic crisis by means of a comparative analysis of Romania and Slovenia. I conclude with a discussion of the main findings and their implications for our understanding of how protest action repertoires are reconfigured in post-communist societies and their consequences for democratic governance and stability in the region.

Conceptualising and explaining protest participation: theoretical perspectives

Protest politics is understood as the deliberate use of protest actions by groups or organisations (and sometimes by individual citizens) to influence a political decision or process they perceive as having negative consequences for themselves, another group, or society as a whole (Dalton 2013: 52–56). Political protest can refer to any political and social issue that is debated and contested, ranging from single-issue protests to broad reformist or revolutionary plans to shape society. Some groups use protest as a key mechanism to make their voice heard, whereas others use it to a much lesser extent or not at all (Rucht 2007: 708). Besides variation in actors and aims, the levels and forms of political protest vary widely. Protest can take different forms, ranging from legal methods (legal strikes and demonstrations, petitions, complaints, etc.) to illegal and sometimes violent ones (illegal strikes, violent demonstrations, occupying buildings, blocking roads, etc.). These distinctions are important both for studying the degree of protest participation and for understanding the motivational dynamics underlying various forms of protest (Opp and Kittel 2010). In terms of the degree of participation, a significant part of the population might approve and even participate in actions that comply with the norms of the existing social system, such as petitioning or taking part in peaceful demonstrations. On the other hand, usually only an extreme minority will engage in actions that violate social rules, such as violent protests, occupying buildings or public spaces, and blocking roads (Guérin et al. 2004; Tătar 2015). Moreover, different motivational attitudes may explain participation in different forms of protest (Uslaner 2004).

The question as to why people engage in political protest has generated significant interest among scholars from various disciplines, such as political science,

Are the Balkans different? Mapping protest politics 133

sociology, political economy, social psychology and history. Responses to this question are divided between macro- and micro-level approaches, which belong to different scholarly traditions (Norris et al. 2006). Macro accounts, derived mainly from historical sociology and comparative politics, seek to explain the cycles of protest mobilisation and processes of contentious politics as systemic phenomena. Among macro approaches, political process theories are prominent, contending that, to protest, aggrieved people need not only strategic resources, but also certain suitable political contexts (McAdam 1982; McAdam et al. 1996; Tarrow 1998) that guarantee more open structures of political opportunity (Tilly and Tarrow 2007). Compared to authoritarian regimes, democracies further collective action by relaxing repression, encouraging associational life, and opening channels of popular participation (Johnston and Almeida 2006). In this sense, democracies tend to lower the cost of protest participation, while at the same time increasing its potential benefits. Alternatively, micro approaches focus on individual-level behaviour, linking specific characteristics of social background, social networks and attitudinal orientations to one's propensity to engage in protest actions (Rosenstone and Hansen 1993; Verba et al. 1995; Dalton 2013; van Stekelenburg and Klandermans 2013).

Initially, radical disaffection theories viewed protest politics as an irrational outburst of potentially discontented classes, such as the poor, youth, and uneducated and unemployed, that threaten public order (Norris et al. 2006; Rucht 2007). However, subsequent studies have found little empirical evidence that the most politically alienated and deprived people are those who protest more (Dalton 2013). On the contrary, relative deprivation theories convincingly explain that the objectively most deprived people were not necessarily those that made their voice heard through protest (Rucht 2007). Although the conclusion of relative deprivation theories is that there are grievances at the heart of every protest (van Stekelenburg and Klandermans 2013), not all aggrieved people protest. Only when additional factors come into play do grievances result in actual protest (Rucht 2007). Supporters of modernisation theory (Inglehart 1977, 1990, 1997) suggest that protest politics are used more often by middle-class and university-educated people with post-materialist values (Dalton 2013) because these segments of the population have the resources and cognitive skills required for this kind of elite-challenging activism. At country-aggregate levels, previous research has pointed out that citizens tend to engage more in both conventional and protest forms of political activity in socio-economically more developed countries (Norris 2002; Bernhagen and Marsh 2007; Blais 2007; Newton and Montero 2007).

Individual-level explanations of political participation often focus on resources that facilitate political action and lay the groundwork for the civic voluntarism model (Verba et al. 1995). This model includes status variables such as age, socio-economic status, education, class and residence (Pattie and Johnston 1998). Education is one of the strongest predictors of participation because it provides cognitive and civic awareness, helping citizens to better understand politics (Norris 2002). The main thesis of the socio-economic model is that people with higher

134   *Marius I. Tatar*

economic status – higher education, higher incomes and better occupational positions – are more active in politics. In addition to skills and other resources that can facilitate civic involvement, motivation is also necessary for individuals to become active in politics. Among the most prominent motivational attitudes and values mentioned in the literature as influencing activism are political interest, support for the political system, and confidence in the main political institutions of representative democracy such as the parliament, government or political parties (Schussman and Soule 2005; Quintelier and van Deth 2014). Besides instrumental motivations, some people may protest based on ideological (leftist or rightist) or expressive considerations (Klandermans 2004). Persons expressing several values associated with a democratic culture, such as lifestyle tolerance, tolerance towards immigrants and gender role egalitarianism (Guérin et al. 2004; Kirbiš 2013), or those having more inclusive views on nationality and a cosmopolitan sense of belonging (Tarrow 2012), are expected to be more engaged in protest activities. Political socialisation (Petrovic et al. 2014) and a willingness to affect changes in society (Martin 2015) are also factors associated with more activism and protest movements.

Most protest events are not spontaneous and solitary acts, but rather organised collective actions (Fillieule 1997). Therefore, both the propensity to protest and the repertoire of protest actions is highly contingent on a person's belonging to various social networks and organisations that create the availability of opportunities for collective action (van Stekelenburg and Klandermans 2013). Moreover, the influence of being embedded in social networks on the propensity to participate in politics depends on the degree of political discussion that occurs in these social networks, and the information that people are able to gather about politics as a result (McClurg 2003). Organisational approaches emphasise the mobilising role of agents and social networks, including political parties, unions, religious organisations (churches) and voluntary associations, in activating political engagement. Following Putnam (2000) and Putnam et al. (1993), a plethora of studies emphasise the role of voluntary associations in fostering social and political participation (Levi 1996; Newton 2001; van Deth 2006; Kriesi 2008; Alexander et al. 2012). According to Putnam's social capital theory, a wide range of heterogeneous organisations and social groups enable face-to-face meetings of members and contribute to the production of dense civic networks that strengthen community bonds and social trust. The literature on social capital and civil society highlights that proximity to an organisation (political or otherwise) has the effect of channelling individuals more or less directly into politics (Diani 2009; Lambright et al. 2009; Uhlin 2009; Wallace et al. 2012; Zakaria 2013). In most direct ways, a person who belongs to more groups has higher odds of being politically involved, as s/he has higher chances to be recruited or invited to participate politically. Moreover, socially involved people are more likely to recognise the relevance of politics to their lives, and eventually become involved in politics, simply because they contact, meet and converse with more people than socially isolated persons, who are most often marginalised and politically alienated (Woshinsky 2008).

Trends of protest politics in Southeastern Europe: a comparative perspective

I use European Values Survey (EVS) and World Values Survey (WVS) datasets to measure the involvement of citizens in elite-challenging activities. Respondents to these public opinion polls were asked whether they have participated in the following activities: signing petitions, attending lawful demonstrations, joining boycotts, joining unofficial strikes, or occupying buildings or factories (see Table 8.1). However, these five protest activities differ in the risk involved and violence inherent to each act – and also in the extent to which an individual is prepared to use these actions. In this sense, relatively innocuous behaviour, such as signing a petition or attending a peaceful demonstration, are practiced by more people compared to increasingly severe forms of protest, such as occupations and riots. This general pattern of what we might call *the civility of protest politics* holds in each of the five European regions, although Western European citizens are more active on all five items, including the more contentious ones.

To aggregate protest participation into a variable more readily comparable across countries, I constructed a summary measure of protest activism. The last column in Table 8.1 reports the percentages of respondents who said they have engaged in at least one of the five protest actions. I use this summary measure in Figure 8.1 to present the dynamics of protest politics in each of the 10 Southeastern European countries analysed in this paper. There are divergent trends of protest politics in the two decades that preceded the economic crisis. In some countries, such as Romania, the number of protesters has dramatically decreased in all five forms of protest presented in Table 8.1, as well as on the aggregate measure of protest participation. By contrast, in Macedonia, there has been a substantial increase of the share of protesters on all five items, whereas in Slovenia,

Table 8.1 Protest participation in Europe 2008; regional variation in a comparative perspective

	Signing a petition	Attending lawful demonstrations	Joining boycotts	Joining unofficial strikes	Occupying buildings or factories	Summarised protest activity (at least 1)
Post-communist SEE	23.7%	12.1%	8.6%	4.1%	1.8%	29.1%
Western Europe	52.0%	25.1%	12.5%	5.8%	2.9%	58.0%
Post-communist CEE	21.3%	7.8%	2.9%	1.5%	0.5%	25.2%
Former Soviet countries	10.2%	12.3%	5.6%	5.3%	1.9%	23.3%
Other	12.8%	11.3%	4.5%	1.6%	1.1%	18.3%

Data source: EVS 2008

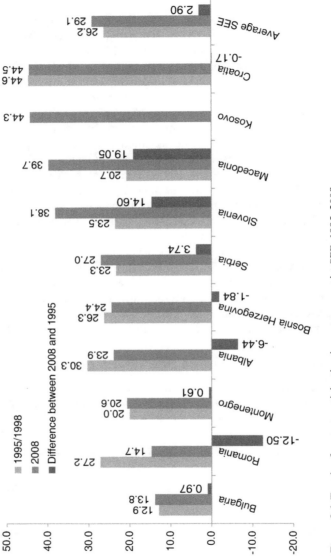

Figure 8.1 Trends of protest participation in post-communist SEE, 1995–2008

Data source: Inglehart et al. 2014a; EVS 2008

Are the Balkans different? Mapping protest politics 137

significant increases are recorded particularly in terms of signing petitions and attending demonstrations (see Table 8.2). On the other hand, the aggregate share of protesters remained virtually the same in Croatia, at almost 45% of the adult population. However, it should be noted that petitioners, representing around 41% of the population both in 1996 and 2008, make up the bulk of protesters in Croatia (see Table 8.2). Nevertheless, the share of Croatians joining boycotts increased from 4.3% to 9.1%, and the proportion of those attending demonstrations grew from 6.5% to 8.4% from 1996 to 2008. However, these figures do not weigh considerably in the aggregate share of protesters, as shown in Figure 8.1.

Besides divergent trends, Figure 8.1 also reveals a high variation between countries in the share of protesters: from less than 15% in Romania and Bulgaria to almost 45% in Croatia and Kosovo and almost 40% in Macedonia and Slovenia. What factors can account for these significant differences? Two expected factors may be, first, the level of democratic development suggested by the political opportunity structure theory, and second, the level of economic development suggested by modernisation theory. Figure 8.2 reveals that, contrary to expectations derived from political opportunity structure theory, there seems to be no significant relationship between the level of democracy and the levels of protest activity in these countries. In other words, countries that are more democratically developed and presumably provide greater opportunity for protest (increasing the benefits and lowering the costs of protest) are not necessarily those in which citizens protest more. For instance, at the onset of the economic crisis,

Table 8.2 Dynamics of petitioning and demonstrating in SEE, 1998–2008

	Signing a petition			Attending lawful demonstrations		
	1998	2008	Difference 1998–2008	1998	2008	Difference 1998–2008
Bulgaria	5.7%	8.8%	3.1	9.0%	7.6%	−1.4
Romania	14.3%	10.3%	−4.0	18.1%	6.8%	−11.3
Montenegro	13.8%	17.5%	3.7	10.8%	9.2%	−1.6
Albania	23.0%	18.6%	−4.4	16.1%	10.1%	−6.1
Serbia	18.3%	21.1%	2.8	7.0%	12.9%	5.9%
Bosnia-Herzegovina	22.6%	22.0%	−0.6	7.8%	6.2%	−1.5
Kosovo*	–	29.5%	–	–	28.1%	–
Slovenia	17.6%	33.0%	15.4	8.7%	12.7%	3.9
Macedonia	14.3%	34.6%	20.3	9.9%	18.2%	8.2
Croatia	41.1%	41.9%	0.8	6.5%	8.4%	1.9

Note: Data represent the % of respondents who, respectively, have signed a petition and attended a lawful demonstration. Cells marked in grey represent a decrease in signing petitions and attending demonstrations in a specific country. *Data is not available for Kosovo in the 1995–1998 wave of the World Values Survey.

138 *Marius I. Tatar*

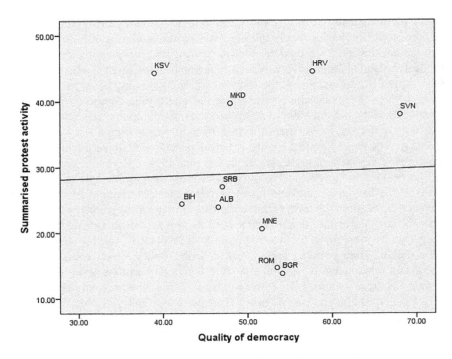

Figure 8.2 Quality of democracy and protest activity in SEE Europe, 2008
Data source: EVS 2008; World Bank WGI 2008

EU member countries like Slovenia, Romania and Bulgaria, which scored higher on democratic development as measured by the World Bank's worldwide governance indicators[3] in 2008, had lower levels of protest compared with Kosovo and Macedonia. These findings suggest that protest politics in the Balkans may be explained by other factors not accounted for by theories mainly developed based on empirical data collected in advanced democracies.

However, when we include economic development in the equation, we note two divergent trends (see Figure 8.3). First, economic and democratic developments strongly correlate. Thus, higher levels of GDP per capita are associated with a higher quality of democracy, and this confirms expectations derived from modernisation theories. Slovenia and Croatia particularly stand out in this regard. Second, protest activity is very poorly related to economic development in postcommunist Southeast Europe, contrary to what modernisation theory would suggest. For instance, less developed states like Macedonia and Kosovo have much higher protest rates than more developed countries in the region. Previous studies have linked increased citizen participation in economically less developed post-Yugoslav states to a growing politicisation of these societies along deep-rooted cleavages (such as those based on ethnic and religious fragmentation) that have

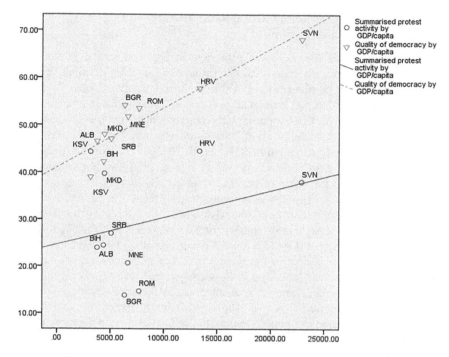

Figure 8.3 Economic development, quality of democracy and protest activity in SEE, 2008
Data source: EVS 2008; World Bank WGI, 2008

structured political conflict and competition (see Kirbiš 2013 for a synthesis on post-Yugoslav citizen participation). Nevertheless, our data suggest more complex patterns of relationships between various factors and protest participation in this region. For instance, a country marked by relatively low levels of ethnic and religious diversity, such as Croatia, also records higher levels of protest participation than its economic development would predict (see Figure 8.3). As shown in Table 8.2, petitioners represent the largest share of Croatian protesters, whereas in Kosovo and Macedonia, along with petitioners, there are relatively high numbers of demonstrators and boycotters.

Overall, country-aggregated levels of economic development and quality of democracy do not offer satisfactory explanations for the variation in the share of protesters in this region. It seems that other factors come into play when explaining protest participation at the country-aggregate level (Krajnc et al. 2012). In the following sections, I move from a country-aggregate to individual-level analysis, which highlights the characteristics of protesters in each of the 10 countries of post-communist Southeast Europe. This is done by comparing the determinants of petitioning and demonstrating – two of the most commonly used forms of protest action.

140　*Marius I. Tatar*

Who protests in Southeast Europe? Comparing determinants of petitioning and demonstrating across countries and regions

This section outlines the profile of protesters in post-communist Southeastern Europe by comparing the individual determinants of signing petitions and participation in lawful demonstrations. Although an increasing number of studies investigate how the Internet influences political activism (Gibson and Cantijoch 2013; Cantijoch et al. 2016), particularly among young people (Xenos et al. 2014), many point to a digital divide that reinforces traditional socio-economic inequalities in online participation (Oser et al. 2013). For instance, the spread of the Internet may have reduced the cost of signing petitions, but this does not necessarily increase the share of petitioners in all countries. In fact, as data in Table 8.2 show for 1998 to 2008, the proportion of those who signed a petition has decreased in three countries and increased in another six countries. This suggests that, besides a simple cost-benefit rationale, there are other relevant factors that influence signing petitions (see Table 8.3 in Appendix). The most spectacular increases in terms of shares of petitioners occurred in Macedonia, rising from about 14% to more than 36%, and in Slovenia, from 17% to 33%. In the same period, the proportion of those who attended a lawful demonstration dropped in five countries and increased in four. The most dramatic decrease in the share of demonstrators occurred in Romania, from 18% to 6.8%, whereas the most significant increase is registered in Macedonia, from 9.9% to 18.2%.

The propensity to participate in these two forms of protest is compared based on 25 socio-demographic and attitudinal factors, which have been introduced as predictor variables in logistic regression statistical models (see Appendix, Tables 8.3, 8.4 and 8.5). Overall, in Southeast Europe, men tend to participate more than women, both in petition signing and demonstrations. For instance, in Macedonia and Romania, men are respectively 1.75 and 1.56 times more likely to sign petitions compared to women, all other factors being equal. Moreover, gender is a particularly influential predictor of attending demonstrations in countries like Macedonia, Slovenia, Bosnia-Herzegovina, Bulgaria and Kosovo. However, in some countries, the effect of gender on protest participation seems to be mediated by attitudinal factors (among which interest in politics is probably the most prominent), which may account for differences between men and women. Overall, the gender gap seems to be smaller in terms of petition signing compared to demonstrating, suggesting women's propensity to engage in less confrontational forms of protest action.

Age is the second socio-demographic variable used in statistical models to predict protest. When we control for other variables such as education, employment status and political values and attitudes, age seems to have no clearly discernible effect on participation in lawful demonstration. However, some variation does occur when we analyse the relationship between age and petitioning. In general, young and adult persons seem to be more prone to sign petitions in Southeast Europe, although this pattern does not hold in every country. For instance, in

Are the Balkans different? Mapping protest politics 141

Montenegro, persons between 18–29 years old are 1.54 times more likely to have signed a petition compared to persons over 50 years old. On the other hand, in Macedonia, younger persons are 0.64 times less likely to have signed petitions than their older counterparts, whereas in Croatia and Slovenia, middle-age individuals seem to have a higher propensity to sign petitions. Further longitudinal studies might better elucidate if these differences are due to simple life-cycle effects or if they originate in more profound generational differences resulting from divergent patterns of political socialisation in different socio-political and economic contexts.

Overall, both petitioners and demonstrators tend to have higher levels of education compared to non-protestors. The effect of individuals' level of education on their propensity to sign petitions is, however, more evident in countries like Bulgaria, Slovenia, Romania and Kosovo, with Bulgaria showing the most significant influence of education on the likelihood to demonstrate, controlling for the effect of all other variables included in this statistical model. However, bivariate analyses reveal that, in each of the 10 Southeast European countries, more educated people are more likely to sign petitions and demonstrate than persons with lower levels of education (details not shown here). Despite this fact, the effect of education on protesting seems to lose its statistical significance in the multivariate models presented in Tables 8.3 and 8.4 (see Appendix), most likely because the impact of education on citizen participation is mediated by other intervening variables.

People with higher family incomes, relative to their fellow citizens, tend to engage more in signing petitions and this pattern holds in 6 out of 10 Southeast European countries. However, household revenues seem to have a much lower, and sometimes contradictory, influence on demonstrating. For instance, in only two countries (Albania and Slovenia) does income have a statistically significant effect on participation in peaceful demonstrations. However, in these two cases, the patterns are divergent: whereas in Albania, persons with higher family incomes tend to demonstrate more, in Slovenia, they are less prone to be involved in street protests. Regardless of income, in general, people living in bigger cities tend to sign petitions and demonstrate more than persons living in smaller localities. Students tend to have a higher propensity to sign petitions compared to their compatriots, particularly in Bosnia-Herzegovina, Slovenia and Croatia, and they demonstrate more in countries like Bulgaria, Bosnia-Herzegovina, Slovenia and Serbia. Being employed is also associated with a higher probability of signing petitions and demonstrating, suggesting that having a job plays an important role in social integration that can provide an individual with the resources and incentives needed to participate.

Members of various organisations tend to engage more often in protest actions. However, membership and participation in different organisations such as trade unions, political parties, civil society organisations and churches seem to have uneven influences on people's repertoires of protest action. Overall, data in Tables 8.3 and 8.4 (see Appendix) indicate that in Southeast Europe, trade unionists are more prone to participate in demonstrations. On the other hand, members of civil society organisations tend to engage in more legalist methods of protest

142   *Marius I. Tatar*

such as petition signing, whereas political party members are more inclined to participate both in petitioning and demonstrations, compared to the general public. Yet these patterns vary significantly across countries. For instance, trade union membership is a particularly strong predictor of attending lawful demonstrations in Bulgaria, Croatia and Montenegro, but is insignificant in Albania and Kosovo. Similarly, civil society membership has an important effect on the propensity to sign petitions in Albania, Bosnia-Herzegovina, Romania, Kosovo, Slovenia and Macedonia, but it does not reach statistical significance in the rest of the Southeast European countries. Party members are more prone to sign petitions in Bulgaria, Serbia, Montenegro and Macedonia, and to demonstrate in Bosnia-Herzegovina, Bulgaria, Croatia, Romania, Serbia and Macedonia, whereas in Kosovo, they tend to engage less in street protests compared to their compatriots. In fact, in Kosovo, civil society membership and the frequency of church attendance (of those belonging to a Muslim religious denomination) seem to be more important mobilising factors for engagement in demonstrations than party or union membership. In the pooled sample, fervent churchgoers in Southeast Europe have a slightly higher probability of participating in demonstrations, although the frequency of church attendance reaches statistical significance as a predictor of demonstrating only in Bulgaria and Kosovo. Overall, people who discuss politics with their friends are more likely to sign petitions and demonstrate, whereas trust in fellow citizens has a minimal effect on petition signing and no significant effect on demonstrating.

Values and attitudes also represent important predictors of protest participation. On average, people who display post-materialist values (i.e. prioritising giving people more say in governance and protecting freedom of speech over maintaining order and fighting rising prices), have an inclusive view on nationality (i.e. believe that place of birth, ancestry, knowledge of official language or long-time residency in a country are not really important for being 'truly a national' of a country) and have a cosmopolitan sense of belonging (i.e. those who say they first belong to the world as a whole or to Europe and not to their country/region/locality) are more likely to sign petitions and demonstrate in Southeast Europe. On the other hand, those who have less positive views on immigration tend to protest more. Lifestyle tolerance (measured here as the belief that homosexuality, abortion and divorce can be justified) and more egalitarian views on gender roles (operationalised here as the belief that men do not have more rights to jobs than women) are also positively associated with a higher propensity to sign petitions, but not to attend demonstrations. Moreover, petitioners (and, in some countries, demonstrators) tend to favour social change to a higher degree than their compatriots. For instance, those who believe that their society should be changed (more radically through revolution or more moderately through reforms) are on average more likely to have signed petitions compared to those who consider that their society should be 'valiantly defended against all change' (EVS 2011).

What is less clear from this analysis, however, is the direction of social change (i.e. ideological orientation) towards which petitioners believe their society should move. In Southeast Europe, those who place themselves at the extremes

Are the Balkans different? Mapping protest politics 143

of the Left-Right ideological axis tend to sign petitions and to demonstrate more, compared to those who place themselves at the centre of this axis. In addition, those who have a clear ideological identification with either the Left or Right tend to display higher levels of support for democracy as a legitimate political regime, but are not necessarily more trusting in particular political institutions or organisations (parliament, government, parties). Placing oneself ideologically at the extremes of the Left-Right axis is particularly salient for attending demonstrations in Romania, Montenegro and Macedonia, and for petition signing in Croatia, Bosnia-Herzegovina and Montenegro. However, further studies should elucidate and compare citizens' interpretations of Left-Right ideological identifications in Western and Eastern Europe. It is very plausible that, in the post-communist context, people might interpret ideological self-identifications differently compared to their Western counterparts.[4]

Petition signing and participation in demonstrations are, on average, higher among persons who have been more exposed to political socialisation within the family. Thus, both forms of protest are more frequent among persons who, during their adolescence, discussed politics with their parents and grew up in families in which parents followed the news frequently. In general, those who have higher levels of support for democracy as a legitimate form of governance, and who are interested in politics, are more likely to have signed petitions and joined demonstrations in all the countries and regions analysed here.

Although citizens of post-communist Southeast Europe protest less than their Western counterparts, most of the predictors of elite-challenging actions analysed here perform similarly in East and West. Yet there are several notable differences between protesters living in these regions. For instance, in Southeast European countries, men are more likely to sign petitions, whereas in Western Europe, women are more prone to petitioning. Younger persons (15–29 years old) are less likely to sign petitions in Western Europe, whereas in Southeast Europe, they have a higher probability of doing so compared to older persons (above 50 years old). In Southeast Europe, the larger the size of the locality in which one lives, the higher the chances the person has signed a petition, whereas in Western Europe, this predictor is statistically insignificant. Overall, students from Western countries are more prone to demonstrate compared to the rest of the population of their countries. Overall, in Southeast Europe, this is not necessarily the case, although in some countries from this region, students are substantially more prone to protest than the general public. In addition, in Southeast Europe, fervent churchgoers tend to protest more compared to those who attend religious services less often or not at all. The situation is reversed in Western Europe where, on average, attending religious services seems to decrease one's likelihood to protest. In terms of ideological positioning, overall both in Southeast Europe and Western Europe, right wingers tend to be more frequent churchgoers than leftists. Tolerant attitudes towards immigration also have potentially divergent effects on one's propensity to demonstrate. In Western Europe, demonstrators tend to have a somewhat more positive attitude towards immigration compared to their fellow citizens, whereas in Southeast Europe, the situation seems to be reversed. Overall, Western

144 *Marius I. Tatar*

demonstrators tend to have a stronger belief that their societies should be changed, compared to demonstrators in Southeast Europe.

In terms of the relationship between ideological self-placement on the Left-Right axis and protest participation, one can note divergent patterns between Southeastern and Western citizens. In Southeast Europe, those who identify themselves with either the Left or Right tend to sign petitions and demonstrate more than those who place themselves at the centre of the Left-Right axis. On the other hand, in Western Europe, 'leftists' tend to demonstrate more than 'centrists', whereas, in their turn, 'rightists' tend to demonstrate less than 'centrists'. In general, Western Europeans who distrust political institutions are more prone to protest compared to their fellow citizens who have higher levels of institutional trust. Overall, in Southeastern Europe, there seems to be no significant relationship between trust in political institutions and the propensity to protest.

Developments during the economic crisis: a closer look at Romania and Slovenia

I have selected Romania and Slovenia for a closer comparative analysis of protest dynamics in the recent economic crisis. The two countries differ significantly in several control variables, including institutional set-up, trajectories and speed of transition to democracy, and levels of economic development, yet are similar in terms of the severity with which the recent economic contraction hit their economies and their social and political responses to the crisis. These characteristics qualify Slovenia and Romania for a comparative analysis of 'most different' cases, which aims to explore patterns of protest participation during the economic crisis.

Post-socialist transformations in Slovenia have been frequently qualified as a success story due to a steady pace of democratisation and increased economic prosperity compared with other former communist countries (Bukowski 1999; Feldmann 2006). By contrast, post-communist Romania has often been considered a regional 'laggard' (along with Bulgaria) in terms of building and consolidating liberal democracy, developing prosperity, and the process of joining the EU (Noutcheva and Bechev 2008). Despite different levels of economic development at the outset of the crisis, after 2008, Romania and Slovenia experienced an equally dramatic economic contraction. According to Eurostat data,[5] the GDP of Slovenia declined by 7.8% in 2009 compared with 2008, and the GDP of Romania decreased by 7.1%. Unemployment data follows somewhat similar trends in both countries. In Romania, unemployment rates increased from 5.8% in 2008 to 6.9% in 2009, and then to 7.3% in 2010, and in Slovenia, unemployment rates grew from 4.4% in 2008 to 6.9% in 2009 and 7.3% in 2010. Not only was the severity of the crisis comparable in Slovenia and Romania, but the episodes of political instability and relatively long periods of social unrest that followed the economic contraction were also similar. Although the two countries had divergent trends of protest mobilisation during their post-socialist transition, protest mobilisation patterns seem to have converged during the economic crisis. These developments may provide evidence that countries that have been hit equally hard by the crisis

Are the Balkans different? Mapping protest politics   145

tend to experience similar political and social developments, regardless of previous differences between them. This could be the case because, as Bellinger and Arce (2011) have pointed out, literature on contentious politics suggests that societal forces react to changes in economic conditions (i.e. decline) and economic policy (i.e. austerity) rather than overall levels of economic development or economic liberalisation policy in general.

Indeed, in 2012, Romania recorded a revival of citizen activism after a relatively long period of political apathy. Massive demonstrations erupted in January 2012 in most major cities in Romania. In February 2012, these protests eventually led to the resignation of the centre-right government that had adopted austerity measures in 2010. Other protests began in spring 2012 against shale gas drilling projects, and summer 2012 witnessed further street demonstrations. Similarly, a new wave of protests swept through Slovenia in late 2012 and 2013 after the centre-right coalition government adopted a package of austerity measures in May 2012, including cuts in public sector wages and benefits. Although both in Romania and Slovenia the first social reactions to austerity measures were economic protests organised by trade unions, after a period of accumulated grievances, new social movements animated mass demonstrations against wider political issues, including political corruption and lack of governmental efficiency and responsiveness.

To compare the profile of petitioners and demonstrators before and during the economic crisis and show the robustness of results, the logistic regression statistical models contained similar predictor variables[6] from the EVS 2008 and WVS 2010–2014 datasets (Inglehart et al. 2014b). The results are presented in Tables 8.3 and 8.4 (see Appendix), which contain the Exp (B) logistic regression coefficients (odds ratio) for the determinants of signing petitions and attending demonstrations in Romania in 2008 and 2012 and Slovenia in 2008 and 2011.

The strongest predictor for petition signing and attending demonstrations in Romania in 2012 was interest in politics, whereas in 2008, this variable was a significant predictor only for demonstrating and not for petitioning. This indicates a potential increase in the explanatory power of this factor, meaning that during the economic crisis, Romanians more interested in politics were increasingly more likely to protest than those who were not interested in politics, controlling for all other factors in the model. In Slovenia in 2011, interest in politics was also the strongest predictor for attending demonstrations and the second strongest (after education) for signing petitions, whereas in 2008, it was a significant determinant only for petitioning.

Civil society membership is another factor that seems to have gained more leverage, particularly in explaining participation in demonstrations during the economic crisis. In Romania in 2011–2012, members in civil society organisations were 1.7 times as likely to demonstrate, and in Slovenia, they were more than twice as likely to participate in demonstrations than non-members, controlling for other factors in the model. On the other hand, civil society membership was a non-significant predictor of attending demonstrations before the economic crisis, when in both countries members of civil society organisations (CSOs) were only more prone to sign petitions than non-members. Although, initially, protests

146   *Marius I. Tatar*

might have been animated by unions that were voicing discontent over economic hardships and austerity measures, it seems that, subsequently, other social agents, such as CSOs, started to mobilise people for protests targeting broader issues (e.g. political corruption, environmental protection, urban planning, etc.). Although the economic downturn could have imposed constraints on the funding resources of many of these organisations and networks, both in Slovenia and Romania, the mobilisation capacity of CSOs seems to have increased after 2008. Overall, membership in CSOs significantly grew in both countries. Data from the WVS/EVS surveys show that, in Romania, the share of respondents who reported membership in at least one CSO[7] rose from 19% in 2008 to almost 30% in 2012, and in Slovenia, it grew from 46% in 2008 to more than 55% in 2011. Students were also increasingly more likely to participate in street demonstrations during the economic crisis in both countries. However, data from Romania reveals that, among younger cohorts, only students and those connected with various social networks and organisations and having certain motivations were particularly more prone to participate in protests. In addition, those living in large cities have higher chances of both signing petitions and attending demonstrations than those living in small rural localities in Romania. On the other hand, in Slovenia, employed persons were almost three times more likely to demonstrate than the rest of the adult population, all other things being equal.

Education is the strongest predictor of signing petitions in Slovenia, and the second most important (after interest in politics) in Romania, controlling for all other variables in the model. In both countries, those expressing higher levels of support for the democratic system of governance during the economic crisis were also more likely to report signing petitions than those supporting authoritarian or technocratic forms of governance. In 2008, this factor had no statistically significant effect on petitioning in either of the two countries. Overall, the predictors of joining street demonstrations and signing petitions seem to perform in a rather similar way before and during the economic crisis in Slovenia and Romania. However, in the context of an overall increase in protest mobilisation, the effects of some predictors appear to have been elevated.

Conclusion

The main results of the analyses carried out in this paper suggest three interwoven pathways to understanding protest action in post-communist Southeast Europe. First, within the instrumental path manifested mainly through attentiveness to and interest in politics, protest is seen as a means to achieve certain goals, such as to protect or increase specific rights. Second, following the logic of identification, manifested in data used here mainly through the self-identification of ideology and values, people protest to express their indignation when their values have been violated (van Stekelenburg et al. 2009). The two logics are not mutually exclusive, but rather complementary. Third, mobilising contexts are needed to create actual opportunities for protest action. Membership in various civil society organisations and belonging to different politicised social networks provide the mobilising context in which both instrumental and ideological motives can lead to protest action.

Although, in Southeast Europe, people protest less than citizens living in Western Europe, protesters in both regions tend to have similar socio-demographical and attitudinal profiles. Contrary to what radical disaffection theories might suggest, protesters in post-communist Southeast Europe are on average democratically oriented citizens of their countries. They tend to support democracy as a form of government and generally ask for more open, responsive and accountable democratic governance. However, this finding should not be interpreted as deterministic, but rather in probabilistic terms. In other words, the results by no means imply that only democratically oriented citizens protest and authoritarian-minded people do not. Without excluding the participation in protest by some extremist segments of the population (sometimes highly publicised in the media), the results do suggest, however, that in this region, as well in as Western Europe, those who tend to support democracy as the only legitimate system of governance are more likely to protest than those who prefer authoritarian alternatives to democracy. This positive relationship between what Easton (1975) has called 'diffuse democratic support' and protest participation holds even after controlling for the effect of various socio-demographic and attitudinal factors. At the same time, protesters in this region also tend to have stronger ideological identifications on the Left-Right axis compared to non-protesters, although the Left-Right semantics may have different meanings in Western and Eastern Europe. Moreover, they usually do not come from the lower strata of the society, as disaffected radicalism theories would predict, but rather from higher-income, better-educated and post-materialist segments of the population who are more open to the idea of social change. In this sense, protesters from Southeast Europe resemble their Western counterparts to a certain degree.

Although the data on public opinion used in this chapter (i.e. World Values Surveys and European Values Surveys) are useful in analysing the general characteristics of protesters by comparing those who have demonstrated or signed petitions with those who have not, this kind of data does not tell us much about what people were protesting against (van Stekelenburg and Klandermans 2014). Despite these limitations, the findings presented in this paper explore some of the factors that can account for citizens' preferences for certain forms of protest action over others. Furthermore, because this research shows that people are more likely to engage in protest when they are more interested in politics, have certain values and ideological orientations and are socially embedded in various mobilising networks, it opens new opportunities for research that can test the robustness of these findings in different contexts, such as the recent economic crisis. This paper has taken a first step in this direction by exploring the patterns of protest politics during the economic crisis through a comparative analysis of Slovenia and Romania. As some research suggests, economic hardships and employment insecurities 'generate political apathy as people's efforts are devoted to participating in the market, and they have less time to become politically active' (Oxhorn 2009, 228). However, worsening economic conditions and governmental policies that

148   *Marius I. Tatar*

imposed austerity programs during the recent economic recession created new opportunities for mobilisation both by existing and newly emerging social actors that have politically activated increasing segments of the population. The cases of Slovenia and Romania seem to support this pattern of anti-government mobilisation because, in both countries, social movements spread during the economic crisis, and protests became an increasingly used means to voice popular discontent both against austerity as well as corruption and bad governance in general.

Notes

1 The states included in this analysis offer significant cross-country variation in terms of protest patterns: Albania, Bosnia-Herzegovina, Bulgaria, Croatia, Kosovo, FYR Macedonia, Montenegro, Romania, Serbia and Slovenia.
2 A notable example in this sense is the Albanian economic crisis of 1997, which was accompanied by unprecedented institutional, political and social turmoil, leading to a spiral of violence and chaos (Vaughan-Whitehead 1999).
3 The World Bank provides aggregate and individual governance indicators for 215 countries and territories over the period 1996–2012 for six dimensions of governance. Available at: http://data.worldbank.org/data-catalog/worldwide-governance-indicators.
4 For instance, in post-communist countries, a right-wing ideological identification might simply mean having a more liberal, anti-communist orientation.
5 Available at: http://ec.europa.eu/eurostat/tgm/table.do?tab=table&plugin=1&language=en&pcode=tec00115
6 Four items included in EVS 2008 were not asked in WVS 2010–2014, namely: frequency of political discussions, index of inclusive views on nationality, scale of opposition to social change, and the index of political socialisation within the family. Despite these limitations, the overall explanatory power of the statistical models employed to predict both petitioning and demonstrating in 2008 and 2011–2012 is comparable.
7 The EVS and WVS ask about membership in an extensive list of voluntary organisations, ranging from environmental, consumer, religious, sport, art and recreational organisations to professional associations, humanitarian or charitable organisations and mutual aid groups.

References

Alexander, D.T., J. Barraket, J.M. Lewis, and M. Considine. 2012. Civic Engagement and Associationalism: The Impact of Group Membership Scope versus Intensity of Participation. *European Sociological Review* 28(1): 43–58.
Bellinger, P.T. and A. Moises. 2011. Protest and Democracy in Latin America's Market Era. *Political Research Quarterly* 64(3): 688–704.
Bernhagen, P. and M. Marsh. 2007. Voting and Protesting: Explaining Citizen Participation in Old and New European Democracies. *Democratization* 14(1): 44–72.
Blais, A. 2007. Turnout in Elections. In: *Political Behavior*, eds. R.J. Dalton and H-D. Klingeman. Oxford: Oxford University Press, pp. 621–635.
Bukowski, C. 1999. Slovenia's Transition to Democracy: Theory and Practice. *East European Quarterly* 33(1): 69–99.
Cantijoch, M., D. Cutts, and R. Gibson. 2016. Moving Slowly Up the Ladder of Political Engagement: A 'Spill-over' Model of Internet Participation. *The British Journal of Politics & International Relations* 18(1): 26–48.

Dalton, R.J. 2013. *Citizen Politics: Public Opinion and Political Parties in Advanced Industrial Democracies*. Washington, DC: CQ Press.

Dalton, R.J. and C. Welzel. 2014. *The Civic Culture Transformed: From Allegiant to Assertive Citizens*. Cambridge: Cambridge University Press.

van Deth, J.W. 2006. Democracy and Involvement: The Benevolent Aspects of Social Participation. In: *Political Disaffection in Contemporary Democracies: Social Capital, Institutions, and Politics*, eds. M. Torcal and J.R. Montero. New York: Routledge, pp. 101–129.

Diani, M. 2009. The Structural Bases of Protest Events: Multiple Memberships and Civil Society Networks in the 15 February 2003 Anti-War Demonstrations. *Acta Sociologica* 52(1): 63–83.

Easton, D. 1975. A Re-Assessment of the Concept of Political Support. *British Journal of Political Science* 5(4): 435–457.

EVS. 2011. *European Values Study 2008: Integrated Dataset (EVS 2008)*. GESIS Data Archive, Cologne.

Feldmann, M. 2006. Emerging Varieties of Capitalism in Transition Countries: Industrial Relations and Wage Bargaining in Estonia and Slovenia. *Comparative Political Studies* 39(7): 829–854.

Fillieule, O. 1997. *Stratégies de la rue: Les manifestations en France*. Paris: Presses de Science Po.

Gibson, R. and M. Cantijoch. 2013. Conceptualizing and Measuring Participation in the Age of the Internet: Is Online Political Engagement Really Different to Offline? *The Journal of Politics* 75(3): 701–716.

Guérin, D., F. Petry, and J. Crête. 2004. Tolerance, Protest and Democratic Transition: Survey Evidence From 13 Post-Communist Countries. *European Journal of Political Research* 43(3): 371–395.

Inglehart, R. 1977. *The Silent Revolution: Changing Values and Political Styles Among Western Publics*. Princeton: Princeton University Press.

Inglehart, R. 1990. *Culture Shift in Advanced Industrial Society*. Princeton: Princeton University Press.

Inglehart, R. 1997. *Modernization and Postmodernization: Cultural, Economic, and Political Change in 43 Societies*. Princeton: Princeton University Press.

Inglehart, R., C. Haerpfer, A. Moreno, C. Welzel, K. Kizilova, J. Diez-Medrano, . . . B. Puranen. eds. 2014a. World Values Survey: Round Three (1995–1998) – Country-Pooled Datafile Version. Madrid, JD Systems Institute. Available at: www.worldvaluessurvey.org/WVSDocumentationWV3.jsp.

Inglehart, R., C. Haerpfer, A. Moreno, C. Welzel, K. Kizilova, J. Diez-Medrano, . . . B. Puranen. eds. 2014b. World Values Survey: Round Six – Country-Pooled Datafile Version. Madrid: JD Systems Institute. Available at: www.worldvaluessurvey.org/WVS DocumentationWV6.jsp.

Johnston, H. and P. Almeida. eds. 2006. *Latin American Social Movements: Globalization, Democratization and Transnational Networks*. Lanham: Rowman & Littlefield.

Kirbiš, A. 2013. Political Participation and Non-Democratic Political Culture in Western Europe, East-Central Europe and Post-Yugoslav Countries. In: *Democracy in Transition: Political Participation in the European Union*, ed. K.N. Demetriou. Heidelberg: Springer, pp. 225–251.

Klandermans, B. 2004. The Demand and Supply of Participation: Social Psychological Correlates of Participation in Social Movements. In: *The Blackwell Companion to Social*

150   *Marius I. Tatar*

Movements, eds. D. Snow, S.A. Soule and H. Kriesi. Oxford: Blackwell Publishers, pp. 360–379.

Krajnc, M.T., S. Flere, and A. Kirbiš. 2012. Is Protest Participation in Post-Yugoslav Countries Motivated by Pro-Democratic Political Culture? A Cross-National Study. *The Western Balkans Policy Review* 2(2): 95–117.

Kriesi, H. 2008. Political Mobilisation, Political Participation and the Power of the Vote. *West European Politics* 31(1–2): 147–168.

Lambright, K.T., P.A. Mischen, and C.B. Laramee. 2009. Building Trust in Public and Nonprofit Networks: Personal, Dyadic, and Third-Party Influences. *The American Review of Public Administration* 40(1): 64–82.

Levi, M. 1996. Social and Unsocial Capital: A Review Essay of Robert Putnam's Making Democracy Work. *Politics Society* 24(1): 45–55.

Martin, G. 2015. *Understanding Social Movements*. London: Routledge.

McAdam, D. 1982. *Political Process and the Development of Black Insurgency, 1930–1970*. Chicago: Chicago University Press.

McAdam, D., J.D. McCarthy, and M.N. Zald. 1996. *Comparative Perspectives on Social Movements*. Cambridge: Cambridge University Press.

McClurg, S.D. 2003. Social Networks and Political Participation: The Role of Social Interaction in Explaining Political Participation. *Political Research Quarterly* 56: 448–464.

Newton, K. 2001. Trust, Social Capital, Civil Society, and Democracy. *International Political Science Review/Revue internationale de science politique* 22(2): 201–214.

Newton, K. and J-R. Montero. 2007. Patterns of Political and Social Participation in Europe. In: *Measuring Attitudes Cross-Nationally: Lessons from the European Social Survey*, eds. V.R. Jowell et al. Los Angeles: Sage Publications, pp. 205–238.

Norris, P. 2002. *Democratic Phoenix: Reinventing Political Activism*. Cambridge: Cambridge University Press.

Norris, P., S. Walgrave, and P. Van Aelst. 2006. Does Protest Signify Disaffection? Demonstrators in a Postindustrial Semocracy. In: *Political Dissafection in Contemporary Democracies: Social Capital, Institutions, and Politics*, eds. M. Torcal and J.R. Montero. London: Routledge, pp. 279–307.

Noutcheva, G. and D. Bechev. 2008. The Successful Laggards: Bulgaria and Romania's Accession to the EU. *East European Politics and Societies* 22(1): 114–144.

Opp, K.D. and B. Kittel. 2010. The Dynamics of Political Protest: Feedback Effects and Interdependence in the Explanation of Protest Participation. *European Sociological Review* 26(1): 97–109.

Oser, J., M. Hooghe, and S. Marien. 2013. Is Online Participation Distinct From Offline Participation? A Latent Class Analysis of Participation Types and Their Stratification. *Political Research Quarterly* 66(1): 91–101.

Oxhorn, P. 2009. Beyond Neoliberalism? Latin America's New Crossroads. In: *Beyond Neoliberalism in Latin America? Societies and Politics at the Crossroads*, eds. J. Burdick, P. Oxhorn, and K. Roberts. New York: Palgrave Macmillan, pp. 217–234.

Pattie, C. and R. Johnston. 1998. Voter Turnout at the British General Elections of 1992: Rational Choice, Social Standing or Political Efficacy? *European Journal of Political Research* 33(2): 263–283.

Petrovic, I., J. van Stekelenburg, and B. Klandermans. 2014. Political Socialisation and Social Movements: Escaping the Political Past? In: *The Palgrave Handbook of Global Political Psychology*, eds. P. Nesbitt-Larking, C. Kinnvall, T. Capelos and H. Dekker. Basingstoke: Palgrave Macmillan, pp. 403–422.

Putnam, R. 2000. *Bowling Alone: The Collapse and Revival of American Community*. New York: Simon & Schuster.

Putnam, R.D., R. Leonardi, and R. Nanetti. 1993. *Making Democracy Work: Civic Traditions in Modern Italy*. Princeton: Princeton University Press.

Quintelier, E. and J.W. van Deth. 2014. Supporting Democracy: Political Participation and Political Attitudes: Exploring Causality Using Panel Data. *Political Studies* 62: 153–171.

Rosenstone, S.J. and J.M. Hansen. 1993. *Mobilization, Participation and Democracy in America*. New York: Palgrave Macmillan.

Rucht, D. 2007. The Spread of Protest Politics. In: *The Oxford Handbook of Political Behavior*, eds. R. Dalton and H.D. Klingemann. Oxford: Oxford University Press, pp. 708–723.

Schussman, A. and S.A. Soule. 2005. Process and Protest: Accounting for Individual Protest Participation. *Social Forces* 84(2): 1083–1108.

van Stekelenburg, J., B. Klandermans, and W.W. van Dijk. 2009. Context Matters: Explaining How and Why Mobilizing Context Influences Motivational Dynamics. *Journal of Social Issues* 65(4): 815–838.

Tarrow, S. 1998. *Power in Movement: Social Movements and Contentious Politics*. Cambridge: Cambridge University Press.

Tarrow, S. 2012. *Strangers at the Gates: Movements and States in Contentious Politics*. Cambridge: Cambridge University Press.

Tătar, M.I. 2015. Selective or Generic Activism? Types of Participants, Political Action Repertoires and Mobilisation Capacity in a Post-Communist Society. *Europe-Asia Studies* 67(8): 1251–1281.

Tilly, C. and S. Tarrow. 2007. *Contentious Politics*. Boulder: Paradigm.

Uhlin, A. 2009. Which Characteristics of Civil Society Organizations Support What Aspects of Democracy? Evidence from Post-communist Latvia. *International Political Science Review/Revue internationale de science pol* 30 (3): 271–295.

Uslaner, E.M. 2004. *Bowling Almost Alone: Political Participation in a New Democracy*. ECPR Joint Sessions of Workshops, Emerging Repertoires of Political Action: Toward a Systematic Study of Postconventional Forms of Participation, Uppsala, Sweden, 13–18 April 2004.

van Stekelenburg, J. and B. Klandermans. 2013. The Social Psychology of Protest. *Current Sociology* 61(5–6): 886–905.

van Stekelenburg, J. and B. Klandermans. 2014. Fitting Demand and Supply: How Identification Brings Appeals and Motives Together. *Social Movement Studies* 13(2): 179–203.

Vaughan-Whitehead, D. 1999. *Albania in Crisis*. Cheltenham: Edward Elgar Publishing.

Verba, S., K. Schlozman, and H.E. Brady. 1995. *Voice and Equality: Civic Voluntarism in American Politics*. Cambridge, MA: Harvard University Press.

Wallace, C., F. Pichler, and C. Haerpfer. 2012. Changing Patterns of Civil Society in Europe and America 1995–2005. *East European Politics & Societies* 26(1): 3–19.

World Bank WGI. 2008. World Bank Worldwide Governance Indicators (WGI). Available at: www.govindicators.org.

Woshinsky, O.H. 2008. *Explaining Politics: Culture, Institutions and Political Behavior*. New York: Routledge.

Xenos, M., A. Vromen, and B.D. Loader. 2014. The Great Equalizer? Patterns of Social Media Use and Youth Political Engagement in Three Advanced Democracies. *Information, Communication & Society* 17(2): 151–167.

Zakaria, P. 2013. Is Corruption an Enemy of Civil Society? The Case of Central and Eastern Europe. *International Political Science Review* 34: 351–371.

Table 8.3 Explaining the signing of petitions in post-communist SEE (Exp (B) logistic regression coefficients)

	Albania 2008	Bosnia Herz. 2008	Bulgaria 2008	Croatia 2008	Montenegro 2008	Romania 2008	Romania 2012	Serbia 2008	Slovenia 2008	Slovenia 2011	Macedonia 2008	Kosovo 2008	SEE[a] 2008	WE[b] 2008	CEE[c] 2008	FSU[d] 2008
Gender (men)	1.16	0.99	1.12	0.98	0.96	1.56*	1.04	1.32	0.79	0.64**	1.75***	1.01	1.14**	0.88***	1.08	1.09
Age 50+ (ref.)	–	–	–	–	–	–		–	–	–	–	–	–	–	–	–
18–29	0.94	1.29	0.77	1.19	1.54*	0.70	1.39	1.22	1.53	0.84	0.64*	0.88	1.16*	0.72***	0.87	0.55***
30–49	0.80	1.07	0.96	1.42*	0.96	1.33	1.19	0.98	1.46*	1.43	0.81	1.11	1.16**	0.97	1.01	0.82*
Level of education	1.10	1.18*	1.33**	1.08	1.04	1.31**	1.32***	1.13	1.38***	1.27***	1.01	1.21**	1.17***	1.16***	1.04	1.06
Household income	1.12*	1.19*	1.24*	0.99	1.34**	1.12*	0.99	1.02	1.07	0.88**	1.14*	1.09	1.14***	1.07***	1.07**	0.94*
Size of locality	1.01	1.07*	0.97	1.12***	1.14**	0.94	1.13**	1.09**	1.03	1.01	1.17***	1.24***	1.07***	0.99	1.02	1.05***
Student	1.00	3.26***	1.54	1.89*	1.66	2.07	1.14	1.46	1.99*	2.85**	1.25	0.78	1.48***	1.16*	0.79	1.01
Employed	1.26	1.64**	1.76*	1.02	1.34	1.63*	1.22	1.24	1.45*	1.51*	1.08	1.35	1.18**	1.16***	0.95	1.23**
Trade unionist	0.59	1.11	1.63	1.71*	2.76**	1.31	2.30**	1.45	1.12	1.16	2.37**	0.42*	1.10	1.18***	1.62***	0.95
Political party member	1.47	1.70	4.53***	1.29	2.02*	1.53	0.83	2.19**	1.75	0.99	1.67*	1.05	1.51***	1.20*	1.25	1.93***
Civil society member	3.29***	1.83**	1.44	1.25	1.08	1.60*	2.09***	1.21	1.41*	1.35	1.37*	1.58*	1.56***	1.54***	1.71***	1.37***
Frequency of church attendance	1.00	1.06	0.98	1.03	1.11*	0.98	0.98	1.03	0.99	1.06	0.96	0.99	1.03*	0.94***	1.05***	1.03
Political discussion	1.99**	0.84	1.00	1.38*	1.22	1.47	NA	1.49*	1.41*	NA	0.93	1.04	1.20***	1.27***	1.03	1.37**
Scale of trust in other people	0.96	1.01	1.02	1.02	0.99	1.12**	1.01	1.02	1.04	1.05	1.00	1.02	1.02**	1.04***	1.01	0.97*
Index of immigration tolerance	0.99	0.99**	1.01	1.00	0.99*	0.98**	0.84	1.00	1.00	0.82	0.99**	1.02**	0.99***	1.00	1.00	1.00
Index of lifestyle tolerance	1.05***	1.05***	1.02	1.04***	1.02*	1.01	1.02	1.02	1.05***	0.60	1.01	1.03*	1.02***	1.03***	1.04***	1.02**
Scale of gender role traditionalism	0.73**	0.82*	0.74*	0.85	0.96	0.69**	0.93	1.06	1.03	0.80	0.96	1.31***	0.92**	0.87***	0.87***	1.10**
Index of post-materialism	1.25	0.96	1.28	1.05	1.61**	1.97***	1.35	0.97	0.95	1.17	0.77*	1.08	1.09*	1.15***	1.27***	1.22**
Cosmopolitan sense of belonging	1.15	1.57	1.00	1.12	1.55	1.88	1.33	1.74**	1.09	1.31	0.95	3.22***	1.52***	1.00	0.93	1.31*

		1	2	3	4	5	6	7	8	9	10	11	12	13	14	15	16
Index of inclusive views on nationality		0.95	1.06**	1.14**	1.01	0.97	1.08*	NA	1.10***	1.01	NA	1.06*	1.12***	1.06***	1.03***	1.01	0.99
Scale of opposition to social change		1.28	1.24	0.61*	0.65**	0.65*	1.26	NA	0.89	0.96	NA	1.06	0.62**	0.86**	0.84***	0.89	0.88
Ideological self-placement on the Left-Right scale	*Centre (ref.)*	–	–	–	–	–	–	–	–	–	–	–	–	–	–	–	–
	Left	0.56**	1.71*	0.82	1.66**	1.22	1.56	1.70*	1.02	1.34	0.98	1.07	1.04	1.26**	1.41***	1.32***	0.97
	Right	0.66	1.79*	1.21	2.10***	2.62***	0.94	1.54	1.59*	1.38	0.60	1.08	1.59*	1.42**	1.08	1.34***	1.60***
Index of trust in political institutions		0.96	0.99	0.99	0.99	0.82***	1.08	0.97	1.03	0.95	0.91	1.02	1.01	1.02	0.97***	1.00	1.03*
Index of political socialisation within family		1.09**	0.95	1.04	1.04	1.03	0.97	NA	1.11***	1.02	NA	1.05*	1.05*	1.05***	1.05***	1.03**	1.04***
Scale of political interest		2.25***	1.44***	1.16	1.23**	1.97***	1.19	1.54***	1.31**	1.29**	1.29**	1.73***	1.57***	1.40***	1.35***	1.45***	1.42***
Index of democratic support		1.01	1.24***	1.06	1.01	1.01	0.98	1.19**	1.03	1.02	1.12*	0.96	1.02	1.06***	1.02**	1.24***	1.05**
Nagelkerke R^2		.331	.260	.204	.214	.262	.216	.246	.214	290	.223	.243	.282	.191	.257	.154	.082
N		1534	1512	1500	1498	1516	1489	1495	1512	1366	1055	1494	1601	15022	24980	10817	10528

Note: Data represent Exp (B) coefficients of a binomial logistic regression model with the dependent variable *Signing a petition* having two categories: 1 = Yes and 0 = No (non-petitioners is the reference category). Exp (B) coefficients are odds ratios: values higher than 1 represent a positive effect; values below 1 represent a negative effect of a predictor variable on the dependent variable, controlling for the effect of all other variables included in the statistical model. The statistical significance of coefficients is presented as: *p<0.05, **p<0.01, ***p<0.001. For nominal or ordinal predictors, the reference category's parameter is set to 0 because it is redundant. Example of reading data: *men*, compared to *women*, are 1.14 times more likely to have signed a petition, all other things being equal (see column 12, line 2 in this table).

[a] SEE here includes: Albania, Bosnia-Herzegovina, Bulgaria, Croatia, Montenegro, Romania, Serbia, Slovenia, FYR Macedonia and Kosovo.
[b] WE here includes: Austria, Belgium, Denmark, Finland, France, Malta, Germany, Greece, Iceland, Ireland, Italy, Luxembourg, Netherlands, Norway, Portugal, Spain, Sweden, Switzerland, Great Britain and Northern Ireland.
[c] CEE here includes: Czech Republic, Estonia, Hungary, Latvia, Lithuania, Poland and Slovak Republic.
[d] FSU here includes: Armenia, Azerbaijan, Belarus, Georgia, Moldova, Russia and Ukraine.

Data source: EVS 2008 for all SEE countries and WVS 2010–2014 (Inglehart et al. 2014b) for Romania (2012) and Slovenia (2011)

Table 8.4 Explaining participation in lawful demonstrations in post-communist SEE (Exp (B) logistic regression coefficients)

		Albania 2008	Bosnia Herz. 2008	Bulgaria 2008	Croatia 2008	Montenegro 2008	Romania 2008	Romania 2012	Serbia 2008	Slovenia 2008	Slovenia 2011	Macedonia 2008	Kosovo 2008	SEE[a] 2008	WE[b] 2008	CEE[c] 2008	FSU[d] 2008
Gender (men)		1.51*	1.84*	1.66*	1.17	1.24	1.51	2.16***	1.34	2.01***	1.14	2.10***	1.31*	1.58***	1.18***	1.18*	1.17*
Age	**50+ (ref)**																
	18–29	1.36	0.71	0.41	0.85	1.06	0.56	0.22***	0.87	0.52	0.51	0.66	1.04	1.06	0.91	0.44***	0.56***
	30–49	0.78	0.82	0.88	1.30	0.75	0.78	0.55*	0.93	1.29	0.71	0.68*	0.92	1.01	0.95	0.69***	0.69***
Level of education		1.05	0.99	1.39*	1.15	1.05	1.13	1.18*	1.16	0.96	1.10	1.09	1.04	1.11***	1.10***	1.19***	1.16***
Household income		1.20**	1.24	1.15	0.95	1.03	0.94	0.99	0.95	0.87*	0.88	1.01	0.95	0.97	0.99	0.93*	0.96
Size of locality		1.05	1.13*	0.89*	1.11*	1.06	0.99	1.17*	1.15***	1.06	1.11	1.14***	1.30***	1.12***	1.04***	1.14***	1.07***
Student		1.15	3.17**	6.70**	0.78	1.48	1.02	3.20*	2.65*	3.17*	5.63**	0.65	0.75	1.10	1.62***	1.06	0.95
Employed		1.32	1.23	2.35**	0.95	1.28	1.80*	1.25	1.83**	1.01	2.94**	1.06	1.32	1.14*	1.17***	0.98	0.99
Trade unionist		0.52	2.02	4.02***	4.04***	3.88***	1.93	1.20	1.27	1.88**	2.02*	2.59**	0.81	1.84***	1.26***	1.90***	1.11
Political party member		1.60	3.94***	2.40*	2.97*	0.71	2.39*	1.70	2.76***	1.93	0.43	1.67*	0.41*	1.42***	1.41***	1.32	2.12***
Civil society member		2.66***	2.04*	1.27	0.94	0.69	1.52	1.70*	1.87**	1.06	2.07**	1.25	2.18***	1.23**	1.32***	1.50***	1.13
Frequency of church attendance		1.07	1.02	1.22*	1.08	1.09	1.15	1.03	0.92	0.99	1.02	0.92	1.31***	1.10***	0.98**	0.98	1.02
Political discussion		2.75**	0.54*	0.97	1.32	1.00	1.05	NA	1.17	1.62*	NA	1.00	1.48*	1.24**	1.40***	1.43**	1.15
Scale of trust in other people		0.97	1.04	1.11*	0.99	1.04	1.08	1.03	1.01	1.10*	0.96	1.00	0.96	1.01	0.97***	1.04*	1.02
Index of immigration tolerance		1.02	1.00	0.98	0.99	1.00	1.00	0.95	1.00	1.01	0.91	0.98***	0.98***	0.98***	1.01***	1.00	1.00
Index of lifestyle tolerance		0.99	0.99	1.03	1.04*	0.98	0.98	1.01	1.04*	1.04*	0.99	1.02	0.99	1.00	1.02***	1.00	1.01*
Scale of gender role traditionalism		0.85	1.13	0.99	0.71	0.96	0.89	0.98	0.93	0.83	0.91	0.94	1.21**	1.02	1.02	1.00	0.98
Index of post-materialism		1.15	1.40	1.29	1.13	1.78**	1.29	1.31	0.98	1.29	1.46	0.97	0.85	1.19***	1.13***	1.45***	1.32***
Cosmopolitan sense of belonging		0.81	1.45	1.08	1.07	1.32	1.76	1.83**	1.68*	1.37	1.01	1.18	2.71***	1.72***	1.16**	1.09	1.44**
Index of inclusive views on nationality		0.97	1.15***	1.05	1.02	0.98	1.17**	NA	1.01	1.00	NA	1.03	1.05	1.05***	1.04***	1.02	0.96**
Scale of opposition to social change		1.65*	0.98	0.55*	0.73	0.47***	1.36	NA	1.00	0.90	NA	0.94	0.79	0.93	0.76***	0.93	0.79**

Ideological self-placement on the Left-Right scale	*Centre (ref.)*																
	Left	0.85	1.96*	1.11	1.84*	1.78*	4.78***	1.38	1.17	1.33	0.95	2.22***	1.41	1.52***	2.33***	1.15	0.84
	Right	1.83*	1.43	1.61	1.40	2.43**	1.70	1.87**	1.76*	0.65	0.80	1.97***	1.71**	1.54***	0.78***	1.48***	1.47***
Index of trust in political institutions		0.96	1.04	0.79*	0.94	0.79***	0.98	1.02	0.93	0.93	0.99	0.96	0.93**	1.02	0.97***	0.89***	0.96**
Index of political socialisation within family		1.09*	1.00	1.06	1.01	1.09*	1.15**	NA	1.07*	1.05	NA	1.00	1.08**	1.08***	1.04***	1.05***	1.04**
Scale of political interest		1.97***	1.37*	1.66**	1.46**	2.02***	1.64***	1.53***	1.59***	1.26	1.75***	1.72***	1.20*	1.52***	1.41***	1.38***	1.49***
Index of democratic support		0.96	1.13	1.15*	1.09	0.91	1.08	1.01	1.17**	0.95	1.09	1.05	1.16***	1.09***	1.11***	1.03	1.08***
Nagelkerke R^2		.293	.189	.296	.192	.238	.251	.211	.284	.166	.151	.262	.268	.172	.229	.127	.106
N		1534	1512	1500	1498	1516	1489	1495	1512	1366	1055	1494	1601	15022	24980	10817	10528

Note: Data represent Exp (B) coefficients of a binomial logistic regression model with the dependent variable *Participation to lawful demonstrations* having two categories: 1 = Yes and 0 = No (non-demonstrators is the reference category). Exp (B) coefficients are odds ratios: values higher than 1 represent a positive effect; values below 1 represent a negative effect of a predictor variable on the dependent variable, controlling for the effect of all other variables included in the statistical model. The statistical significance of coefficients is presented as: *$p<0.05$, **$p<0.01$, ***$p<0.001$. For nominal or ordinal predictors, the reference category's parameter is set to 0 because it is redundant. Example of reading data: in Southeastern Europe (SEE), *men*, compared to *women*, are 1.58 times more likely to have attended a lawful demonstration, all other things being equal (see column 12, line 2 in this table).

[a] SEE here includes: Albania, Bosnia-Herzegovina, Bulgaria, Croatia, Montenegro, Romania, Serbia, Slovenia, FYR Macedonia and Kosovo.
[b] WE here includes: Austria, Belgium, Denmark, Finland, France, Malta, Germany, Greece, Iceland, Ireland, Italy, Luxembourg, Netherlands, Norway, Portugal, Spain, Sweden, Switzerland, Great Britain and Northern Ireland.
[c] CEE here includes: Czech Republic, Estonia, Hungary, Latvia, Lithuania, Poland and Slovak Republic.
[d] FSU here includes: Armenia, Azerbaijan, Belarus, Georgia, Moldova, Russia and Ukraine.

Data source: EVS 2008 for all SEE countries and WVS 2010–2014 (Inglehart et al. 2014b) for Romania (2012) and Slovenia (2011)

Table 8.5 The measures

Variable/Index	Measures and methods of recoding/building variables/indices	
	European Values Survey, wave 4, 2008	*World Values Survey, wave 6, 2010–2014*
Gender	1 = Male, 0 = Female	1 = Male, 0 = Female
Age	Recoded into three interval categories 1 = 18–29, 2 = 30–49, 3 = 50+	Recoded into three interval categories 1 = 18–29, 2 = 30–49, 3 = 50+
Level of education	Highest level of education attained by respondent. Missing values replaced with mean.	Highest level of education attained by respondent. Missing values replaced with mean.
Household income	Scale ranging from 1 to 12	Scale ranging from 1 to 10
Size of locality	Scale ranging from 1 to 8, i.e. 1 = under 2,000 to 8 = 500,000 and more	Scale ranging from 1 to 8, i.e. 1 = under 2,000 to 8 = 500,000 and more
Student	Dummy variable (recoded from v337): 1 = yes, 0 = no	Dummy variable (recoded from v229): 1 = yes, 0 = no
Employed	Dummy variable (recoded from v337): 1 = yes, 0 = no	Dummy variable (recoded from v229): 1 = yes, 0 = no
Trade unionist	Recoded variable (v13): 1 = yes, 0 = no	Recoded variable (v28): 1 = yes, 0 = no
Political party member	Recoded variable (v14): 1 = yes, 0 = no	Recoded variable (v29): 1 = yes, 0 = no
Civil society member	Recoded variable for membership in at least one CSO (v10–12, v15–20): 1 = yes, 0 = no	Recoded variable for membership in at least one CSO (v25–27, v30–35): 1 = yes, 0 = no
Frequency of church attendance	v109 scale ranging from 1 (more than once a week) to 7 (never)	v145 scale ranging from 1 (more than once a week) to 7 (never)
Political discussion	Recoded variable for engagement in political discussions with friends (v7): 1 = yes, 0 = no	Not asked
Scale of trust in other people	Scale ranging from 1 = 'Most people would try to take advantage of me' to 10 = 'Most people would try to be fair' (v63). Missing values replaced with country mean.	Scale ranging from 1 = 'People would try to take advantage of you' to 10 = 'People would try to be fair' (v56). Missing values replaced with country mean.
Index/Scale of immigration tolerance	Additive index based on variables v268–272, and v274–275. Cronbach's Alpha = 0.861	v46 'When jobs are scarce, employers should give priority to people of this country over immigrants': 1 = agree, 2 = neither, 3 = disagree

Variable/Index	Measures and methods of recoding/building variables/indices	
	European Values Survey, wave 4, 2008	*World Values Survey, wave 6, 2010–2014*
Index of lifestyle tolerance	Additive index based on variables v242–244 regarding the degree to which homosexuality, abortion and divorce are justifiable	Additive index based on variables v203–205 regarding the degree to which homosexuality, abortion and divorce are justifiable
Scale of gender role traditionalism	v103, 'When jobs are scarce, men have more right to a job than women': 1 = disagree, 2 = neither, 3 = agree	v45, 'When jobs are scarce, men should have more right to a job than women': 1 = disagree, 2 = neither, 3 = agree
Index of post-materialism	1 = Materialist, 2 = Mixed, 3 = Post-materialist	1 = Materialist, 2 = Mixed, 3 = Post-materialist
Cosmopolitan sense of belonging	The feeling of belonging to the world (v253): 1 = yes, 0 = no	'I see myself as a world citizen' (v212): 1 = yes, 0 = no
Index of inclusive views on nationality	Additive index based on scores from variables v276, v278, v279, v280	Not asked
Scale of opposition to social change	v200, 1 = 'The entire way our society is organised must be radically changed by revolutionary action'; 2 = 'Our society must be gradually changed by reforms'; 3 = 'Our present society must be valiantly defended against all changes'	Not asked
Ideological self-positioning on the Left-Right scale	Recoded variable (v193): 1 = Left, 2 = Right, 3 = Centre	Recoded variable (v95): 1 = Left, 2 = Right, 3 = Centre
Index of trust in political institutions	Additive index measuring trust in national government, parties and parliament (v211, v221, v222 reverse coded)	Additive index measuring trust in national government, parties and parliament (v115, v116, v117 reverse coded)
Index of political socialisation within family	Additive index based on reversed scores from variables v361, v362, v365, v366	Not asked
Scale of political interest	Recoded variable (v186): 'How interested are you in politics?' 1 = not at all, 2 = not very interested, 3 = somewhat interested, 4 = very interested	Recoded variable (v84): 'How interested are you in politics?' 1 = not at all, 2 = not very interested, 3 = somewhat interested, 4 = very interested
Index of democratic support	Additive index based on v225–228 (scores reversed)	Additive index based on v127–130 (scores reversed)

9 The international context of mass political unrest in the Balkans – conceptual issues and perspectives

Mark Kramer

Introduction

This chapter draws on relevant bodies of literature in political science, sociology and economics to explore how the calculations and efforts of anti-regime protesters can be influenced by external actors. The chapter focuses in particular on the impact of external actors on mass political protests in Bulgaria, Romania and Turkey in 2013 – protests that were part of a wave of unrest in the Balkans that year.[1] The external actors who influenced the protests in one way or another included foreign governments, foreign media outlets, international organisations, transnational movements, foreign individuals and groups, and other entities. Some of them affected the protests only inadvertently, without deliberately setting out to do so. Others took steps that were bound to instigate or fuel protests, and still others sought to prevent or curb unrest. The bodies of theoretical literature discussing these topics share some important characteristics, particularly their focus on mass unrest and collective action, but in other respects, they diverge. This chapter distils from the various strands of literature the themes that are most helpful in understanding the impact of external actors on mass political protests in Bulgaria, Romania and Turkey.

Throughout the chapter, I use the terms 'protesters', 'challengers' and 'insurgents' interchangeably for the most part. This is not because protesters necessarily perceive themselves as rebelling against the entire system. In most cases, protesters focus only on a particular grievance or set of grievances and seek 'within-system' redress of those grievances, usually by non-violent means. Nonetheless, the terms 'insurgents' and 'challengers' are widely used in the contentious politics literature because, under some circumstances, protesters can evolve into rebels and insurgents even if they do not start out that way. For example, in some of the republics of the USSR in the late 1980s and early 1990s, newly formed protest movements that had initially focused solely on environmental and ecological grievances soon developed into radical separatist movements that sought to exit from the Soviet system, rather than work within it.

To be sure, political protests are very common, whereas full-scale rebellion is relatively rare. The likelihood that any particular protest will evolve into a rebellion is minuscule. Indeed, up to a point, protest can actually help to bolster, rather

The international context of mass political unrest in the Balkans 159

than destabilise, an authoritarian regime. In China, for example, tens of thousands of protests have occurred over the past several years, especially against local officials (see O'Brien 2008; Cai 2010; Tang 2016: 100–117). But these protests, far from threatening the communist dictatorship in Beijing, have served as a kind of 'safety valve' that dissipates popular discontent and helps to keep any kind of larger movement from arising that would be directed against the communist regime itself. The central authorities have skilfully used the local protests to their advantage, cracking down on egregious local cases of corruption and thus appearing to be the 'saviour' to which discontented people in the countryside can and must turn. The central authorities also have pursued a divide-and-rule strategy, playing the localities off against each other. The high incidence of protest in the Chinese countryside has thus, ironically, helped to strengthen the communist dictatorship. When peasants in China become profoundly dissatisfied with corrupt and abusive local officials, they look to the communist authorities in Beijing to set things right.[2]

Nonetheless, in using the terms 'insurgents' or 'challengers' to refer to protesters, as is commonly done in the literature on contentious politics, I do not mean to imply that a political protest in a Balkan country, or even a spate of protests as in 2013, are likely to evolve into full-scale rebellions against the governments. One aim of this chapter, in fact, is to determine under what conditions the people who collectively take part in such protests – whether described as 'protesters', 'challengers' or 'insurgents' – potentially could develop into a larger movement that would destabilise the regime and cause wider social and political turmoil. The specific task of the chapter is to draw on relevant bodies of literature in political science and sociology to explore how the calculations and efforts of insurgents are likely to be influenced by external actors.

Until recently, most of the contentious politics literature omitted the international context or came close to doing so.[3] Tilly's (1978) seminal work *From Mobilization to Revolution*, published in 1978, treats internal upheavals as mostly a self-contained phenomenon influenced only indirectly, if at all, by the international environment. Lichbach's (1995) acclaimed *The Rebel's Dilemma*, a 500-page rational-choice analysis of the interactions between rebels and the ruling authorities, fails to consider how the decisions and actions of participants on both sides are affected by foreign actors (see also Lichbach 1998). An influential essay by McAdam, Tarrow and Tilly (1997), proposing 'an integrated perspective on social movements and revolution', almost totally excludes the international dimension of mass protest within particular societies. As Tarrow (1999: 3) pointed out two years later, 'much of the work [in the literature on contentious politics] has been cordially indifferent to what happens beyond the water's edge until quite recently'.

The separate but related literature on ethnic and civil warfare has tended to pay greater attention to the international context, but even in this literature, the impact of external actors on internal conflicts has often been neglected. Although case studies of individual ethnic or civil conflicts touched on the role of foreign states in supporting one side or the other, no real effort was made until recently

160   *Mark Kramer*

to study this phenomenon or other aspects of the external environment in a more systematic, theoretical way. That gap has been at least partly filled over the past 15–20 years with the publication of theoretical works on such topics as interstate signalling and the outbreak and duration of internal conflicts, the 'marketing of rebellion' by insurgent groups to enlist foreign support, the 'boomerang effect' as domestic actors try to gain the cooperation of transnational movements in promoting their cause, and the impact of various global forces on separatist and national self-determination movements (see Bob 2006; Carment et al. 2006; Thyne 2009). A comparative study of armed internal conflicts published in 2006, which noted that most scholars in the field had focused almost exclusively on domestic actors, emphasised that 'the global dimension is a critical component [of the insurgent movements] and must be factored into the analysis of contemporary internal conflicts' (Fitzgerald et al. 2006: 247). Much the same is true about the study of non-violent protest movements and collective action. A few scholars, such as Doug McAdam, had earlier taken at least some account of the role of foreign actors and cross-country influences in political protest movements, but even these scholars rarely ascribed great importance to the external environment (see McAdam and Rucht 1993). Only in recent years has the international dimension come to play a much more salient role in the literature on contentious politics.

Although the discussion here of the role of external actors in domestic protests and conflicts is general and somewhat abstract, the chapter offers tangible illustrations and scenarios relevant to Bulgaria, Turkey, Romania, and Ukraine. The framing of protests in foreign media coverage, the support offered by transnational groups and organisations, the spill-over effect from protests in one country into neighbouring countries, the inspiration protesters can gain from unrest overseas, and the facilitating role of diaspora communities are among the many ways the international environment can affect protest movements – in some cases, fuelling and supporting protests and spurring them on, and in other cases, helping to deter unrest or quell it wherever it occurs.

Framing of political protests by foreign media

Studies in numerous fields, such as contentious politics, social movements and mass communications, have long stressed the singular role of the mass media in framing the goals and activities of protest movements or of combatants in an ethnic or civil conflict (see Entman and Rojecki 1993; McLeod and Hertog 1998). Entman (1993: 52) has pointed out that 'to frame is to select some aspects of a perceived reality and make them more salient in a communicating text, in such a way as to promote a particular problem definition, causal interpretation, moral evaluation, and/or treatment recommendation for the item described'.

The media's framing of protests, strikes and other contentious action can decisively shape public perceptions of the movements' grievances, helping to provoke responses by governments, non-governmental organisations (NGOs) and individuals. Depictions in the media also can affect the protesters themselves, helping to foster what McAdam (1995: 227–230, 1999) describes as 'insurgent

The international context of mass political unrest in the Balkans   161

consciousness'. In some cases, the media's framing of grievances and of efforts by protesters to remedy them can generate new recruits for the protest groups, but in other cases, it might discredit the groups, deter people from joining, and cause existing members to leave. If the perceived grievances are severe and remedies are non-existent, the media's framing might cause key groups and individuals to conclude that the existing order is illegitimate (and indeed intolerable) and the only way to change it fundamentally is through collective rebellious action.

In societies in which the mass media are not entirely state-controlled, the insurgents do their best to sway the media's framing of events, trying to ensure that it overlaps with their own (Oliver and Maney 2000). During what Tarrow (1998: 154) described as a 'protest cycle' (an extended phase in which protest spreads from active segments of society to previously dormant segments), the rebels' efforts to produce 'new or transformed collective action frames' become particularly intense. To the extent that this process tends to radicalise the 'master frame' of the protests as reflected in the mass media, it narrows the leeway for moderates and increasingly polarises the society between radicals on the one hand and the regime and its supporters on the other.[4] If the media's framing of the situation shifts steadily in favour of the radicals, this is almost always a tell-tale sign that the regime is losing crucial support at high levels. The authorities from then on will have a much more difficult time trying to avoid far-reaching concessions or even outright capitulation to the rebels.

Most of the literature concerning the mass media's framing of protests has focused on the media within the society in which the protests or conflicts are taking place. But the basic conceptions can be extended to encompass foreign media as well.[5] The foreign media's framing is especially important when protests arise in countries in which the mass media are either state-controlled or heavily influenced by the state. If political protests erupt, the ruling authorities will undoubtedly seek to restrict citizens' access to foreign media coverage of the unrest, but in only a few pervasively tyrannical countries like North Korea can the regime completely deny access to foreign media. Although press freedom in Turkey has been highly problematic during the prolonged tenure of Recep Tayyip Erdoğan (initially as prime minister and then as president), the Turkish government has not emulated China and Iran in permanently blocking access to popular Internet content, including all Google-related products. Similarly in Bulgaria and Romania, despite the extensive influence the state often wields over the mass media (particularly television), access to foreign media coverage has generally been limited only by financial and linguistic considerations, not by overt censorship. Although the percentage of regular Internet users in the Balkan countries until recently was a good deal lower than in Western Europe, and linguistic obstacles further circumscribe the reach of foreign media in both countries, elites and many ordinary citizens in these countries have at least some exposure to foreign media. Hence, they can gauge how protests in their own countries are interpreted by the foreign media.

The most important foreign media outlets for Bulgaria and Romania are those in major Western countries, especially the United States, Germany, Great Britain

162 *Mark Kramer*

and France, and also (for Bulgaria) media outlets in Russia. Western television and wire services and Russian television are the dominant sources of external coverage of internal protest events in Bulgaria. The salient role of Western media outlets is replicated around the world. Even in highly authoritarian countries like Iran, the state-controlled media often find themselves drawing on coverage in the Western media, which is then re-framed in accordance with the preferences of the Iranian authorities (Motamed-Nejad et al. 1992: 99–103). The influence of Russian television in Bulgaria tends to be much more limited than the influence of Western media, but in certain instances, the Russian media's coverage of protest events in Bulgaria (such as the anti-fracking demonstrations funded by Gazprom) can reach sizable numbers of Bulgarians via a cable or satellite link or over the Internet.

In Turkey and other Balkan countries with sizable Muslim populations, the most important foreign media outlets are the Balkans service of Al Jazeera (a branch of Al Jazeera created in 2011, with headquarters in Sarajevo) and Western television and wire services. Because of Turkey's size and importance in the Islamic world, Al Jazeera has tried to attract large numbers of viewers in Turkey and has achieved some success in major urban areas, but the reach of the station has been limited. The network launched an Al Jazeera Türk station in 2010, but the station never reached full operational status before it and its associated website were ended in May 2017. With a fully operating Turkish service, Al Jazeera would have the potential for even greater influence during future protests in Turkey. Western media and wire services, including CNN Türk (started in 1999), also enjoy considerable influence in Turkey with both elites and the wider public, but under pressure from the Turkish authorities, CNN Türk eschewed coverage of the Gezi Park protests in May–June 2013 (Fleishman 2013). However, CNN International, received by many households in Turkey, did cover the protests extensively, filling in the conspicuous gap left by CNN Türk. Al Jazeera Balkans, which broadcasts in Bosnian, Serbian and Croatian, has attained a large following in Bosnia-Herzegovina (where it is routinely available via cable) and other former Yugoslav countries, and Al Jazeera has also attracted viewers in Albania and Bulgaria.

The role of foreign mass media in framing grievances, protests and violent conflicts in Bulgaria, Romania and Turkey can produce diverse effects. When the foreign media decide what to cover, how much salience to give it and what to exclude, their framing of the events often departs from the local government's own interpretation. This pattern was conspicuous with foreign television and press coverage of mass protests in 2013. The Erdoğan government repeatedly objected to foreign coverage of the surge of political unrest in Turkey. Because links to the coverage were spread far and wide in Turkey by social network sites and web portals that rebroadcast foreign media, official attempts to keep people from learning about the protests were circumvented.

Protesters and government officials alike in Bulgaria, Romania and Turkey have vied to influence the foreign media's portrayal of the unrest in their countries. The conflicting media frames of the protests in the three countries in 2013

The international context of mass political unrest in the Balkans 163

reflected underlying divergences of views about the nature of the local governments and opposition forces, and the appropriate repertoires of contention. Because foreign media coverage is usually crucial in determining the level of external support for (or opposition to) mass unrest in a given country, the way protests are framed by foreign media is seen as especially important – and thus becomes a matter of intense contestation – in countries in which external actors matter most or at least are perceived to matter. Erdoğan himself acknowledged as much when he denounced Twitter at the height of the Gezi Park protests, sparking vigorous efforts by Twitter users in Turkey to guard against a potential crackdown and ensure that service would continue without interruption.

Transnational assistance for contentious action

Government agencies, NGOs and social groups in the United States and the EU have provided a good deal of training and assistance to NGOs, informal groups and individuals in Bulgaria, Romania and Turkey. Some of this training and assistance could potentially be of use to anti-government protesters during periods of unrest. For example, assistance furnished by Western advocacy groups and some Western NGOs has specifically included training in the conduct of non-violent protests, the recruitment and mobilisation of protesters, and the framing of grievances and goals. When I interviewed protest organisers in both Bulgaria and Turkey in mid-2013 and again in December 2013, they emphasised the importance of their receipt of this aid.

The theoretical literature pertaining to this aspect of external influences on domestic protest movements has encompassed several issues, including the role of transnational advocacy networks (TANs) in facilitating collective protest action within countries and in creating a 'boomerang effect' (when citizens of State A appeal through a TAN to citizens of States B and C, urging them to demand that their governments as well as international organisations pressure the government of State A to respect human rights and adopt democratic reforms), the impact of international norms on the framing and conduct of political protests, the role of external 'norm entrepreneurs' (individuals, groups, organisations or governments that promote normative concepts such as human rights, democracy and political freedom) in the development and outlook of indigenous protest movements, the extent to which transnational protest groups have eroded the sovereignty of states, and the way major recipients of transnational assistance are chosen or try to get chosen ('transnational marketing' and the 'marketing of rebellion').

The literature on TANs traces its genealogy back to concepts developed by scholars such as James Rosenau, Robert Keohane and Joseph Nye in the 1960s and 1970s regarding linkages in international politics, international interdependence and transnational relations (Rosenau 1969; Keohane and Nye 1973, 1979). However, the main theoretical works that fully laid out the concept did not begin to appear until the 1990s, inspired by the wave of democratisation engulfing countries in Latin America, East Asia and Eastern Europe in the 1980s and early 1990s and the subsequent proliferation of international NGOs.[6]

164　*Mark Kramer*

In seeking to elucidate the spread of democracy to formerly autocratic states and the rapidly growing salience of international NGOs on the world scene, numerous scholars such as Margaret Keck, Thomas Risse, Kathryn Sikkink and Martha Finnemore have highlighted what they see as the crucial role of TANs, which they define as 'networks of individuals in nongovernmental organizations [who] conduct substantial transnational campaigns to persuade others of the importance and value of norms' (Sikkink 1998: 519; see also Della Porta and Mattoni 2014). A TAN, as they characterise it, includes all 'relevant actors working internationally on an issue, who are bound together by shared values, a common discourse, and dense exchanges of information and services' (see Keck and Sikkink 1998: 2; Keck and Sikkink 1999: 89; Risse and Sikkink 1999: 18). The wave of democratic transformation in the 1980s and 1990s, they claim, was greatly expedited by networks of human rights advocates who organised protests and brought pressure to bear 'from below' and 'from above' on authoritarian regimes (Keck and Sikkink 1998: 79–120, Sikkink 1998). The work conducted through these networks, as they see it, inhibited efforts by authoritarian rulers to continue resorting to mass repression.

Evangelista (1999) has made a similar argument about the role of transnational anti-nuclear movements in contributing to the end of the Cold War. These activists, Evangelista contends, generated a political climate in which the two superpowers felt under pressure both at home and abroad to begin significantly reducing their nuclear arsenals. This trend, as he depicts it, eventually permitted a sharp break with the past, resulting in far-reaching nuclear arms control treaties.

The literature on TANs reflects diverse outlooks and approaches to the topic, but the most useful strands of the literature show, if only implicitly, how transnational activism affects and is affected by domestic political opportunity structures (POS). In the 1960s and 1970s, the literature on political protest movements and collective action depicted grievances and relative deprivation as the major stimuli, but over the past 35 years (especially after the appearance of Tilly's *From Mobilization to Revolution*), most scholars studying the origins, nature and actions of political protest movements have come to rely on a political process framework emphasising POS.

Even though the POS approach has been criticised on several grounds – that it has tended to be more useful in understanding the emergence of protest movements than in tracing their subsequent evolution and activities, that it has been too static in its characterisation of protest groups, that it has not always facilitated comparisons of political protests with other forms of mass upheavals – the framework has been adapted over the years to take account of many of the critiques.[7] At least a few problems remain, but cumulative research over some three decades has underscored the fruitfulness of the political process theory, which focuses on changes in opportunities available to formal and informal groups as they struggle for influence on the issues of greatest concern to them. Most of the recent literature on contentious politics has depicted POS not as unified entities (the way they were characterised in the early work) but as varying in accordance with the specific issues raised by each social movement (Kriesi et al. 1995). In some circumstances, the structure of political opportunities could remain relatively uniform,

The international context of mass political unrest in the Balkans   165

but much of the time, its contours are at least partly contingent on the political sensitivity of the issues in question.

From at least some of the TAN literature, one can infer how advocacy networks focusing on human rights and democratisation have helped social movements in the Balkans overcome obstacles or promote change in their own structures of political opportunities, giving them greater leeway to vie for influence. Keck and Sikkink (1998: 2–3) write:

> [A]dvocacy networks often reach beyond policy change to advocate and insti-gate changes in the institutional and principled basis of international interac-tions. [. . .] What is novel in these networks is the ability of nontraditional international actors to mobilize information strategically to help create new issues and categories and to persuade, pressure, and gain leverage over much more powerful organizations and governments. Activists in networks try not only to influence policy outcomes, but to transform the terms and nature of the debate. [. . .] Simultaneously strategic and principled actors, they 'frame' issues to make them comprehensible to target audiences, to attract attention and encourage action, and to 'fit' with favorable institutional venues. Net-work actors bring new ideas, norms, and discourses into policy debates, and serve as sources of information and testimony.

According to Smith's (2002) surveys of TAN activists, specifically those focusing on human rights and environmental issues, the networks have three chief goals when dealing with affiliate groups. First, they frame the issues and correspond-ing pressure tactics and protest actions in a way that is relevant to local affiliates but also makes clear that many others around the world share the same concerns and face the same problems. This is largely equivalent to what McAdam, Tarrow and Tilly (1997: 142) have termed 'brokerage' – the 'linking of two or more cur-rently unconnected social sites by a unit that mediates their relations with each other and/or with yet another [social] site'. Second, the TANs try to convince local affiliates that they can influence global political events relating to the issues of greatest concern to them. Third, the network organisers stress to local groups that their own efforts will be matched and reinforced by others around the world, another aspect of 'brokerage'. In short, by 'relating the immediate concerns of potential movement supporters to global level agendas and political processes', the human rights TANs, according to Smith (2002: 520), are striving to encourage 'activists to develop a shared language of resistance' along with common 'objec-tives, collective action strategies, and symbols'.

These themes come together in the reworking of the TAN framework under-taken by Sidney Tarrow and others in accordance with the political process model. Tarrow (2001) had been dissatisfied with some of the early TAN literature, which gave the impression that a 'global civil society' was forming and an untethered 'cosmopolitan' identity was emerging among supporters of local and national protest movements, who supposedly were coming to identify mainly with trans-national protest networks acting against globalisation. Tarrow began challenging

166   *Mark Kramer*

some of the TAN arguments in the late 1990s and then put forth his own conception of transnational contentious politics in a series of publications, culminating in his wide-ranging 2005 book, *The New Transnational Activism*. In the book, he views TANs through the prism of the political process theory, arguing that the networks consist mainly of 'actors whose interests continue to be framed by domestic political opportunities and constraints' and whose transnational activism 'is shaped by changes in the opportunity structure of international politics', not by globalisation:

> Acting collectively requires activists to marshal resources, become aware of and seize opportunities, frame their demands in ways that enable them to join with others, and identify common targets. If these thresholds constitute barriers in domestic politics, they are even higher when people mobilize across borders. Globalization is not sufficient to explain when people will engage in contentious collective action and when they will not.
>
> (Tarrow 2005: 6)

Tarrow argues that globalisation serves only as 'a source of interest, ideology, and grievances' (Tarrow, 2005: 19) for some transnational activists but does not provide the institutional framework within which transnational activism occurs. Grievances and frustration alone are not enough to give rise to social movements and collective protest actions. Tarrow sees 'internationalisation' as the phenomenon that actually 'constrains and creates opportunities for citizens to engage in collective action' on a transnational scale. The term *internationalisation* in his scheme encompasses an 'increasing horizontal density of relations across states, governmental officials, and nonstate actors' and a simultaneous proliferation of 'vertical links among the subnational, national, and international levels', which together have given rise to 'an enhanced formal and informal structure that invites transnational activism and facilitates the formation of networks of nonstate, state, and transnational actors' (Tarrow 2005: 25, 42–43). Nearly all transnational activists, Tarrow argues, are 'rooted' in their local and national POS, which determine when and where they can most easily organise mass protests that are of direct relevance to their members' concerns. Hence, the large majority of 'cosmopolitan' activists still identify first and foremost with their local and national 'roots'.

Tarrow (2005) devises a taxonomy of three sets of paired 'processes of transnational contention': (1) global framing and internalisation; (2) diffusion and scale shift; and (3) externalisation and transnational coalition formation. The first set consists of the mobilisation of global symbols and themes 'to frame domestic conflicts'. The second set refers to two ways of connecting domestic and international political issues – one involving a 'transfer of claims or forms of contention' from one setting to another (diffusion), and the other involving the shift of collective action from one level – domestic or international – to the other (scale shift). The third pair of processes refers to the 'vertical projection of domestic claims onto international institutions or foreign actors' (externalisation) and the 'horizontal

The international context of mass political unrest in the Balkans   167

formation of common networks among actors from different countries with similar claims' (transnational coalition formation) (Tarrow 2005: 32). Tarrow (2005: 209) avers that even if we take account of the importance of these six processes of transnational contention, the reality is that transnational activists still live in a 'state-centered world'.

The concept of a 'boomerang effect', as developed by Keck and Sikkink, stipulates that activists in State A who are blocked from making claims against their own government are able to bring pressure to bear on the government indirectly by enlisting support from activists in States B and C, who use 'informational pathways' (pressure campaigns by advocacy groups and individuals) to spur their own governments and international organisations to demand that the government of State A change its behaviour (Keck and Sikkink 1998: 13–14). Numerous international human rights NGOs such as Human Rights Watch, Amnesty International and Global Rights have had affiliates in the Balkans and Turkey. These affiliates are usually unable to pressure their own governments directly, but can seek the assistance of the larger human rights network to try to influence the governments. This concept has become especially germane to Turkey amid the sweeping crackdown against scholars, journalists and other intellectuals in the wake of the failed coup in 2016.

Tarrow (2005: 145–160) expands the concept of a boomerang effect to include two other routes of externalisation: institutional access and direct action. This expanded conception is particularly useful in analysing the boomerang effect in Bulgaria, Romania and Turkey with regard to the European Court of Human Rights (ECHR), which has played an important role not only in dealing with cases of rights violations of individuals from ethnic minorities in these countries but also as a potential outlet of last resort for the adjudication of cases relating to mass protests.

Clifford Bob (2006) recasts the boomerang concept as he explores how a few marginalised social groups (out of the vast number of such groups that exist) manage to gain external support for their struggle against their government. Like Tarrow, Bob (2006, 2010) is sceptical of accounts that depict a 'global civil society', and he convincingly argues that the real focus should be on the political 'marketing' strategies that enable a few select groups to enlist international support even as a multitude of other groups (equally or more deserving) fail to win backing and eventually cease to exist.

In a refreshingly clear-eyed take on transnational advocacy, Bob (2006) avers that insurgent groups' success in attracting external support stems not from need or merit but from savvy marketing and public relations techniques that can win over international NGOs and the international media. Insurgent marketers deliberately invoke ideological precepts and highlight certain grievances (real or otherwise) that are likely to appeal to the NGOs and media outlets whose support they seek. If the insurgents believe that violent struggle is the best way to gain attention and earn international support, they will be more inclined to engage in it. Bob (2006) shows that the international NGOs and foreign media often

168   *Mark Kramer*

have little interest in understanding the details of the local groups' struggles and instead are wont to re-frame the groups' objectives and actions to suit their own purposes. Often the movements that gain TAN support are the ones that already have substantial material and organisational resources at their disposal (and are therefore best able to embark on the sorts of projects and publicity campaigns that draw attention).

Bob's argument is fully consonant with the thesis put forward by Kuperman (2008) and other scholars regarding the 'moral hazard' of humanitarian intervention in the Balkans and elsewhere (Crawford and Kuperman 2006). This thesis suggests that an insurgent group might try to gain international military intervention on its behalf by stepping up its violence against government forces and thereby provoking grisly reprisals that can be 'marketed' as evidence of the cruelty inflicted on the local populace and as justification for outside humanitarian intervention. Repeated attacks launched by the Kosovo Liberation Army (KLA) against Serb positions in 1997–1999 and by separatist guerrillas in Darfur in 2006–2008 were deliberately aimed at prodding government forces into carrying out severe reprisals, which in turn (the insurgents hoped) would trigger external 'humanitarian' intervention. The KLA succeeded in this goal, whereas the Darfuri rebels did not.

Experience with mass protests in the Balkan countries underscores the complexities of the marketing of rebellion. In Turkey more so than in the other Balkan countries, the authorities over the past decade have taken steps to try to prevent indigenous human rights and pro-democracy NGOs from 'marketing' their work to TANs. Not only has Erdoğan castigated and cast aspersions on NGOs that receive foreign assistance, but the Turkish government has also erected a dense array of legal restrictions and penalties to deter many indigenous NGOs from having extensive contact with foreign activists. Erdoğan has curtailed Turkey's links with democratic countries in the European Union (EU) and established close ties with authoritarian rulers in Russia and elsewhere. Some activist groups in Turkey still receive foreign support, but they have to be constantly on their guard, lest their leaders or activists be accused of working against Turkey. Such tactics by the Erdoğan regime stifled the 'marketing' of protest groups in mid-2013.

Among the many virtues of Bob's marketing framework is the attention it gives, as does Tarrow's notion of three routes of 'externalisation', to international NGOs (and governments) as the vehicles that exert pressure on State A. Tarrow (2001: 15) maintains that an institutionalist approach illuminates how 'domestic activists can find one another, gain legitimacy, form collective identities, and go back to their countries empowered with alliances, common programs, and new repertoires of collective action'. The Turkish government has taken steps to ward off this pressure and thwart the participation of domestic groups in TANs, but future changes in domestic political opportunity structures could afford a larger role for transnational activism. Even now, when the main impact of transnational channels has been in facilitating individual rather than collective claims, the channels might become crucial in times of domestic political flux.

Diffusion of protests through external 'demonstration effects'

The international dimension of mass political unrest is brought out clearly in recent academic literature on the cross-national spread of social movements and collective action, the external diffusion of contentious repertoires, the reciprocal transfer of policies and institutions from core to periphery, and the potential for cross-border 'demonstration effects' from mass protests (Soule 2004; Weyland 2009; Kolins Givan et al. 2010). The importance of these topics has been repeatedly highlighted over the past three decades, especially by the upheavals in Eastern Europe and the USSR in 1989–1991, the 'coloured' revolutions in Serbia in 2000 and several former Soviet republics (Georgia, Ukraine, Kyrgyzstan) in 2003–2005, and the wave of turbulence in North Africa and the Middle East in 2011.

The concepts of 'diffusion', 'demonstration effects' and 'spill-over' have at times been used loosely or ambiguously in the literature, and it is therefore important to clarify them here. Diffusion occurs within countries as well as across borders, but the chief focus here is on *international* diffusion, which encompasses the spread of ideas, events, institutions, procedures, innovations, identities, customs or policies from one country to another, whether directly or indirectly. Specifically, international diffusion refers to a process whereby an event in State A (the adoption of an innovation, onset of a financial crisis, outbreak of ethnic unrest, etc.) affects the likelihood that a similar event will occur in State B. This process can be either planned or spontaneous, and the 'adopters' of a practice are not necessarily aware they are assimilating it from a 'source' abroad. The process of diffusion characterises many social phenomena, including the spread of mass political unrest and political turmoil from one country to another.

The probabilistic phrasing of this definition leaves open the possibility that the occurrence of an event in State A will reduce rather than increase the likelihood that a similar event will occur in State B – a point emphasised by Midlarsky (1970: 75) in an early study of international diffusion. In several articles on international diffusion published in the 1980s and 1990s, Most and Starr (1990: 394) likewise stressed the importance of considering 'negative diffusion' as well as 'positive diffusion', arguing that 'inhibitory effects [are] as exemplary of diffusion processes as various forms of emulation'. They acknowledged that negative diffusion is 'difficult to deal with because the researcher is placed in the awkward position of trying to analyse "events" that do not occur', but they stressed that 'it is [. . .] entirely plausible that such processes operate' (Most and Starr 1980: 933). Although my earlier work on the collapse of East European Communism and its impact on the USSR focused mainly on positive diffusion, I noted that inhibiting effects (or what I termed an 'anti-demonstration effect') at times played a crucial role (Kramer 2003, 2004, 2005).

Much of the theoretical and empirical literature on international diffusion (and diffusion in general) seeks to explain why and how it happens. Wejnert (2002: 300) has rightly pointed out that 'the manner of channeling information from an innovation's source to an adopter differs depending upon the innovation's consequences' and that 'different mechanisms of interaction between the source of

170　Mark Kramer

an innovation and an adopter result in diffusion processes that differ in nature'. The distinction rests on whether the consequences of the diffused phenomena are mainly public or private. Phenomena that have public consequences involve collective actors (governments, social movements, etc.) and public goods, or at least goods that affect large parts of society. Phenomena that have private consequences affect mainly the well-being of individuals or small private groups. The topics explored in this chapter – collective action, protest movements, political unrest and rebellion – are all clearly phenomena that have public consequences.

Sociologists and political scientists have proposed numerous explanations of the cross-border diffusion of these sorts of activities (and of others with public consequences). The explanations can be grouped into six broad categories that are likely to be relevant when analysing the potential diffusion of mass unrest in Eurasia:

(1) Rational learning (sometimes called 'lesson-drawing') whereby actors in one country observe events or policies in another country and modify their own behaviour and ideas accordingly (see Rose 2005; Evans 2006; Meseguer 2006). Individuals, groups or government organisations in State A may decide to emulate a successful tactic used in State B, or, conversely, avoid certain policies or practices that seem, on the basis of State B's experience, to be risky, ineffective or unduly costly to adopt. Most of the literature emphasises state policy, but the basic dynamic is just as relevant to protest movements, which can learn specific protest tactics or larger strategies from the experiences of their foreign counterparts. More fundamentally, the diffusion of collective protest can stem from 'demonstration effects' linked with a process of rational learning.

(2) Social constructivist notions of the spread of international norms through social mobilisation and social learning. From the social constructivist perspective, cross-border diffusion becomes possible when the collective identities of important actors in State A change in response to an international norm (a shared set of expectations about proper standards of behaviour and proper attitudes) (see Finnemore and Sikkink 2001; Hopf 2002; Wiener 2003). Once this identity change occurs, the norm can spread to State A either from the bottom up or from the top down, depending on the specific actors involved.[8] In the bottom-up version, which is of greater relevance to this chapter, diffusion occurs when non-state actors unite in support of the norm and are successful in pressuring government elites to comply with it. In the top-down version, diffusion occurs when high-level government officials themselves come to internalise the norms independently and modify State A's policies accordingly. Diffusion of political contention usually reflects the bottom-up spread of norms, as government elites come under pressure from protest movements to make policies conform with basic norms (e.g. racial equality, gender equality, freedom of speech). If over time the government elites come to internalise the norm fully, the process of diffusion no longer is merely a

The international context of mass political unrest in the Balkans 171

process of emulation or political pressure; instead, it involves a deeper social learning that transforms intersubjective understandings of the world.

(3) Spatial-diffusion models emphasising the importance of 'neighbourhood effects' (geographic proximity) in the spread of democratisation, which can be readily adapted to focus on the spread of collective protest action. Statistical analyses covering many decades of experience have shown that if State A is an authoritarian regime surrounded by democratising (or democratic) states and State Z is an authoritarian regime surrounded by non-democratic states, State A will be far more likely than State Z to undergo democratisation (Gleditsch 2002; Starr and Lindborg 2003; Doorenspleet 2004). The larger the number of democratic states in the 'neighbourhood', the greater the odds that State A will embark on democratic reforms. In principle, the spread of democracy will gradually encompass the whole of State A's neighbourhood. Although most advocates of this view have not clearly specified the mechanisms of diffusion, the notion seems to be that democracy will spread to neighbouring states through a demonstration effect and through deliberate actions taken by key actors in newly democratising states – either government elites or protest movements – to promote democracy in their 'neighbourhood'. At one time, geographic propinquity was crucial to facilitate communications between protest movements in State A and those in State B, but this factor is no longer as relevant in an era of wireless telecommunications and the Internet. Nevertheless, the unrest in the Arab world in 2011 and Southeastern Europe in 2013 suggests that other aspects of the spatial diffusion model, especially demonstration effects, do remain salient.

(4) Realist conceptions of a powerful state (or international organisation) that induces weaker states to embrace its own preferred policies or practices. The dominant state or organisation may do this by forcibly imposing its preferences on weaker states (as the Soviet Union did in Eastern Europe under Stalin) (Kramer 2013), demanding that certain policies be adopted as a quid pro quo for the provision of coveted 'goods' (as the US government and International Monetary Fund have done when setting conditions for foreign aid recipients, or as the EU has done when setting terms for prospective new members) (see Henderson 1999; Crawford 2001), serving as a focal point for the harmonisation of policies (as the United States has often done in key areas of commercial, transportation and financial regulation, and as the EU has done with regard to the monetary, social and fiscal policies of its member-states) (Bulmer et al. 2007; Dobbin et al. 2007; Kerber and Eckardt 2007), or establishing a hegemonic international order embodying the dominant state's preferred institutions and ideas, which are then adopted and come to be taken for granted by other states in the system (as the United States was able to do after World War II when it ensured that liberal capitalism became the basis of the global economic order with the exception of the Soviet bloc) (see Kil Lee and Strang 2003; Elkins and Simmons 2004; Jordana and Levi-Faur 2005). This line of thought is relevant to the diffusion of protest activity when strong

172   *Mark Kramer*

external actors are supporting contentious political movements against their national governments.

(5) Structural realist conceptions of a diffusion/emulative mechanism inherent in the competitive nature of international relations. In this depiction, states come to pursue similar military, economic and technological policies to prevent other states from gaining a military or economic edge (Waltz 1979: 76–77, 92, 127). The great powers, according to this school, will seek to deny advantages to their rivals and may even strive for military or economic superiority of their own.[9] Perhaps the best-known proponent of this view is Waltz (1979: 127), who has argued that 'contending states imitate the military innovations contrived by the country of greatest capability and ingenuity. And so the weapons of the major contenders, and even their strategies, begin to look much the same the world over'. Waltz's argument implies that even if some states might prefer, *ceteris paribus*, to go their own way, the competitive pressures of the international system induce them to emulate one another. This process is the international analogue of what Hannan and Freeman (1977) have described as the 'competitive isomorphism' of government and corporate organisations. In some instances, Waltz's notion could be relevant to the international diffusion of protest when governments are mindful of structural pressures in responding to collective action.

(6) Concrete spill-over from one state to another. Even without any process of emulation, learning or identity change, an event can diffuse from one state to another if the concrete by-products of the event spread either deliberately or inadvertently to neighbouring states. This dynamic has been cited as a possible reason for the diffusion of phenomena such as ethnic conflict (see Weiner 1996; Collier et al. 2003; Stedman and Tanner 2003). Violence between ethnic groups often produces outpourings of refugees from one or more of the warring groups. The flight of these refugees from State A to neighbouring State B can lead to ethnic imbalances and large congregations of displaced, angry people in State B, increasing the likelihood that ethnic conflict will occur there as well (Newland 1993). Similarly, some of the perpetrators of ethnic attacks in State A may pursue refugees across the border into State B, further increasing the chance that the sort of ethnic conflict under way in State A will be replicated in State B. This approach to diffusion is relevant to the spread of contentious politics in several respects, particularly in highlighting the potential for protesters in State A to travel to States B or C to help galvanise incipient protest movements in those neighbouring states or foment supportive action.

In addition to explaining how and why international diffusion occurs, scholars have highlighted numerous factors that, in their view, are conducive to the process. Among the circumstances that are thought to facilitate cross-border diffusion is extensive media coverage of innovative actions or events in foreign countries, such as the coverage of Mahatma Gandhi's campaign of non-violent protest (*satyagraha*) against the British presence in India. Rightly or wrongly, the tactics of

The international context of mass political unrest in the Balkans   173

satyagraha were depicted as having played a decisive role in spurring the British to pull out of India and grant it independence (Brown 2009). The US press coverage of the protests in India had a far-reaching impact on future civil rights leaders in the United States such as Martin Luther King, who adopted a similar approach in their own struggle for racial equality and an end to institutionalised racial segregation and discrimination (Chabot 2013). Rejecting the violence and murderous intimidation advocated by rival black leaders such as Elijah Muhammad and Malcolm X, King insisted on sticking to non-violent tactics even in the face of harsh repression from police and white segregationists in Alabama, Mississippi and other states across the American South.

Other circumstances that have been highlighted in the literature as contributors to cross-border diffusion from protest groups in State A to groups in State B include cultural and political similarities between the 'adopters' and 'sources'; use of the same (or a closely related) language in States A and B to facilitate the transmission and sharing of information; interpersonal ties between the adopters and sources; inexpensive means of direct communication between the protest groups; the outbreak of a political or economic crisis that creates opportunities for collective action and departures from existing policies; a decision-making structure that encourages (or at least does not impede) innovative policies and tactics; temporal contiguity; shared cultural understandings that a particular action is both effective and morally right to pursue; relatively low transaction costs involved in adopting an innovative approach; and direct encouragement by authoritative, trusted actors in either State A or B or, better yet, in both.

To the extent that diffusion is the most important factor in the emergence and cross-border spread of collective protest – as leading scholars in the field have argued in recent years (McAdam et al. 2001: 17–19; Tarrow 2005: 102–103; Myers and Oliver 2008) – the literature on this topic provides a valuable framework for understanding mass political unrest in the Balkans. Many of the factors that are seen as promoting international diffusion played an important role in the wave of 'coloured' unrest in the former USSR in 2003–2005 and the spread of mass protest in the Arab world in 2011. These same factors are present in the Balkans and helped fuel the protests there in 2013. If contentious politics remains a fact of life in the Balkans in the future, the process of diffusion is likely to be the chief means by which it spreads.

By the same token, the spread of protest from country to country can be abruptly halted through the use of merciless repression. If those who might engage in collective action in State A see that protesters in neighbouring States B and C are being met with ruthless violence, the 'anti-demonstration effect' will tend to deter contentious action in State A. This counter-diffusion was evident after the brutal crackdown in Andijon in May 2005 and again with the atrocities perpetrated by the Libyan and Syrian regimes in 2011, which spawned devastating civil wars in those countries and largely put an end to the diffusion of protest to other Arab countries. The role of repression in the international context of mass political unrest was significant in Turkey in 2013. Although Erdoğan's harsh deployment of repressive violence against the Gezi Park protesters did not cause mass fatalities,

174 *Mark Kramer*

it set an ominous precedent for subsequent brutal repression in Turkey against anti-Erdoğan protesters, notably in 2016–2017. Elsewhere in the Balkans in 2013, repression played much less of a role. A crackdown in Bulgaria in February 2013 was so limited that it merely emboldened the protesters rather than cowing them. The resulting escalation of protests in central Sofia quickly led to the collapse of Boyko Borisov's government. Throughout the year, the prospect of repression in both Bulgaria and Romania was much less salient than in Turkey, which helps to explain why protests lasted a good deal longer there.

Uncompromising repression is not the only option available to an authoritarian regime if it is confronted by the international spread of protest. During bouts of popular unrest, the Turkish government has relentlessly used propaganda to discredit protesters, depicting them as 'tools of foreign interests', 'Gülenists', and 'traitors' to the nation and Islam. Propaganda can be an effective instrument, but it may not be sufficient to halt diffusion. Hence, when a cross-country wave of destabilising protests is under way, an authoritarian regime seeking to deter or crush an anti-regime protest movement is apt to clamp down decisively at the outset to let opposition activists know it is willing to do whatever is necessary to preserve itself in power.

National diasporas and 'long-distance nationalism'

Collective protests in some countries have been fuelled by 'long-distance nationalism', a concept first proposed by Benedict Anderson in the early 1990s and then developed in a quite different way by Anderson (1992) and other scholars (see Anderson 1998; Skrbis 1999). The term in its current sense refers to 'a set of identity claims and practices that connect people living in various geographical locations to a specific territory that they see as their ancestral home. Actions taken by long-distance nationalists on behalf of this reputed ancestral home may include voting, demonstrating, contributing money, creating works of art, fighting, killing, and dying' (Schiller 2008: 570). Anderson and most other scholars have viewed long-distance nationalism in a strictly negative light, regarding it as a baleful source of instability and violent domestic conflict. However, at least a few analysts have argued that 'long-distance nationalism cannot be summarily classified as more pernicious than other kinds of nationalism' (Schiller 2008: 580).

Regardless of how one assesses long-distance nationalism, theoretical and empirical studies have shown that in some circumstances, the long-distance nationalism of diaspora communities in State X and State Y can increase the likelihood that collective protest movements in State Z will adopt bold tactics in pursuit of far-reaching political change. The notion that long-distance nationalism is directed from States X and Y towards State Z is the way the concept has usually been understood, but the same basic process exists if the direction of the instigating relationship is reversed – that is, if the central national leaders in State Z try to inflame the sentiments of their compatriots in States X and Y, exhorting them to resort to mass contentious action.

The concept of long-distance nationalism illuminates the role of external actors in inciting, fuelling or even – in some instances – dampening and deterring political protests in Balkan countries. Nearly all Balkan states have ethnic compatriots living in other Southeastern European countries or in the West. Some of these diaspora communities – Turks, Albanians, Serbs, Croats, Greeks – are relatively large and potentially restive. The extent to which they are integrated into their countries of residence varies from case to case. The interaction between these diaspora communities and their nominal 'homelands' can trigger political unrest in two very different ways that reflect the 'two faces' of long-distance nationalism.

On the one hand, members of a diaspora community can help create or at least support protest movements and political insurgents in their native land, as Turkish communities in Western Europe did in providing aid directly or indirectly to pro-democracy protesters in Turkey in 2013. In some cases, the support may be inadvertent (skimmed off from remittances), but in other cases, it is deliberately targeted towards opposition groups. During the two major rounds of protests in Bulgaria in 2013, Bulgarian citizens living abroad helped organise social network websites and computer support for their compatriots who were taking part in daily protests.

On the other hand, ethnic Turkish diaspora communities in EU countries can serve as a vehicle of influence for the Turkish government to try to keep the governments in those countries off-balance. This is the reverse 'face' of long-distance nationalism. In Germany, France and other West European countries, the presence of large Turkish minorities who feel at least some degree of loyalty to Turkey gives the Turkish government a quasi-lobbying group it can use to push for support of the government's stance against protests and its campaign against purported Gülenists.

The internal reach of international organisations

International organisations can have important effects on political protests in member-states and aspiring member-states. All Balkan countries are members of the Council of Europe and the Organization for Security and Cooperation in Europe (OSCE). Most Balkan states are members of the North Atlantic Treaty Organization (NATO), and the three countries that do not belong to NATO have shown at least some interest in joining. (A fourth country, Macedonia, has been invited to join NATO but has not yet formally gained entry because of objections by Greece.) The EU includes a smaller number of Balkan countries, but the ones that have not yet been admitted are intent on eventually gaining membership. Even though Erdoğan has apparently concluded that the EU will never grant membership to Turkey, especially after the European Commission (backed by the European Parliament) effectively halted its accession negotiations with Turkey in late 2016 and 2017 in light of serious human rights concerns, a large majority of Turks still favour membership in the EU.[10] Moreover, despite deep resentment in Ankara about the de facto termination of the accession talks in 2017, the Turkish

176 *Mark Kramer*

government avoided indicating that it would permanently abandon its long-standing bid to join (Ash 2017: 7; Connolly and Rankin 2017: 3).

NATO and the EU have been crucial external actors for the Balkan countries because both organisations expect and require their members (and aspiring members) to adhere to democratic norms. Although deviations from these norms have occurred from time to time in some members of both organisations, the two bodies have come to be seen as democratic clubs. Their external presence therefore is bound to affect the political opportunity structures for protest movements not only in the countries that are members of the organisations but also in those that aspire to join. The Council of Europe and OSCE have also been important external actors insofar as they have significantly expanded institutional access for protest movements in the Balkans. If protesters encounter repression, they are entitled to seek redress in the European Court for Human Rights and attempt to gain overt support from the Council of Europe and the OSCE.

Moreover, to the extent that the EU and NATO have promoted democratisation and the rule of law in the Balkan countries (if only with mixed success), they have helped to expand the political opportunities there. What this has meant is that (1) disaffected citizens in Balkan countries have greater leeway than in the past to take part in mass contentious action, and (2) when large-scale protest movements do arise in these countries, the protesters have a greater incentive than in the past to stick with non-violent action. Although EU officials might not be able to reduce the ethnic and political cleavages in the Balkan countries, they can try to ensure that all major aspirants for power see it as in their interest to abide by the norms the EU expects.

Conclusions

This chapter has shown that the likelihood and specific nature of political unrest and violent upheaval in a given country can be influenced in a wide variety of ways by external actors, including other states, international organisations, NGOs and prominent individuals. Until recently, the social science literature on contentious politics, rebellion and civil unrest had not given due weight to the international context of these phenomena. But over the past 20 years, a sizable body of scholarship has been produced that looks squarely at the impact of external actors on political protests and anti-regime unrest. This literature enhances our understanding of an important dimension of the wave of political protests in Balkan countries in 2013.

One of the two main goals of this chapter was to consider how a wide variety of external actors can affect the structure of political opportunities facing activists and other potential protesters in Balkan countries.[11] Tarrow (1998: 71–90) has pointed to several 'dimensions of opportunity' – institutional access, fluctuations in political alignments, cleavages among elites, the presence of supportive and allied groups, and diminished levels of repression – that can facilitate mass protests. To varying degrees, external actors can affect all of these areas.

The international context of mass political unrest in the Balkans 177

Tarrow (1998) juxtaposes the dimensions of opportunity with what he calls the three 'dimensions of the state', namely, state strength, prevailing state strategies, and repressiveness, all of which help to shape the government's response to mass political unrest. These dimensions, too, can be influenced by external actors.

In all the Balkan countries, the most important external actors vis-à-vis protest movements have been the EU and NATO, along with the Council of Europe, the ECHR, the European Court, and the OSCE. Non-governmental actors of various sorts (foundations, NGOs, universities, think-tanks, corporations) and transnational NGOs have also had a far-reaching impact on the POS in Balkan countries, particularly in increasing the potential for like-minded protest groups to emerge (through the Western media's framing of issues, the provision of democracy assistance, and the encouragement of overseas educational programs and exchanges), and in encouraging fluctuations in political alignments (mostly indirectly through the provision of democracy assistance and exchanges). Although the Erdoğan government has sought to keep out the influence of Western entities during periods of unrest and tried to undermine attempts by indigenous opposition groups and individuals to receive meaningful support from Western governments and non-state actors (NGOs or foundations) and international organisations, the Turkish government's ability to counter these unwanted influences has often fallen short. Hence, Western actors still exert considerable influence on the 'dimensions of opportunity' in Turkey.

The other main goal of this chapter was to evaluate how external actors can affect the likelihood that a protest movement succeeds. Measuring 'success' is no easy task, in part because the aims of a protest group are apt to change over time, shifting in either a more radical or conciliatory (within-system) direction (see Giugni 1998; Kolb 2007: 22–25; Saeed 2009). The protest group's own criteria for success are rarely static, as the experience of Bulgaria in 2013 made clear. The task of evaluating the 'success' of a protest movement is further complicated by the need to take account of the movement's long-term impact as well as its short-term results. When assessing either type of outcome, scholars of contentious politics must provide concrete evidence that the protest movement itself caused or at least contributed to the changes that occurred (or helped to prevent certain undesired events from occurring) and did not simply witness the changes.

In some instances, the members of a protest movement might believe they were successful (or unsuccessful), whereas scholars using objective criteria might come to the opposite conclusion, especially with the passage of time (Suh 2001; Meyer 2006). Some researchers have claimed that it is pointless to judge the 'success' or 'failure' of a protest group and it is better to focus on the 'consequences' or 'impact' of the group (see Giugni 1999). Other scholars disagree, arguing that the difference between these sets of criteria is mainly one of semantics and that 'most critiques being raised against the concept of success and failure are directed against flawed benchmarks rather than against the concept itself' (Kolb 2007: 23). So long as analysts carefully specify the benchmarks they are using, evaluations of a protest group's 'success' are methodologically sound and illuminating.

178 *Mark Kramer*

For the purposes of this chapter, which has focused on anti-government protest movements that seek (either from the outset or eventually) to change how a country is ruled, one can define success as the posing of a sustained, grave threat to a government's survival in power, culminating in the downfall of the government. What occurs afterwards is of no relevance to the discussion here unless the displaced rulers return to power quickly through non-electoral means. If that does not happen, the precise nature of who ultimately takes power after the ouster of the government does not have a direct bearing on a protest movement's 'success' (as defined here). Whether in countries such as Bulgaria and Romania that hold genuine national elections, or in a country such as Turkey where elections have become increasingly problematic and ritualistic under Erdoğan, the ouster of a government is the foremost prerequisite of a protest movement's success.

Even if the downfall of a government is a necessary condition for characterising an anti-government protest movement as 'successful', it is not a sufficient condition. One must also demonstrate that the outcome was at least partly attributable to the actions of the protest movement – a difficult but not necessarily impossible task. A protest movement can be deemed 'successful' if the available evidence shows that the movement helped dislodge the government from power.

Given this definition of success, what are the factors that increase the chances of an anti-government protest group's success, and how can external actors affect the chances? To answer these questions, we need to proceed in three stages. First, we need to specify which factors increase the likelihood that an anti-government protest movement will emerge. Second, we need to consider which tactics an anti-government protest movement should use to maximise its chances of ousting the existing rulers, in particular whether it should rely exclusively on non-violent resistance. Third, we need to consider how external actors can affect these conditions and tactics.

Cumulative research has identified many structural and individual factors that are conducive to protest mobilisation, bolstering the odds that an anti-government movement will emerge.[12] Three are worth stressing here: (1) 'suddenly imposed grievances', the term coined by Walsh (1981: 1–21) to refer to 'dramatic, highly publicised, and often unexpected events – man-made disasters, major court decisions, official violence – that serve to dramatise and therefore increase public awareness of and opposition to particular grievances'. Such events underscore the need for collective remedial action and become a catalyst for mass unrest; (2) geographic concentration of the society (to permit a high 'ecological density' of recruits for mass protests); and (3) the relative absence of cross-cutting social cleavages (e.g. ethnicity, race, regional identity) that would more easily permit the authorities to rely on a divide-and-rule strategy.

External actors can have at least a modicum of influence on each of these factors, even the question of geography. The government or other actors in State Z might provoke or publicise the events that dramatically highlight grievances among groups in State A. Price increases for heating and electricity in Bulgaria – services provided by foreign companies – were the catalyst for the first round of

The international context of mass political unrest in the Balkans   179

contention in 2013, and the Bulgarian Socialist Party's appointment of Delyan Peevski (a wealthy crony of senior officials in the party) to a high-ranking national security post for which he was totally unqualified was the catalyst for the second round, which soon resulted in the removal of Peevski from his position (Gigova 2013). Foreign media coverage of these developments, especially on the Internet, helped to spread awareness of the protesters and their goals.

With regard to geography, the ecological density of recruits for protest movements in State A can increase if refugees, members of diaspora communities, and other sympathetic groups and individuals in neighbouring States Y and Z travel to State A. In Turkey and the former Yugoslavia, protest movements were strengthened by recruits from other Balkan countries. In Ukraine during the Orange Revolution in late 2004 and again during the Euromaidan Revolution in 2013–2014, recruits for protest rallies streamed in from neighbouring Poland (which also was the source of recruits for the anti-regime demonstrations in Belarus in 2006). Some protesters also came to Ukraine from Russia in defiance of the Russian government, which in both 2004 and 2013–2014 was strongly opposed to the pro-democracy movements in Ukraine and dispatched officials to Kyiv in a futile attempt to spur a decisive crackdown.

External actors can deepen or diminish the cross-cutting cleavages in neighbouring countries. The Albanian government's ties with ethnic Albanians in neighbouring countries have at times intensified social cleavages. Much the same is true about the Turkish government's links with Turkish diasporas in nearby countries and further afield. An increasingly bitter cleavage in Turkey between those who favour secularism and those who favour Erdoğan's drive to establish an Islamist polity can also be significantly affected by external actors on either side of the issue.

Once an anti-government protest movement has emerged, the choice of tactics can be influenced by external actors. If the movement wants to get rid of the government, one obvious question is whether the use of violence increases the protesters' chance of success. In the 1970s and 1980s, research on the efficacy of violence in protest movements yielded contradictory results. Gamson's (1975) examination of collective protests in the United States indicated that the use of violence resulted in 'a higher than average success rate', but work done by other researchers on strikes and student protests in both North America and Western Europe was far less conclusive (Shorter and Tilly 1974; Snyder and Kelly 1976). Some researchers found that the use of violence increased the likelihood of protesters' success, whereas others found the opposite. Still others concluded that the choice of whether to use violence had no systematic bearing on the outcomes of contentious politics (Steedly and Foley 1979; Giugni 1998).

One drawback to nearly all of this literature is that it has dealt entirely (or at least mostly) with narrowly focused protests in liberal democratic countries of long standing. Whether the findings are equally applicable to mass protests in newly democratising or increasingly authoritarian countries aimed at destabilising the government and removing it from power is doubtful.

180   *Mark Kramer*

Recent work done by Chenoweth and Stephan (2011), as well as several other political scientists, has focused squarely on the question of protest movements striving to oust non-democratic governments (a situation that in the Balkans would be most relevant to Turkey) (see also Schock 2005; Stephan and Chenoweth 2008; Roberts and Ash 2009). Relying on a database of some 323 resistance campaigns in the 20th and early 21st centuries, Stephan and Chenoweth make a laudatory attempt to support their view that non-violent resistance is more effective (i.e. more likely to succeed) than armed struggle. But the problem is that their database unavoidably omits countless non-violent resistance campaigns that never begin (because they are deterred) or are crushed at a very early stage before they become widely known.[13] Hence, the database is heavily biased towards successful cases of non-violence, leaving ample room for doubt about the authors' conclusions. Moreover, even if we assume, for the sake of argument, that Stephan and Chenoweth are correct in their aggregate analysis of non-violent resistance campaigns unadjusted for size, the existence of crucial outliers – China in 1989, Burma in 2007, Zimbabwe in 2005 and 2008, and Iran in 2009 – raises further questions about the validity of their argument. Suffice to say, more research is needed.

For now, the question of whether the use of violence by a protest movement is likely to contribute to the ouster of a government remains open. The downfall of regimes in numerous countries after non-violent protests over the past four decades makes this an exceptionally timely and important issue, but it has by no means resolved the matter in favour of the use of non-violence. In many instances, including China in 1989, Uzbekistan in 2005, Burma under its military junta, Zimbabwe under Robert Mugabe, Iran in 2009, and Belarus in 2006 and 2010, among others, autocratic governments have been willing to rely on ruthless violence to crush mass non-violent protests and prevent further challenges. In Turkey in 2013, violent repression (albeit on a much less deadly scale) in Gezi Park also helped quell peaceful anti-government demonstrations and deter renewed protests. Since 2013, especially in the aftermath of the abortive military coup in Turkey in July 2016, Erdoğan's security forces have continued to use overwhelming force against individuals or groups that even consider posing a challenge to the regime.

On the other hand, the inefficacy of non-violence in many cases does not necessarily mean that the use of violence would have been more conducive to success. Clearly, in some cases, the use of violence would simply have made things worse. In the Baltic republics of the Soviet Union in the late 1980s and early 1990s, separatist movements that sprang up remained scrupulously non-violent, knowing that if they turned to violence, the Soviet Army and state security organs would have a pretext for using brutal force against them (Kramer 2003, 2009). Even when the Soviet authorities tried to goad the Baltic protesters into using violence and sent provocateurs to stimulate rash action, the Baltic separatist movements sedulously eschewed violence. For a few years, their reliance on peaceful tactics seemed to achieve little, but after a failed coup in August 1991 fatally weakened the Soviet regime, the Baltic protesters achieved everything they had been seeking.

The international context of mass political unrest in the Balkans 181

The potential for external influence in the Balkans could increase over the next several years with the possible emergence of conflicts among local elites, the prospect of a severe, prolonged downturn of the region's economies, and the chance that destabilising unrest will emerge in one or more of the Balkan countries and spread to others. In such circumstances, Western actors would very likely be able to influence the situation, possibly shifting the balance in favour of opposition groups that want to adhere to Western democratic norms and do away with the corruption, cronyism and arbitrariness that still characterise political life throughout the region.

Notes

1 In this chapter, I use the term 'Balkans' to refer to European countries that were at one time part of the Ottoman Empire. I use the term interchangeably with 'Southeastern Europe', although I am aware of the disagreements about precisely what these rubrics should include.
2 The only exceptions to this pattern are outbursts of mass unrest among ethnic Uighurs in Xingjiang province or ethnic Tibetans in Tibet. The Chinese authorities swiftly and brutally crack down on ethnic minority protests, aiming to suppress them before they escalate out of control.
3 For an early exception, see Marx (1979).
4 On the nature of 'master frames' in protest cycles, see Snow and Renford (1988).
5 One of the few focused studies of this topic is Kern (2010).
6 On the rapidly burgeoning number of international NGOs in the 1990s, see Smith et al. (1997: 47–52).
7 For extensive self-criticism (and proposed solutions) by the three chief architects of the POS framework, see McAdam et al. (2001: 3–191).
8 For a thoughtful explication of the social constructivist perspective on norm diffusion, see Checkel (1999). Checkel relies, at least implicitly, on this same framework in some of his subsequent analyses of European integration; see, for example, Checkel (2001). Similar perspectives focusing on the international spread of democratisation can be found in Schmitz (2004) and Cortell and Davis (1996). For a critique of the constructivist emphasis on norm diffusion, see Tarrow (2001).
9 Structural realists are divided on the question of whether states actively pursue superiority or are content to maintain their existing position in the international order. 'Defensive' realists like Waltz (1979) argue that states seek to maintain their current position and ensure their survival but are not driven by aggressive motivations or a desire for global or regional domination. 'Offensive' realists like Mearsheimer (2001: 33–35) argue that because 'states quickly understand that the best way to ensure their survival is to be the most powerful state in the system', they continually seek to increase their power. On the offensive-defensive realist split, see Zakaria (1992: 190–196) and Schweller and Priess (1997).
10 See German Marshall Fund (2015) and its October 2017 supplement. In contrast to Turkish citizens' attitudes, Eurobarometer surveys over the past several years have shown that a significant majority in every important EU country is opposed to the prospect of Turkey's accession to the organisation.
11 For a somewhat related analysis, assessing the probable link between a state's place in international political and economic hierarchies and the nature of its POS, see Maney (2001).
12 The discussion here draws on Lofland (1996: 204–256).

182   *Mark Kramer*

13 On the nature and means of compilation of their Nonviolent and Violent Conflict Outcomes database, see Stephan and Chenoweth (2008: 15–19).

References

Anderson, B. 1992. The New World Disorder. *New Left Review* 193: 3–13.

Anderson, B. 1998. Long Distance Nationalism. In: *The Spectre of Comparisons: Nationalism, Southeast Asia, and the World*, ed. B. Anderson. New York: Verso, pp. 58–74.

Ash, T. 2017. Turkey's EU Accession: The Way Forward. *Financial Times*, 20 September.

Bob, C. 2006. *The Marketing of Rebellion: Insurgents, Media, and International Activism.* Cambridge: Cambridge University Press.

Bob, C. ed. 2010. *The International Struggle for New Human Rights*. Philadelphia: University of Pennsylvania Press.

Brown, J.M. 2009. Gandhi and Civil Resistance in India, 1917–47: Key Issues. In: *Civil Resistance & Power Politics: The Experience of Non-Violent Action from Gandhi to the Present*, eds. A. Roberts and T.G. Ash. Oxford: Oxford University Press, pp. 45–61.

Bulmer, S., D. Dolowitz, P. Humphreys, and S. Padgett. 2007. *Policy Transfer in European Union Governance*. London: Routledge.

Cai, Y. 2010. *Collective Resistance in China: Why Popular Protests Succeed or Fail*. Stanford: Stanford University Press.

Carment, D., P. James, and Z. Taydas. 2006. *Who Intervenes? Ethnic Conflict and Interstate Crisis*. Columbus: Ohio State University Press.

Chabot, S. 2013. *Transnational Roots of the Civil Rights Movement: African American Explorations of the Gandhian Repertoire*. Lanham: Lexington Books.

Checkel, J. 1999. Norms, Institutions, and National Identity in Contemporary Europe. *International Studies Quarterly* 43(1): 83–114.

Checkel, J. 2001. Why Comply? Social Learning and European Identity Change. *International Organization* 55(3): 553–588.

Chenoweth, E. and M.J. Stephan. 2011. *Why Civil Resistance Works: The Strategic Logic of Nonviolent Resistance*. New York: Columbia University Press.

Collier, P., V.L. Elliott, H. Hegre, A. Hoeffler, M. Reynal-Querol, and N. Sambanis. 2003. *Breaking the Conflict Trap: Civil War and Development Policy*. Washington, DC: The World Bank.

Connolly, K. and J. Rankin. 2017. Turkey Hits Back After Merkel Says EU Should Scrap Accession Talks. *The Guardian*, 4 September.

Cortell, A.P. and J.W. Davis. 1996. How Do International Institutions Matters? The Domestic Impact of International Rules and Norms. *International Studies Quarterly* 40(3): 451–478.

Crawford, G. 2001. *Foreign Aid and Political Reform: A Comparative Analysis of Democracy Assistance and Political Conditionality*. New York: Palgrave Macmillan.

Crawford, T.W. and A.J. Kuperman. eds. 2006. *Gambling on Humanitarian Intervention: Moral Hazard, Rebellion, and Civil War*. London: Routledge.

Della Porta, D. and A. Mattoni. eds. 2014. *Spreading Protest: Social Movements in Times of Crisis*. Colchester: ECPR Press.

Dobbin, F., B. Simmons, and G. Garrett. 2007. The Global Diffusion of Public Policies: Social Construction, Coercion, Competition, or Learning? *Annual Review of Sociology* 33: 449–472.

Doorenspleet, R. 2004. The Structural Context of Democracy. *European Journal of Political Research* 43(3): 309–335.

The international context of mass political unrest in the Balkans   183

Elkins, Z. and B.A. Simmons. 2004. The Globalization of Liberalization: Policy Diffusion in the International Political Economy. *American Political Science Review* 98(1): 171–189.

Entman, R.M. 1993. Framing: Toward Clarification of a Fractured Paradigm. *Journal of Communication* 43(4): 51–58.

Entman, R.M. and A. Rojecki. 1993. Freezing Out the Public: Elite and Media Framing of the Anti-Nuclear Movement. *Political Communication* 10(2): 155–173.

Evangelista, M.A. 1999. *Unarmed Forces: The Transnational Movement to End the Cold War.* Ithaca: Cornell University Press.

Evans, M. 2006. At the Interface Between Theory and Practice: Policy Transfer and Lesson-Drawing. *Public Administration* 84(2): 479–489.

Finnemore, M. and K. Sikkink. 2001. Taking Stock: The Constructivist Research Program in International Relations and Comparative Politics. *Annual Review of Political Science* 4: 391–416.

FitzGerald, V., F. Stewart, and R. Venugopal. 2006. Conclusions. In: *Globalization, Violent Conflict, and Self-Determination,* eds. V. FitzGerald, F. Stewart, and R. Venugopal. Basingstoke: Palgrave Macmillan, pp. 247–259.

Fleishman, C. 2013. CNN Turk Airs Penguin Documentary During Istanbul Riots. *The Daily Dot,* 2 June.

Gamson, W. 1975. *The Strategy of Social Protest.* Homeward, IL: Dorsey Press.

German Marshall Fund of the United States. 2015. *Turkish Perceptions Survey, 2015.* Washington, DC: German Marshall Fund.

Gigova, Irina. 2013. Delyan Peevski veche ne e shef na DANS. *Fakti,* 19 July.

Giugni, M. 1998. Was It Worth the Effort? The Outcomes and Consequences of Social Movements. *Annual Review of Sociology* 24: 371–393.

Giugni, M. 1999. How Social Movements Matter: Past Research, Present Problems, Future Developments. In: *How Social Movements Matter,* eds. M. Giugni, D. McAdam, and S. Tarrow. Minneapolis: University of Minnesota Press, pp. xi–xxxiii.

Givan, R.C., K.M. Roberts, and S.A. Soule. eds. 2010. *The Diffusion of Social Movements: Actors, Mechanisms, and Political Effects.* Cambridge: Cambridge University Press.

Gleditsch, K.S. 2002. *All International Politics is Local: The Diffusion of Conflict, Integration, and Democratization.* Ann Arbor: University of Michigan Press.

Hannan, M.T. and J.H. Freeman. 1977. The Population Ecology of Organizations. *American Journal of Sociology* 82(5): 929–964.

Henderson, K. ed. 1999. *Back to Europe: Central and Eastern Europe and the European Union.* London: UCL Press.

Hopf, T. 2002. *Social Construction of International Politics: Identities & Foreign Policies, Moscow 1955 and 1999.* Ithaca: Cornell University Press.

Jordana, J. and D. Levi-Faur. 2005. The Diffusion of Regulatory Capitalism in Latin America: Sectoral and National Channels in the Making of a New Order. *Annals of the American Academy of Political and Social Sciences* 598: 102–124.

Keohane, R. and J.S. Nye. eds. 1973. *Transnational Relations and World Politics.* Cambridge, MA: Harvard University Press.

Keohane, R. and J.S. Nye. 1979. *Power and Interdependence.* Boston: Little, Brown.

Keck, M. and K. Sikkink. 1998. *Activists Beyond Borders Advocacy Networks in International Politics.* Ithaca: Cornell University Press.

Keck, M. and K. Sikkink. 1999. Transnational Advocacy Networks in International and Regional Politics. *International Social Science Review* 51(1): 89–101.

184   *Mark Kramer*

Kerber, W. and M. Eckardt. 2007. Policy Learning in Europe: The Open Method of Co-ordination and Laboratory Federalism. *Journal of European Public Policy Research* 14(2): 227–247.

Kern, H.L. 2010. Foreign Media and Protest Diffusion in Authoritarian Regimes: The Case of the 1989 East German Revolution. *Comparative Political Studies* 43(3): 203–224.

Kil Lee, C. and D. Strang. 2003. *The International Diffusion of Public Sector Downsizing.* Ithaca: Center for the Study of Society and Economy, Cornell University.

Kolb, F. 2007. *Protests and Opportunities: The Political Outcomes of Social Movements.* Chicago: University of Chicago Press.

Kolins Givan, R., K. Roberts, and S.A. Soule. eds. 2010. *The Diffusion of Social Movements: Actors, Mechanisms, and Political Effects.* Cambridge: Cambridge University Press.

Kramer, M. 2003. The Collapse of East European Communism and the Repercussions Within the Soviet Union (Part 1). *Journal of Cold War Studies* 5(4): 178–256.

Kramer, M. 2004. The Collapse of East European Communism and the Repercussions Within the Soviet Union (Part 2). *Journal of Cold War Studies* 6(4): 3–67.

Kramer, M. 2005. The Collapse of East European Communism and the Repercussions Within the Soviet Union (Part 3). *Journal of Cold War Studies* 7(1): 3–96.

Kramer, M. 2009. The Dialectics of Empire: Soviet Leaders and the Challenge of Civil Resistance in East-Central Europe, 1968–91. In: *Civil Resistance and Power Politics: The Experience of Non-Violent Action from Gandhi to the Present*, eds. A. Roberts and T.G. Ash. Oxford: Oxford University Press, pp. 91–109.

Kramer, M. 2013. Stalin, Soviet Policy, and the Establishment of a Communist Bloc in Eastern Europe, 1941–1949. In: *Imposing, Maintaining, and Tearing Open the Iron Curtain: The Cold War in East-Central Europe, 1945–1990*, eds. M. Kramer and V. Smetana. Lanham: Rowman & Littlefield, pp. 3–37.

Kriesi, H., R. Koopmans, J.W. Duyvendak, and M.G. Giugni. 1995. *New Social Movements in Western Europe: A Comparative Analysis.* Minneapolis: University of Minnesota Press.

Kuperman, A.J. 2008. The Moral Hazard of Humanitarian Intervention: Lessons From the Balkans. *International Studies Quarterly* 52(1): 49–80.

Lichbach, M.I. 1995. *The Rebel's Dilemma.* Ann Arbor: University of Michigan Press.

Lichbach, M.I. 1998. Contending Theories of Contentious Politics and the Structure-Action Problem of Social Order. *Annual Review of Political Science* 1: 401–424.

Lofland, J. 1996. *Social Movement Organizations: Guide to Research on Insurgent Realities.* New Brunswick: Aldine Transaction.

Maney, D.G. 2001. Transnational Structures and Protest: Linking Theories and Assessing Evidence. *Mobilization* 6(1): 83–100.

Marx, G.T. 1979. External Efforts to Damage or Facilitate Social Movements: Some Patterns, Explanations, Outcomes, and Complications. In: *The Dynamics of Social Protests*, eds. M.N. Zald and J.D. McCarthy. Cambridge, MA: Winthrop Publishers, pp. 202–231.

McAdam, D. 1995. 'Initiator' and 'Spin-off' Movements: Diffusion Processes in Protest Cycles. In: *Repertoires and Cycles of Collective Action*, ed. M. Traugott. Durham: Duke University Press, pp. 221–240.

McAdam, D. 1999. *Political Process and the Development of Black Insurgency, 1930–1970.* Chicago: University of Chicago Press.

McAdam, D. and D. Rucht. 1993. The Cross-National Diffusion of Movement Ideas. *The Annals of the American Academy of Political and Social Science* 528: 56–74.

The international context of mass political unrest in the Balkans 185

McAdam, D., S. Tarrow, and C. Tilly. 1997. Toward an Integrated Perspective on Social Movements and Revolution. In: *Comparative Politics: Rationality, Culture, and Structure*, eds. M.I. Lichbach and A.S. Zuckerman. Cambridge: Cambridge University Press, pp. 142–173.

McAdam, D., S. Tarrow, and C. Tilly. 2001. *Dynamics of Contention*. Cambridge: Cambridge University Press.

McLeod, D.M. and J.K. Hertog. 1998. Social Control and the Mass Media's Role in the Regulation of Protest Groups. In: *Mass Media, Social Control, and Social Change*, eds. D. Demers and K. Viswanath. Ames: Iowa State University Press, pp. 305–332.

Mearsheimer, J. 2001. *The Tragedy of Great Power Politics*. New York: W.W. Norton.

Meseguer, C. 2006. Rational Learning and Bounded Learning in the Diffusion of Policy Innovation. *Rationality and Society* 18(3): 35–66.

Meyer, D.S. 2006. Claiming Credit: Stories of Movement Influence as Outcomes. *Mobilization: An International Journal* 11(3): 202–218.

Midlarsky, M. 1970. Mathematical Models of Instability and a Theory of Diffusion. *International Studies Quarterly* 14(1): 60–84.

Most, B.A. and H. Starr. 1980. Diffusion, Reinforcement, Geopolitics, and the Spread of War. *American Political Science Review* 74(4): 932–946.

Most, B.A. and H. Starr. 1990. Theoretical and Logical Issues in the Study of International Diffusion. *Journal of Theoretical Politics* 2(4): 391–412.

Motamed-Nejad, K., N. Badii, and M. Mohsenian-Rad. 1992. The Iranian Press and the Persian Gulf War: The Impact of Western News Agencies. In: *Triumph of the Image: The Media's War in the Persian Gulf – a Global Perspective*, eds. H. Mowlana, G. Gerbner, and H.I. Schiller. Boulder, CO: Westview Press, pp. 99–103.

Myers, D.J. and P.E. Oliver. 2008. The Opposing Forces Diffusion Model: The Initiation and Repression of Collective Violence. *Dynamics of Asymmetric Conflict* 1(2): 164–189.

Newland, K. 1993. Ethnic Conflict and Refugees. In: *Ethnic Conflict and International Security*, ed. M.E. Brown. Princeton: Princeton University Press, pp. 143–163.

O'Brien, K.J. ed. 2008. *Popular Protest in China*. Cambridge, MA: Harvard University Press.

Oliver, P.E. and G.M. Maney. 2000. Political Processes and Local Newspaper Coverage of Protest Events: From Selection Bias to Triadic Interactions. *American Journal of Sociology* 106(2): 463–505.

Risse, T. and K. Sikkink. 1999. The Socialization of International Human Rights Norms Into Domestic Practices: Introduction. In: *The Power of Human Rights: International Norms and Domestic Change*, eds. T. Risse, S.C. Ropp, and K. Sikkink. New York: Cambridge University Press, pp. 1–39.

Roberts, A. and T.G. Ash. eds. 2009. *Civil Resistance and Power Politics: The Experience of Non-Violent Action From Gandhi to the Present*. Oxford: Oxford University Press.

Rose, R. 2005. *Learning From Comparative Public Policy: A Practical Guide*. London: Routledge.

Rosenau, J.N. ed. 1969. *Linkage Politics: Essays on the Convergence of National and International Systems*. New York: The Free Press.

Saeed, R. 2009. Conceptualizing Success and Failure for Social Movements. *Law, Social Justice & Global Development* 2: 1–13.

Schiller, N.G. 2008. Long-Distance Nationalism. In: *Encyclopedia of Diasporas: Immigrant and Refugee Cultures around the World*, eds. M. Ember, C.R. Ember and I. Skoggard. New York: Kluwer Academic, pp. 570–580.

186 *Mark Kramer*

Schmitz, H.P. 2004. Domestic and Transnational Perspectives on Democratization. *International Studies Review* 6(3): 403–426.

Schock, K. 2005. *Unarmed Insurrections: People Power Movements in Nondemocracies.* Minneapolis: University of Minnesota Press.

Schweller, R.L. and D. Priess. 1997. A Tale of Two Realisms: Expanding the Institutions Debate. *Mershon International Studies Review* 41(1): 1–32.

Shorter, E. and C. Tilly. 1974. *Strikes in France, 1830–1968.* Cambridge: Cambridge University Press.

Sikkink, K. 1998. Transnational Politics, International Relations Theory, and Human Rights. *PS: Political Science and Politics* 31(3): 516–523.

Skrbis, Z. 1999. *Long-Distance Nationalism: Diasporas, Homelands, and Identities.* Brookfield, VT: Ashgate Publishing.

Smith, J. 2002. Bridging Global Divides? Strategic Framing and Solidarity in Transnational Social Movement Organizations. *International Sociology* 17(4): 505–528.

Smith, J., C. Chatfield, and R. Pagnucco. eds. 1997. *Transnational Social Movements and Global Politics: Solidarity Beyond the State.* Syracuse, NY: Syracuse University Press.

Snow, D. and R. Renford. 1988. Ideology, Frame Resonance, and Participant Mobilization. In: *From Structure to Action: Comparing Social Movements Across Cultures*, eds. B. Klandermans, H.P. Kriesi, and S. Tarrow. Greenwich, CT: JAI Press, pp. 197–218.

Snyder, D. and W.R. Kelly. 1976. Industrial Violence in Italy, 1878–1903. *American Journal of Sociology* 82(1): 151–162.

Soule, S.A. 2004. Diffusion Processes Within and across Movements. In: *The Blackwell Companion to Social Movements*, eds. D.A. Snow, S.A. Soule, and H.P. Kriesi. Oxford: Blackwell Publishing, pp. 294–310.

Starr, H. and C. Lindborg. 2003. Democratic Dominoes Revisited: The Hazards of Governmental Transitions, 1974–1996. *Journal of Conflict Resolution* 47(4): 490–519.

Stedman, S.J. and F. Tanner. 2003. eds. *Refugee Manipulation: War, Politics, and the Abuse of Human Suffering.* Washington, DC: Brookings Institution Press.

Steedly, H.R. and J.W. Foley. 1979. The Success of Protest Groups: Multivariate Analyses. *Social Science Research* 8(1): 1–15.

Stephan, M.J. and E. Chenoweth. 2008. Why Civil Resistance Works: The Strategic Logic of Nonviolent Action. *International Security* 33(1): 7–44.

Suh, D. 2001. How Do Political Opportunities Matter for Social Movements? Political Opportunity, Misframing, Pseudosuccess, and Pseudofailure. *The Sociological Quarterly* 42(3): 437–460.

Tang, W. 2016. *Populist Authoritarianism: Chinese Political Culture and Regime Sustainability.* Oxford: Oxford University Press.

Tarrow, S. 1998. *Power in Movement: Social Movements and Contentious Politics.* Cambridge: Cambridge University Press.

Tarrow, S. 1999. International Institutions and Contentious Politics: Does Internationalization Make Agents Freer – or Weaker? *Working Papers of the American Sociological Association's Section on Collective Behavior and Social Movements* 2(4).

Tarrow, S. 2001. Transnational Politics: Contention and Institutions in International Politics. *Annual Review of Political Science* 4: 1–20.

Tarrow, S. 2005. *The New Transnational Activism.* Cambridge: Cambridge University Press.

Thyne, C.L. 2009. *How International Relations Affect Civil Conflict: Cheap Signals, Costly Consequences.* Lanham: Lexington Books.

Tilly, C. 1978. *From Mobilization to Revolution.* Reading, MA: Addison-Wesley.

Walsh, E.J. 1981. Resource Mobilization and Citizen Protest in Communities around Three Mile Island. *Social Problems* 29(1): 1–21.

Waltz, K.N. 1979. *Theory of International Politics*. Reading, MA: Addison-Wesley.

Weiner, M. 1996. Bad Neighbors, Bad Neighborhoods: An Inquiry Into the Causes of Refugee Flows. *International Security* 17(1): 5–42.

Wejnert, B. 2002. Integrating Models of Diffusion of Innovations: A Conceptual Framework. *Annual Review of Sociology* 28: 297–326.

Weyland, K. 2009. The Diffusion of Revolution: '1848' in Europe and Latin America. *International Organization* 63(3): 391–423.

Wiener, A. 2003. Constructivism: The Limits of Bridging Gaps. *Journal of International Relations and Development* 6(3): 252–275.

Zakaria, F. 1992. Realism and Domestic Politics: A Review Essay. *International Security* 17(1): 190–196.

Index

activism 19–20, 23, 34, 125, 133–134; and civic activism 9, 23; informal activism 14; local 20, 67, 124–125; normalisation of 23; online 20, 102–103, 108; transnational 166–168

actors: external 7–10, 158–160, 163–167, 172, 175–181; informal 9, 18, 163–166; international 10–12, 123–126, 158–160, 163–181; political 1, 7–12, 18, 23–24, 132, 140

Albania 3, 136–137, 141–142, 152–155, 175, 179

austerity 1–4, 6–8, 30, 33–34, 41–43, 48–49, 66–68, 77, 79–80, 114, 118–119, 145–148; anti-austerity 7–8, 41, 49, 79, 124, 127

authoritarianism 131

Borisov, Boyko 2, 49, 52, 107, 174

Bosnia-Herzegovina 3–10, 103–115, 121–128, 136–143, 162; Bosnian Spring 3

Bulgaria 5–8, 48–64, 107, 137–155, 161–163, 174–179

capitalism 72, 75, 85, 87, 171

class 2, 18, 32–34, 36–40, 68, 72, 76, 92, 126, 133

commercial interest 3, 50

corruption 1–2, 9, 17, 38, 42, 60, 80–81, 87, 94, 106, 145–148, 159, 181

democracy: direct democracy 7, 38, 42, 50, 52, 93, 114, 119; democratic transition 4, 6, 30–32, 35–37, 131; grassroots democracy 5, 18, 113, 116, 126–127

Egypt 1, 26, 99, 129

Erdoğan, Recep Tayyip 4, 107, 117, 127, 161–163, 168, 173, 174–175, 177–178

ethnicity 108, 128, 178; ethnic conflict 23–24, 131, 159–160, 172, 181–182

European Union 4, 32, 41–45, 141–142, 149, 156, 168

Gezi Park 1–3, 7, 114, 116–118, 162–163, 173, 180

Greece: 2–7, 40, 43, 49, 66–77, 97, 113–115, 118, 120–129, 153, 155, 175

Istanbul 1–3, 114, 117–118, 128

Kangler, Franc 3, 35, 38, 42, 80–81, 105–106

Macedonia (Former Yugoslav Republic of) 3, 135–143, 152–155, 175

media: outlets 8, 158, 161–162, 167; social media 7–8, 96–109, 116, 118

nationality 12, 45, 134, 142, 148, 153–154, 157

neoliberalism 6, 48, 86, 150

organisations: civil society 10, 13, 27, 125–126, 134, 141, 145–146; international 8, 10–11, 13, 25, 116, 158, 163, 167, 175–177; local 13, 19, 34, 115–116, 125–126; non-governmental 9–16, 19–21, 24, 27–28, 40, 45, 50, 58, 101, 116–117, 125, 145, 160, 163–164, 166–168, 176–177; religious 134, 148

political parties: 4–6, 9, 11–12, 15, 18–19, 23–26, 30–31, 36, 42, 44, 48, 50, 52, 59, 62–63, 125, 134, 141–143, 157

protest forms: banners 7, 34, 50, 79, 90, 119; flags 7, 79, 84, 90, 104; occupation 30, 51, 53, 63, 68, 71, 74, 99, 113, 119–120; posters 7, 73, 79, 81–82,

85–90; riots 99, 131, 135, 141, 142, 174–175; violence 10, 16, 21, 24, 27–28, 35, 52, 58, 70, 76, 135, 148, 168, 172–173, 178–180

Romania 3, 5, 8, 43, 132, 135–155, 158, 161–163, 167, 174, 178

Serbia 136, 137, 141–142, 148, 152–155, 162, 169
Slovenia 2–7, 30–47, 79–88, 90, 92–95, 105–108, 132, 135–148, 152–155
social mobilisation 6, 31, 66–77, 170

socialism 7, 8, 33, 38, 42–43, 85–86, 113–118, 122–130, 158, 160–163, 167–168, 173–182
Syriza 5, 42, 44, 67–68, 76–77, 86, 127

totalitarianism 3, 31, 42–43, 60, 84, 90
trade unions 18, 36, 41–45, 93, 141, 145
Turkey 1–2, 5–8, 43, 107

Ukraine 1, 153, 155, 160, 169, 179

Yugoslavia 30–31, 39, 44–45, 79–80, 83–90, 179